Christian Spirituality *in* Africa

african christian studies series (africs)

This series will make available significant works in the field of African Christian studies, taking into account the many forms of Christianity across the whole continent of Africa. African Christian studies is defined here as any scholarship that relates to themes and issues on the history, nature, identity, character, and place of African Christianity in world Christianity. It also refers to topics that address the continuing search for abundant life for Africans through multiple appeals to African religions and African Christianity in a challenging social context. The books in this series are expected to make significant contributions in historicizing trends in African Christian studies, while shifting the contemporary discourse in these areas from narrow theological concerns to a broader inter-disciplinary engagement with African religio-cultural traditions and Africa's challenging social context.

The series will cater to scholarly and educational texts in the areas of religious studies, theology, mission studies, biblical studies, philosophy, social justice, and other diverse issues current in African Christianity. We define these studies broadly and specifically as primarily focused on new voices, fresh perspectives, new approaches, and historical and cultural analyses that are emerging because of the significant place of African Christianity and African religio-cultural traditions in world Christianity. The series intends to continually fill a gap in African scholarship, especially in the areas of social analysis in African Christian studies, African philosophies, new biblical and narrative hermeneutical approaches to African theologies, and the challenges facing African women in today's Africa and within African Christianity. Other diverse themes in African Traditional Religions; African ecology; African ecclesiology; inter-cultural, inter-ethnic, and inter-religious dialogue; ecumenism; creative inculturation; African theologies of development, reconciliation, globalization, and poverty reduction will also be covered in this series.

SERIES EDITORS
Dr Stan Chu Ilo (St Michael's College, University of Toronto)
Dr Philomena Njeri Mwaura (Kenyatta University, Nairobi, Kenya)
Dr Afe Adogame (University of Edinburgh)

Christian Spirituality *in* Africa

Biblical, Historical, and
Cultural Perspectives from Kenya

∽

SUNG KYU PARK

∽PICKWICK *Publications* · Eugene, Oregon

CHRISTIAN SPIRITUALITY IN AFRICA
Biblical, Historical, and Cultural Perspectives from Kenya

African Christian Studies Series 3

Pickwick Publications
An Imprint of Wipf and Stock Publishers
199 W. 8th Ave., Suite 3
Eugene, OR 97401

www.wipfandstock.com

ISBN 13: 978-1-62032-465-3

Cataloging-in-Publication data:

Park, Sung Kyu.

   Christian spirituality in Africa : biblical, historical, and cultural perspectives from Kenya / Sung Kyu Park.

   African Christian Studies Series 3

   xii + 218 p. ; 23 cm. Includes bibliographical references and index.

   ISBN 13: 978-1-62032-465-3

   1. Christianity and culture—Africa. 2. Christianity—Africa—Western influences. 3. Christianity—African influences. I. Series. II. Title.

BR1360 P245 2013

Manufactured in the U.S.A.

Dedicated
In Loving Memory to
Paul Kyu Young Park
(1964–2009)
My Beloved Brother

Contents

Preface

IT IS A DAUNTING task to describe Christian spirituality in Africa since Africa is diverse and there are more than 3,500 ethnic groups in Africa. To describe Christian spirituality of a certain African nation, Kenya in our case, can also be a challenging task since Kenya is composed of more than forty tribes. However, commonalities exist within tribal African cultures. Trying to avoid generalizations, this book seeks to describe Christian spirituality in Kenya.

Part 1 describes biblical and Christian historical (Western) spirituality as a foundation of Christian spirituality. Both Old and New Testament spirituality provide norms for Christian spirituality. Christian spirituality also developed over two millennia and its expressions are varied according to each specific situation in which unique forms of spirituality developed. Patristic (early church), medieval, and Protestant spirituality all provide us with rich traditions of Christian spirituality. This foundational understanding of biblical and Christian historical spirituality is essential in our study of Christian spirituality.

Part 2 deals with the historical development of Christianity in Kenya. Mission Christianity introduced the Bible to Africans along with Western civilization, thus a unique form of Christian spirituality developed. The East African Revival Movement, the first revival among mainline mission churches, refined the Christian faith that missionaries handed down to Africans. Then the charismatic/Pentecostal revival under which the African church experienced tremendous growth takes the African church in a certain new direction.

Part 3 presents African culture and African Traditional Religion (ATR). As mentioned in the beginning, although African culture and religion are diverse, it is still possible to describe them in a singular term through the eye of a particular culture—here the Kikuyu—because of common characteristics they share. African culture and religion are also discussed in light of their relationship to Christian spirituality. Finally, the secularization of Kenyan society and the necessity of spiritual formation as a vital forward movement are discussed.

As a researcher, a theologian, and a practitioner who has a keen interest in spirituality/spiritual formation, I wanted to provide some foundational material for the discussion of Christian spirituality in Africa (Kenya). Available are many other literatures that deal with each specific topic of this book in more detail, and there should be more publication in the area of Christian spirituality in Africa. However, it is my sincere desire that theological students, pastors, Christian educators and workers, and serious Christians would find this book helpful to understand the basic factors that comprise Christian spirituality in Africa (Kenya). Although Christianity grows at a tremendous speed in Africa, nurturing of Christians is not widely practiced for various reasons. Thus, in order to deepen spirituality of Christians in Africa, one must first of all develop a proper understanding of Christian spirituality. As a non-African, although I have lived in Africa over a decade, my own spiritual, cultural perspectives may be reflected in this book, and I ask for your understanding if it is necessary.

Nairobi, June 2012

Acknowledgements

THERE ARE MANY TO whom sincere gratitude should be expressed for the publication of this book. The research participants, who willingly shared their life stories, the focus group, and students of Nairobi International School of Theology, have all provided invaluable information and insight for this book. Special thanks go to Patrick Mureithi of the Presbyterian Church of East Africa (PCEA), who played a crucial role in the organization of the research participants. Prof. Julian Müller of the University of Pretoria, South Africa, guided the research process with excellence. The chancellor of the Pan African Christian University (PACU), Bishop Bonifes Adoyo, read the manuscript several times and critiqued it from an African perspective. Sally Gradin, a former missionary to Kenya, edited the manuscript with sensitivity and expertise. I also thank the PCEA for permission to use their logos in this book. Finally, I thank my family who gives me their full support for my work in Kenya.

1

The Subject of Spirituality

THE SUBJECT OF SPIRITUALITY is vast, from Christian spirituality to New Age spirituality. Differences exist even within Christian spirituality, such as is displayed by the Catholic, Anglican, Reformed, and charismatic branches of Christianity. Increasingly, people are more interested in personal experience of their belief than in organized religions. Hence, spirituality as a personal experience of faith plays a significant role in people's lives whether they are religious or not.

Dallas Willard defines spirituality as follows: Spirituality is simply the holistic quality of human life as it was meant to be, at the center of which is our relation to God.[1] Francis Schaeffer states that "true spirituality" is a positive inward reality and outward results.[2] Marie McCarthy's definition of spirituality is in-depth and broad: "Spirituality is broader and more encompassing than any religion. It is an expression of one's deepest values and commitments, one's sense or experience of something larger than and beyond oneself."[3] To summarize the above definitions, the subject of spirituality is holistic. It encompasses the whole human experience with God in the center. It includes both inner life and outer manifestations. These elements of spirituality provide us with some initial ideas of spirituality. Our discussion of spirituality in this book is about *Christian* spirituality.

1. Willard, *The Spirit of the Disciplines*, 77.
2. Schaeffer, *True Spirituality*, 14.
3. McCarthy, "Spirituality in Postmodern Era," 196.

Etymology of Spirituality

The English word "spirituality" originated from the Latin term *spiritualitas,* an abstract word derived from the noun *spiritus* and the adjective *spiritalis,* as translations of the Greek *pneuma* and *pneumatikos* respectively. In medieval times, the Latin word *spiritualitas* gave rise to such forms as *esperitalité, espirituauté,* and *espérituaulté* in French, and *spiritualty* or *spirituality* in English.[4]

In Pauline theology, *pneuma* or *spiritus* are not contrasted with *soma* or *corpus (body),* but with *sarx* or *caro (flesh).* In other words, "Spirit" or "spiritual" are not antonyms of "physical" or "material," but of "all that is opposed to the Spirit of God." Therefore, the contrast is between two ways of life or attitudes to life. "The 'spiritual' is what is under the influence of or is a manifestation of the Spirit of God."[5] The "carnal" is what is opposed to the working and guidance of the Spirit of God.[6] The Christian life is "life in the Spirit" (Gal 5:25).

Historical Development of Meaning

In the ninth century, a new meaning of spirituality was introduced by Fulda, most likely a monk, who used the word *spiritualitas* as opposed to *corporalitas* or *materialitas (materiality),* thereby changing the Pauline moral sense of the word to an entitative-psychological sense. This shift of meaning brought in the idea of disdain for the body and matter in the later movement related to spiritual life.[7] Then, in the twelfthth century, scholasticism made a sharp distinction between spirit and matter. The word "spiritual" was applied to intelligent creation, that is, mankind, as opposed to non-rational creation. Losing its original Pauline moral sense, "spirituality" adopted a new meaning more radically opposed to corporeality or matter. However, the new meaning did not replace the old meaning completely, but rather the two meanings co-existed in the thirteenth century.[8] For example, while in the majority of Thomas Aquinas' texts the word *spiritualitas* is related to the Pauline idea of life, according to the Holy Spirit or what is

---

4. Principe, "Toward Defining Spirituality," 44–46.

5. Sheldrake, *Spirituality & History,* 42.

6. Principe, "Toward Defining Spirituality," 45.

7. Ibid., 45.

8. Sheldrake, *Spirituality & History,* 43.

highest in the human, in a good number of texts, it is still used as opposite to corporeality or matter.[9] The thirteenth century was also the time that saw the split between theology and spirituality or between the reasoned expression of faith and its lived experience.[10]

In the seventeenth century the word "spiritualite" became established once again in France in reference to the spiritual life. It was used positively to express a personal, affective relationship with God. However, it was also used pejoratively of enthusiastic or quietistic movements[11] and eventually disappeared from the vocabulary of Roman Catholics in the eighteenth century due to a suspicion of those movements. Free religious groups outside mainline churches were the main users of it in the nineteenth century. In the early decades of the twentieth century, "spirituality" appeared once again among Roman Catholics in France and passed into English through translations. The increased use of it in this period was related to the attempts to distinguish dogma and the study of spiritual life as well as an increasing emphasis on religious consciousness and the experiential dimension of Christian life.[12] Historian Philip Sheldrake points out that in recent decades there has been more emphasis on human experience in the general approach to theology, and this brought about a movement from the static "spiritual theology" to the more fluid "spirituality."[13] Among Protestants, the word "spirituality" came to be used from about 1960.[14]

Spiritual Theology vs. Spirituality

In the early patristic and early medieval periods, before the later split between it and theology, spirituality was the purpose of all study, both sacred and profane. Spirituality was lived theology and theology was articulate spirituality. In the High Middle Ages, however, this integrated approach was destroyed as theology moved from the monastery to the university and became a philosophically elaborated academic and scientific specialization. Mystical theology as an experiential knowledge, and wisdom of God

---

9. Principe, "Toward Defining Spirituality," 46.

10. Schneiders, "Christian Spirituality: Definition, Methods and Types," 2.

11. Sheldrake, *Spirituality & History*, 43; Principe, "Toward Defining Spirituality," 46.

12. Sheldrake, *Spirituality & History*, 43–44.

13. Ibid., 41.

14. Holt, *Thirsty for God*, 8.

acquired in prayer through scriptural meditation, became an exclusively monastic experience. Sheldrake explains the period as follows:

> The period from the twelfth century onwards in the West saw a process of development in the approach to the spiritual life which may be characterised as one of separation and division. There was, first of all, a division of spirituality from theology, of affectivity from knowledge. Secondly, there was a gradual limitation of interest to interiority or subjective spiritual experience. In other words, spirituality became separated from social praxis and ethics. And finally, although it has been touched upon only indirectly, there was a separation of spirituality from liturgy, the personal from the communal, expressed most graphically by a new attention to the structures of personal prayer and meditation. Through these divisions and separations, an interest developed in specific experiences and activities: prayer, contemplation and mysticism.[15]

Protestant orthodoxy became suspicious of the word "mysticism" after the Reformation because of the suggested elitism or paranormal experience not rooted in the Scriptures. "Piety" was preferred, meaning a daily reading of Scriptures and prayer. Anglicans preferred the terms "devotion," "inner life," and "life of perfection" to "piety."[16] From the eighteenth century to the mid-twentieth century, "spiritual theology" as a discipline emerged in Catholic seminaries as a sub-discipline of theology. According to Sandra Schneiders:

> It [spiritual theology] was defined as the "science of perfection" and usually subdivided into "ascetical theology," which dealt with the active stages of the spiritual life (the purgative and illuminative ways) and "mystical theology" which dealt with the higher reaches of contemplation (the unitive way). The discipline of spiritual theology was deductive in method, prescriptive in character, and concerned primarily with the practice of personal prayer and asceticism.[17]

A new discipline that came to be called "spirituality" rather than "spiritual theology" emerged in the academy in the 1970s and '80s. The emergence of this new discipline was due to interest in the search of

15. Sheldrake, *Spirituality & History*, 52.

16. Schneiders, "Approach to the Study of Christian Spirituality," 22; Schneiders, "Christian Spirituality: Definition, Methods and Types," 2

17. Schneiders, "Christian Spirituality: Definition, Methods and Types," 2.

meaning, transcendence, personal integration and social transformation.[18] The transition from spiritual theology to spirituality is well summarized by Sheldrake:

> There has been a major shift in Western theology towards a more serious reflection on human experience in its cultural particularity and therefore pluriformity. This in turn provoked a movement away from a static approach to the Christian life, embodied in an analytical and abstract spiritual theology, and towards a more dynamic and inclusive concept, namely "spirituality." I would also add that this new concept has gained considerable ecumenical acceptance and so spirituality now tends to be eclectic in its approach as it seeks to draw upon the riches of a shared Christian heritage rather than to limit itself to a sectarian understanding of "life in the Spirit." Spirituality, in other words, is far better expression of Catholicity than any previous spiritual theology.[19]

Definition of Spirituality

Besides some definitions given initially, I want to revisit the definition of spirituality here. Spirituality has two levels of definition. First, spirituality can be defined as "the lived experience of Christian faith and discipleship."[20] This definition is an emic view (intrinsic to Christianity's self understanding) rather than etic (derived from outside the phenomenon).[21] The contemporary understanding of Christian spirituality on this level emphasizes the holistic and personal involvement of the person in the spiritual quest.[22] Schneiders asserts:

> It is the way some person understood and lived, within his or her historical context, a chosen religious ideal in sensitivity to the realm of the spirit of the transcendent. For Christians such a life would be one influenced, as Paul taught, by the Holy Spirit or Spirit of God incorporating the person into Jesus Christ as Head, through whom he or she has access to the Father in a life of faith, hope, love, and service.[23]

18. Ibid., 3.
19. Sheldrake, *Spirituality & History*, 57–58.
20. Holder, *The Blackwell Companion to Christian Spirituality*, 5.
21. Ibid.
22. Schneiders, "Christian Spirituality: Definition, Methods and Types," 1–2.
23. Principe, "Toward Defining Spirituality," 48.

The second level of spirituality is spirituality as an academic discipline. Schneiders, one of the most significant figures in the emergence of Christian spirituality as an academic discipline, defines spirituality as "the experience of conscious involvement in the project of life-integration through self-transcendence toward the horizon of ultimate value one perceives." Schneiders further identifies "the horizon of ultimate value" in Christian spirituality as the "*triune God* revealed in *Jesus Christ* to whom *Scripture* normatively witnessed and whose life is communicated to the *believer* by the *Holy Spirit* making her or him a child of God" [emphasis mine]. This academic discipline of spirituality as a research discipline has the expansion of knowledge and understanding of the God-human relationship as its specific objective.[24]

Three Approaches to the Study of Christian Spirituality

Three approaches have been recognized in the study of spirituality as an academic discipline: historical, theological, and anthropological. In addition to approaching the subject matter historically, the first approach supplies the context for and constitutes the positive data upon which other studies exercise their inquiries. As stated, spirituality as lived experience takes place in time and space. It occurs within specific cultural contexts in interacting with the forces operating within the same context and being influenced by what and who preceded it. In some sense, all studies of spirituality can be said to be historical.[25]

Using theological categories to examine the practice of Christian faith, the second approach allows spirituality to be regarded as a form of practical theology. Although this approach is closer to a nineteenth- and early-twentieth century understanding of spiritual theology, it is more holistic and integrated than the dogma and prescription of its predecessor.[26] About the theological approach's contribution to spirituality, Schneiders states:

> The contribution of the theological approach to spirituality is that it keeps the specifically Christian character of the discipline in focus and reminds everyone in the field, whatever their preferred approach, that Christianity is a specific faith tradition that has

24. Schneiders, "Approach to the Study of Christian Spirituality," 16–17.

25. Ibid., 21.

26. Schneiders, *Christian Spirituality*, 4.

content and dynamics it does not share with other traditions, even those with analogous concerns.[27]

Finally, the anthropological approach focuses on the interpretation of Christian religious experience to generate responses to contemporary questions rather than historical or theological ones. This approach uses methodologies that are always interdisciplinary, with different disciplines taking the lead role in different research projects depending on the researcher's primary question.[28] Schneiders explains about this approach:

> Whereas historical and theological approaches frame the questions raised about complex spiritual phenomenon from the standpoint of those particular disciplines, the anthropological approach addresses the phenomenon in terms of what the researcher wants to know about religious experience, which may not be primarily historical or theological.[29]

In the study of spirituality, the three approaches are not mutually exclusive, but complementary to one another. All Christian experience is human, historically situated in a particular socio-cultural setting, and rooted in a theological tradition of Christian faith. In this book all three approaches have been used to deal with the subject of African Christian spirituality. Part 1 deals with biblical and Christian historical data for the subject. Part 2 takes up historical contribution to the current topic, and Part 3 follows with the cultural dimension of African Christian spirituality. The overall approach is theological.

Characteristics of Spirituality

The contemporary understanding of spirituality has several distinctive features. First, spirituality is not simply the prescriptive application of absolute or dogmatic principles to life. Rather, it tries to understand the complex mystery of human growth in the context of a living relationship with God. Second, it does not concern only the interior life but seeks an integration of all aspects of human life and experience, both human and religious values.[30] Third, spirituality is not only informative but transformative. Through

---

27. Schneiders, "Approach to the Study of Christian Spirituality," 25.

28. Ibid., 27–28.

29. Ibid., 28.

30. Sheldrake, *Spirituality & History*, 58–59.

the wisdom gained from texts, traditions, and practices, such questions are asked, "What difference does this make?" or "What could or should our response be?" This transformative dimension of spirituality involves judgment and appropriation.[31] Fourth, spirituality is interdisciplinary, interreligious, ecumenical, and cross cultural. In other words, it is holistic. Therefore, the context within which spiritual experience is studied is anthropologically inclusive.[32] Fifth, Scripture and the history of Christianity are two constitutive disciplines that supply the positive data of Christian religious experience, as well as its norm and hermeneutical context.[33] Finally, I would like to finish this part by quoting Sheldrake:

> A central feature is that spirituality derives its identity from the Christian belief that as human beings we are capable of entering into a relationship with God who is both transcendent and, at the same time, indwelling in the heart of all created things. This relationship is lived out, not in isolation, but in a community of believers that is brought into being by commitment to Christ and sustained by the active presence of the Spirit of God in each and in the community as a whole. . . . In other words, contemporary Christian spirituality is explicitly Trinitarian, Christological, and ecclesial.[34]

---

31. Sheldrake, "Spirituality and Its Critical Methodology," 23.
32. Berling, "Christian Spirituality: Intrinsically Interdisciplinary," 40.
33. Ibid., 39.
34. Sheldrake, *Spirituality & History*, 60–61.

PART ONE

Biblical and Christian Traditional Spiritualities

2

Biblical Spirituality

THE SCRIPTURES AND THE history of Christianity supply the positive data of Christian religious experience as well as its norm and hermeneutical context.[1] The term "spirituality" encompasses both Christian and non-Christian spiritualities. Christian spirituality treats specifically "Christian" spirituality as seen in chapter 1, and it is essentially *biblical*:

> In some sense, for a Christian, all spirituality is fundamentally *biblical*. The life of faith of Christians has been and continues to be inspired and nourished by the encounter with the God mediated by the Scriptures. . . . In short, our faith, our spirituality, is *biblical* because through the Scriptures we are schooled in the ways of the biblical God.[2]

Three meanings of the biblical spirituality are distinguished. The first is biblical spirituality as the "spiritualities that come to expression in the Bible and witness to patterns of relationship with God that instruct and encourage our own religious experience."[3]

> We find in the Bible a variety of biblical spiritualities: the dialogical spirituality of the deuteronomistic tradition in which God intervenes directly and participates in Israel's history, the profoundly Christocentric spirituality of Paul, the contemplative Jesus-centred spirituality of John, the ecclesiastical spirituality of the pastorals, the apocalyptic spirituality of Revelation. In the Psalms we find expressed in prayer and poetry the full range of Old Testament

1. Schneiders, "The Study of Christian Spirituality," 3.
2. Bowe, *Biblical Foundations of Spirituality*, 11.
3. Schneiders, "Biblical Spirituality," 134–36.

spiritualities that have been practiced by Christians in the light of
the mystery of Christ.[4]

The second meaning of biblical spirituality is "a pattern of Christian
life deeply imbued with the spirituality(ies) of the Bible, and the third
meaning as "a transformative process of personal and communal engagement with the biblical text."[5] These second and third meanings of biblical
spirituality are rather contemporary expressions of biblical spirituality. This
chapter will focus on the first meaning of biblical spirituality; that is, the
spiritualities that come to be expressed in the Bible and which instruct our
own religious experience.

Regarding the transformative process of biblical spirituality, John Donahue, following Schneiders, argues for a faithful reading of the text in its
original context, which results in appropriation and transformation based
on the contemporary hermeneutic theory of Georg Gadamar and Paul
Ricoeur. According to Ricoeur, the process of interpretation starts with a
"naïve grasping of the meaning of the text as a whole," moving to the explanation of the text through the historical-critical method, and culminating
in a "second naiveté" (Ricoeurs' term); that is, an informed explanation of
the text. However, the meaning of the text is not limited to the intention of
the original author but engenders a new self-understanding through the
process of appropriation in a dialectical relationship between authorial
intention and subsequent meaning.[6] Schneiders claims that true transformation is delayed until a faith community responds to the preached word
and liturgy and is committed to transformative action. Therefore, biblical spirituality is focused on descriptive studies of biblical texts, issues of
hermeneutics, appropriation, and transformation.[7]

Old Testament Spirituality

It may be the case that historical traditions of spiritual life and theological
treatises serve as a focal point of Christian spirituality, but omitting the Old
Testament is a serious mistake. The Old Testament is an essence of and a rich
source for Christian spirituality. But technically speaking, it is impossible
to talk about *the* Old Testament spirituality because of the multiplicity and

4. Ibid., 135.
5. Ibid., 136.
6. Donahue, "The Quest for Biblical Spirituality," 83–85.
7. Schneiders, "Biblical Spirituality," 137–41.

diversity portrayed in the Old Testament. It is more correct to talk about Old Testament *spiritualities*. It is beyond the scope of this book to describe various spiritualities of the Old Testament's figures, authors, and books, so I would rather discuss a "spirituality which is informed and nourished by the Old Testament." The focus of this kind of spirituality would be on the Old Testament's contribution to a sound spirituality today.[8] A point that needs to be made is the importance of Jewish perspective on the Old Testament: "The fact that the Christian Bible includes texts which originated within and are still shared by the Jewish community is massively significant."[9]

Themes of the Old Testament Spirituality

The following themes provide a skeleton picture of the Old Testament spirituality, which is based on the Torah but extends to the Prophets and the Writings.

Creation

> *The doctrine of creation, affirming the distinction between the Creator and his creature, is the starting point of true religion. There is no existence apart from God, and the Creator can only be known truly through revelation. . . . This creation is properly said to be* ex nihilo, *"out of nothing," thus preserving the distinction of the world in its dependence on God. The Triune God is the author of creation rather than any intermediary. The outgoing works of God are indivisible though it is appropriate to distinguish an economy of tasks in the Godhead so that the Father is spoken of as the first cause, the Son as the one by whom all things are created, and the Holy Spirit as the immanent cause of life and movement in the universe. . . . The creation proceeds from the Father through the Son and in the Spirit. . . . The purpose and goal of creation is to be found solely in God's will and glory. . . . A doctrine of creation is one of the foundational building blocks of a biblical and Christian worldview. Creation is neither to be deified nor despoiled but as the "theatre of God's glory" to be delighted in and used in a stewardly manner. It is God's good creation.*[10]

8. Barton, "The Old Testament," 48.

9. Stevens and Green, *Living the Story*, 52.

10. Bavinck, *Reformed Dogmatics*, 406.

The Old Testament declares that God is the source of all that exists: "The realization of the council of God begins with creation. Creation is the initial act and foundation of all divine revelation and therefore the foundation of all religious and ethical life as well."[11] Creation is divided into a spiritual and a material realm, into heaven and earth, into things in heaven and things on earth, things visible and things invisible, that the spiritual world is in communion with the visible world, and that the deepest cause of all things do not lie within the circle of visible things.[12] A Jewish notion of creation is somewhat different from the Reformed position: "It is not accidental . . . that classical Hebrew lacks such a distinction [between the material world and the realm of the spirit]. For Jewish spirituality, there is only one world that is simultaneously material *and* spiritual."[13]

In creation it is evident that creation is the work of the triune God. "Let us make man in our image" (Gen 1:26). The Scriptures also attribute the act of creation to God exclusively (Gen 1:11; Isa 40:12f; 44:24; 45:12; Job 9:5–10; 38:2f). Although the Jewish notion of God was monotheistic and the doctrine of Trinity is not explicitly asserted in the Old Testament, the Scriptures, especially the New Testament, suggest the unity and the diversity of the three persons of God (Matt 28:19–20; John 1:33–34; 2 Cor 13:14; 1 Pet 1:1–2), and the church formulated the doctrine of Trinity in the patristic era in order to hold on to both the unity and diversity. Thus speaking of creation as an act of the triune God is more of a Christian interpretation of the Old Testament rather than the thoughts of its original writers. Furthermore, Christian theology unanimously attributes the work of creation to all three persons of the Trinity. God created all things through the Son (Ps 33:6; Prov 8:22; John 1:3; 5:17; 1 Cor 8:6; Col 1:15–17; Heb 1:3) and through the Spirit (Gen 1:2; Ps 33:6; Job 26:13; 33:4; Ps 104:30; Isa 40:13; Luke 1:35). The Son and the Spirit are not the secondary forces but independent agents who fulfilled the work of creation with the Father.[14]

The narrative of Genesis 1:26–28 describes how human beings have been created in the image and likeness of God and thus share the divine stamp:

> The fact that Genesis 1:27 explicitly defines *adam* as "male and female" means that our contemporary claims about the mutual

11. Bavinck, *In the Beginning*, 24.

12. Ibid., 61–66.

13. Kushner, *Jewish Spirituality*, 10.

14. Bavinck, *In the Beginning*, 40.

dignity of women and men in their capacity to image God are entirely correct and faithful to the biblical revelation. Moreover, this affirmation of human dignity, male and female, is essential to the very fabric of creation itself and its enduring permanence.[15]

Created in the image of God, humanity is also unique:

> The uniqueness of self and the preciousness of personality are indispensable elements of Old Testament spirituality. This view of life forms the basis for contrasts between the Israelites and pagan culture. It stands behind the ethical-behavioural allowances and prohibitions of the Law. It is the foundation of the prophetic call to justice and mercy for even the "least" persons in a society.[16]

In the creation story, there is an essential relationship factor between God and humans. This relationship and intimacy with God, however, does not violate the mystery of God or the autonomy of man.[17] In his sovereignty God also commanded humans to have dominion over the whole creation (Gen 1:28). Therefore, created in the image of God, human beings have the capacity to relate not only to God but also to others and to all other creation. All these relationships are characterized by love, respect, and service, and in interpersonal relations, morality, fairness, and concern.[18] "*Our* well-being deepens as we learn to reverence the rest of creation and to treat all others with the profound respect due to them as creatures, like us, fashioned in the image of God."[19]

With emphasis on the unity of creation, Harper summarizes creation as one of the main Old Testament spiritualities:

> Old Testament spirituality as revealed in creation is that amazing and awesome mixture of allowance and accountability, liberty and limitation, freedom, and fidelity. Thus our very creation becomes a major element of our spirituality. Such a spirituality saves us from any notions of dualism. Such a spirituality clearly reveals the value and sacredness of life. Through what we might call a spirituality of creation, we see our interconnected-ness, mutual dependency, and moral responsibility. And we recognize that true life is not being

15. Bowe, *Biblical Foundations of Spirituality*, 37.
16. Harper, "Old Testament Spirituality," 316.
17. Barton, "The Old Testament," 56–57.
18. Harper, "Old Testament Spirituality," 317.
19. Bowe, *Biblical Foundations of Spirituality*, 41.

swept along by some kind of cosmic energy, but rather is being sustained by an intimate relationship with a personal God.[20]

Covenant

The creator God, who made persons in the image of God, is not satisfied with general relationship. Through the introduction of covenant, the divine-human relationship is intensified and particularized.[21] Whereas a contract is an agreement to exchange goods or services upon certain terms, a covenant is not about *doing* so much as *being*.[22] The Hebrew word for covenant is *berit*. It is the word that captures the heart of Israel's religious beliefs. Covenants of various kinds existed in the ancient Near East. Some were made between equal partners and others were made between unequal partners, such as those treaties common among the ancient Hittites. The lord promised to protect the vassals, who in turn pledged loyalty to their lord. This type of covenant may have become a model for Israelites' covenant with YHWH.[23] The complex tradition of covenant and commands began when Israel arrived in Sinai. In Exodus 19–24, the proclamation of commands by YHWH is followed by the oath of allegiance to YHWH by Israel, thereby binding Israel to YHWH in obedience.[24]

The covenantal theme of the Old Testament is argued as follows:

> It was at Sinai that God sealed this relationship and established an everlasting covenant with them. . . . Built into the literary structure of the Pentateuch, this covenantal theme applies not only to the encounter between God and Moses at Sinai. It also provides the framework and the theological basis for understanding God's earlier promises made with Noah (Gen 9:8–17) and with Abraham (Gen 12:1–3; 15:5–7, 18–21; 17), as well as the continuing reinterpretation of covenant traditions with David in the period of the monarchy and with those who would rearticulate covenant theology in succeeding generations.[25]

20. Harper, "Old Testament Spirituality," 318.

21. Ibid.

22. Stevens and Green, *Living the Story*, 58.

23. Bowe, *Biblical Foundations of Spirituality*, 70.

24. Brueggemann, *An Introduction to the Old Testament*, 61.

25. Bowe, *Biblical Foundations of Spirituality*, 70.

The covenant between God and man reveals a bonding between God and those who entered into the covenant: "I will be their God and they will be my people" (Exod 6:6–7; Lev 26:12). This bonding that began in Gen 9:16 with Noah continues with the patriarchs and reaches its climax with the nation Israel. Closeness and intimacy are the hallmarks, and various covenantal images are presented in the Old Testament: Shekinah glory in the Tabernacle, intimacy between husband and wife as analogous between God and Israel, and a child nursed at a mother's breast.[26] One thing that is noteworthy is the God who says "the whole earth is mine" (Exod 19:5) is the same covenant-making God who takes Israel as his own. According to Walter Brueggemann, "This 'scandal of particularity' is decisive for faith in the Old Testament."[27]

However, this covenantal bonding is never automatic and guaranteed. Individuals such as David (Ps 30:7) and Jeremiah, as well as the whole nation (Ps 44:23–24), experience the absence of God.[28] The closeness and intimacy must be guarded and maintained with vigilance. Brueggemann lists three appropriate human responsive actions:

> In response to the One who makes all things new, a faithful human action is *hope*: to live in sure and certain confidence of promises, to function each day trusting that God's promises and purposes will not fail. . . . In response to the One who speaks, faithful human action is to *listen* . . . to concede that we are subjects to Another who legitimately addresses us by name and tells us who we are. . . . In response to the God who holds fast to us, who holds us accountable and responsible, faithful human action involves *obedient answering*. Obedient answering consists in action that may be summarized as the doing of justice and righteousness, loyalty and graciousness.[29]

God's act does not end with covenant making, but extends to keeping the covenant. As a result of a covenant relationship with God, human life is redefined. Israel received their identity, personhood, and being from YHWH, who held fast to the covenant. They are in a new context of promise and claim, of surprise and amazement.[30] As a covenant people,

26. Harper, "Old Testament Spirituality," 318.

27. Brueggemann, *An Introduction to the Old Testament*, 65.

28. Barton, "The Old Testament," 51–52.

29. Brueggemann, *The Psalms*, 157–58.

30. Ibid., 156, 164.

therefore, Israel had enough faith content and experience to render any movement toward other religions unnecessary. Seifert puts the position of Israel in perspective, "Going to other world religions for decisively different insights is like carrying a lantern to a neighbor's house to borrow a match. We already have the essential fire in our own keeping."[31] What is crucial to understand, though, is as God's covenant people, Israel had to be engaged in mission. Harper explains this perspective by saying, "The goal has been to incorporate as many as possible into the covenant community. Thus, to be in covenant is to be reaching out."[32]

> Because God is God, there are purposes to which we belong that are larger than our purposes (Isa 55:6–9). Or viewed another way, the Bible never holds to the notion that we exist as prepurpose persons and then may choose a purpose in life. On the contrary, our being called into being as persons already is decisive for our humanness. Biblical anthropology is from the beginning *mission-al*. Biblical faith asserts that being grounded in this other One who has purposes that are not our purposes characterizes our existence as missional, that is, as claimed for and defined by the One who gives us life. The metaphor of covenant thus poses the central reality of our life in terms of vocation. Vocation means we are called by this One, who in calling us to *be* calls us to *service*.[33]

However, Israel was satisfied with their faith content and did not fulfill its mission imperative, thereby God opened up the New Covenant with the Christian church.[34]

The primary intent of the covenant was to ensure blessing upon Israel. Curses are the result of disobedience, Israel's breaking of the covenant relationship. The ruptured relationship between God and human is restored through Israel's acceptance of the covenant and living it out, which results in blessings upon them.[35] Brueggemann talks about "dangerous freedom" of covenant parties, humans and God. God claims the freedom to act without stricture, and the community of faith also has freedom. Neither is free to exercise freedom that does not take the other into account. Covenant

---

31. Seifert, *Explorations*, 16.
32. Harper, "Old Testament Spirituality," 319.
33. Brueggermann, *The Psalms*, 162.
34. Harper, "Old Testament Spirituality," 319.
35. Ibid., 320–21.

reality indicates living by faith in the Other who made the covenant. Covenantal people live on the edge.[36]

> Covenantal people always live at the edge of the curse with real dangers and threats. Covenanted people always live at the brink of blessing, where the break of surprise and gift is about to come. Faith means to place ourselves in that vortex where life is granted, received, and risked.[37]

Community

The Old Testament spirituality treats community as an authentic expression of spirituality. Both the law and the prophets are for the sake of people. There was no such thing as a private spiritual advancement. The patriarchs, judges, prophets, kings, and priests were all for the people. There was no understanding of faith and life apart from the community. Jews are the people who were grounded in the revelation of one God as one nation under one standard.[38] Kushner describes Jewish spirituality:

> Upon waking in the morning and upon retiring each night, Jews recite the passage from Deuteronomy 6:4 known as the *Shema*: "Hear O Israel, the Lord our God, the Lord is one." In so doing, they not only proclaim that God is one; they remind themselves that everything and everyone is connected—that it's all One.[39]

The emphasis on community puts forth some important aspects of spirituality. First, the identity as a Jew is formed in the community from the family outward to the entire nation, even to those living outside of national boundary. Second, this closely-knit community of the king, the priest, prophets, and people requires interdependence. A breakdown anywhere in the line causes the entire nation to suffer. Righteousness and holiness are not only personal characters, but also interpersonal qualities in the community. In this community of mutual interdependence, immorality, injustice, and oppression cannot be tolerated to ensure God's blessing, let alone the survival of community. Third, therefore God raises up judges, priests, kings, and prophets at various times to reveal his will and to sustain the

36. Brueggermann, *The Psalms*, 163–64.

37. Ibid., 165.

38. Harper, "Old Testament Spirituality," 321–22.

39. Kushner, *Jewish Spirituality*, 34

community of his people. Without discernment and will to carry out the will of God, Israel's community is destroyed.[40]

The psalms of the Old Testament also emphasize corporate character:

> A great many psalms and prayers are plainly corporate in character . . . where the speaker, in the first person plural, must be the congregation at worship. . . . [T]his individual is a personification of the community. . . . [M]any of the psalms make much better sense if understood as "cultic" or liturgical poetry, in which the "I" who speaks is the voice of the congregation . . . than if they are treated as religious lyrics for use in private prayers.[41]

The Old Testament teaches us of the necessity of community. There is no sound spirituality which leaves out community. "Community is an essential ingredient for every Christian, regardless of status, maturity, or experience. It is at one and the same time a provider of an essential element in spirituality, and a protector against excesses and pitfalls."[42]

The Presence of God

Through creation, covenant relationships, and in Israelite community, God was present. Through the Law, Prophets, and wisdom tradition, God was there:

> The Torah sets out the terms on which God will be with his people; the histories show from concrete examples how his presence can be forfeited, and how gracious must be the God who never lets his absence from an unworthy people become permanent; the prophets look forward to the day when God will never be or even seem absent again; and the psalms reflect on all these aspects of presence and absence as they affect both the worshiping community and the individual at prayer. Many psalms speak of a sense of God's temporary absence, and of a hope for his reappearance.[43]

A good example of his presence is found in the book of Exodus. The Israelite community experienced the presence of God in wilderness after the exodus. The "priestly tradition" that refers to a community of interpretation in ancient Israel was primarily concerned with practices of holiness

40. Harper, "Old Testament Spirituality," 321–22.
41. Barton, "The Old Testament," 48–49.
42. Harper, "Old Testament Spirituality," 322.
43. Barton, "The Old Testament," 56.

and orderliness that make possible the habitation of YHWH in Israel. To them, hosting the Holy One in the Tabernacle is no small or casual matter, requiring the practice of symmetry, order, discipline, and beauty.[44] As God is present, he is also absent. The God of the Old Testament is a hidden God:

> If even Moses could see only God's back, there was small hope that anyone else could see his face and live! For practical purposes, therefore, the God of the Old Testament is a hidden God, hidden not through any weakness or inadequacy, but because of his very glory and the unworthiness of his human creatures. Yet the God who is hidden from sight in the cloud of his own glory can be *known* by the person who does not seek to *see* him, but rather to obey his will: "Thus says the high and lofty one who inhabits eternity, whose name is holy: 'I dwell in the high and holy place, with him also who is a contrite heart and humble spirit'" (Isa 57:15).[45]

Thus the essentiality of the Old Testament challenges us to a deeper intimacy with God and trust of his absolute faithfulness:

> In creation we are invited to the richness of the cosmos and the sacredness of life made in the image of God. Through the covenant we are encouraged to bond ourselves to the living God, which necessarily calls us into community with all other persons who have done the same. Thus formed, we are challenged to deepen our intimacy with God and to direct our energies toward the service of others.[46]

Prophetic Spirituality

The prophets were people who had an encounter with the living God, so their influence and power were derived from their direct contact with God and the resultant insight. Their concern was mainly the present, not the distant future: present realities, the implications of present actions, and their consequences in the immediate future. They stood on the middle ground between God and the people—crying out to God on behalf of the people and pleading with the people on behalf of God. Prophets also played an essential social function lending divine legitimization to the dominant social-political group or challenging the status quo for social changes.[47]

44. Brueggemann, *An Introduction to the Old Testament*, 65–66.
45. Barton, "The Old Testament," 57.
46. Harper, "Old Testament Spirituality," 324.
47. Bowe, *Biblical Foundations of Spirituality*, 83–85.

The characteristics of prophets were many. They were summoned by God to an irrevocable calling (Ezek 2:1–3, 8) and had lives bathed in prayer (Dan 9:4–16). They had great courage to confront kings and queens and false prophets, risking their own lives (Isa 22:11–12; Ezek 34:1). Prophets sometimes had honest doubts and complained to God (Jer 4:9–10). Sins of their day deeply disturbed them—mainly idolatry, immorality, and injustice. Prophets were people of passion.[48] Abraham Heschel looks into the heart of the prophet:

> The fundamental experience of the prophet is a fellowship with the feelings of God, a *sympathy with the divine pathos,* a communication with the divine consciousness which comes about through the prophet's reflection of, or participation in, the divine pathos. The typical prophetic state of mind is one of being taken up into the heart of the divine pathos. . . . He lives not only his personal life, but also the life of God. The prophet hears God's voice and feels His heart. He tries to impart the pathos of the message together with its logos. As an imparter his soul overflows, speaking as he does out of the fullness of his sympathy.[49]

Justice and Righteousness

Prophets' hearts were aflame for justice and righteousness. The primary way to serve God for them was not in rituals, but through justice, righteousness, and love.[50] Justice here is relational:

> Ancient Israel "does not distinguish between right and duty," and *mishpat,* the word for justice, denotes what a person may claim as well as what he is bound to do to others. In other words, it signifies, both *right* and *duty.* Justice is an interpersonal relationship, involving a claim and a responsibility. . . . In its fundamental meaning, *mishpat* refers to all actions which contribute to maintaining the covenant, namely, the true relation between man and man, and between God and man.[51]

---

48. Stevens and Green, *Living the Story*, 66.

49. Heschel, *The Prophets*, 26.

50. Stevens and Green, *Living the Story*, 68.

51. Heschel, *The Prophets*, 210.

Prophets were those who had breathless impatience with injustice, and their ear perceived the silent sigh.[52] They were convinced that "the most minor violation of the covenant bond was an affront in the eyes of God."[53] The prophet was the one who constantly judged in the daily life because he was expected to continually act so as to uphold the covenant, which was the whole of the common life of the community. Everything in which this kind of judging manifests itself is called *mishpat*.[54]

In Love with God

Prophets were in love with God. Take Hosea for example. Hosea's marriage to Gomer is a proof of the incarnational medium through which he gave and received a message about covenant love. His love for his wife gave him a glimpse of the heart of God, and the unconditional love of God made him look into his own heart with sorrows of an impossible marriage. For Hosea, knowing God meant courting, betrothal, and the renewal of the marriage covenant, and the word used for this covenant love was *hesed* as Hosea says, "For I desire mercy [*hesed*], not sacrifice, and acknowledgment of God rather than burnt offering."[55]

A clear description of the prophets of the Old Testament is as follows:

> They were persons who had been touched by God in profoundly personal and intimate ways. They felt the coal sear their tongues (Isa 6:6), sensed God's hand touch their mouths (Jer 1:9), and felt the fire of God's word within them (Jer 20:9). They saw the world through God's eyes, felt its pain through God's heart, and challenged its abuses as if with God's mighty arm. Like YHWH, they could not be deaf to the cry of people in pain; their sensitivity to evil was raw and uncompromising. These were people who found the courage to hope beyond hope and who spent themselves to convey that hope in the face of despair. These were the poets and dreamers, the ones who could see beyond the surface of things into a deeper reality in the present and into a future time still to come. These were the faithful ones who endured affliction, distress,

---

52. Heschel, *The Prophets*, 4, 9.

53. Bowe, *Biblical Foundations of Spirituality*, 85–86.

54. Pederson, quoted in Heschel, *The Prophets*, 210.

55. Stevens and Green, *Living the Story*, 68–69; Hos 6:6

and persecution and who paid a heavy price for their courageous words.[56]

Wisdom Tradition

In these books, we find a tradition called the blessing tradition, in which God is viewed primarily as the source of blessing and providential care.[57] In the blessing tradition, God does not intervene only at dramatic moments of crisis and need, but is always present in the midst of the world and sustains it, whereas in the saving tradition God acts in history to save and rescue people. The blessing tradition is fascinated with the pursuit of *wisdom* as a central emphasis and is therefore also called the wisdom tradition. Wisdom observes the world and carefully reflects on it to discern the harmony and order in it. It also pursues a practical and comprehensive ethic and behavior consonant with its context.[58]

The book of Proverbs draws its sayings from all different sources to entertain, to instruct, and to edify. They inculcate virtues to live by, such as diligence (Prov 10:4), humility (Prov 11:2), or truthfulness (Prov 12:20). The wise choose the right action among the competing ways and many possibilities of life. The wisdom of Proverbs divides the world between the "wise/righteous" and the "foolish/wicked." The wise show humility, self-discipline, generosity, hard work, and prudence, while the foolish are arrogant, undisciplined, selfish, lazy, and lack judgment. "In the daily rhythms of life each one must choose between the ways of the wise and the ways of the foolish. In choosing the wise path we choose the path of life."[59]

Job represents the gnawing questions of the meaning of suffering by the righteous. The normal theological premise is that the good and righteous actions bring reward while sinful living brings punishment. But in the case of Job, this argument did not work. The righteous can suffer. But

---

56. Bowe, *Biblical Foundations of Spirituality*, 105.

57. The books of the Bible called "the Writing" designate all the books of the Jewish Bible, not part of the "Law and the Prophets." In the Hebrew Bible they are (1) the three great poetic books of Psalms, Job, and Proverbs; (2) the "Five Scrolls" of Ruth, Esther, Ecclesiastes, Lamentations, and the Song of Solomon; (3) a revisionist historical corpus of 1 and 2 Chronicles, Ezra, and Nehemiah; and (4) a single apocalyptic scroll, Daniel (Brueggemann, *An Introduction to the Old Testament*, 5). The Protestant Bible, however, lists Job, Psalms, Proverbs, Ecclesiastes, and Song of Solomon as the Wisdom literature.

58. Bowe, *Biblical Foundations of Spirituality*, 48–49, 109–10.

59. Ibid., 114–15.

God did not answer Job's questions about the meaning of suffering. The only answer was the conviction that God cares for those who suffer and even visits and stays with them. Job's teaching is not about *why* we suffer but about how we must relate to God in our suffering.[60] One of the lessons that Job learns is that the God he thought he knew is different from the God who had been watching over him all along. A new knowledge of God dawned on him. After all, the mystery of God is the mystery of silence and wisdom.[61]

In Ecclesiastes we hear a skeptical believer. The most repeated phrase of this book, "vanity of vanities, all is vanity!" is used thirty-eight times. The speaker recognizes the "ambiguities and contradictions of human experience."[62] Nothing satisfies and nothing fulfils. Only when one has genuinely given up on everything can one become a candidate for growth in grace and be prepared to hear the end of the matter, which is "Fear God, and keep his commandments; for that is the whole duty of everyone" (Eccl 12:13).

Song of Songs gives us yet another element of wisdom in the Bible. It is the wisdom of love. Both Jews and Christians interpreted the Song of Songs as the love between the Lord and the people of God, or between Christ and the church. However, "All scholars today would agree that the author of the text did not write an allegory. He wrote a meditation, in erotic poetic language, celebrating the joy and ecstasy of heterosexual love."[63] This actual, tangible, and passionate human love is a glimpse and reflection of the divine love.[64] Basically, "The Song has a clear and obvious relevance to the divine-human relationship. Throughout the Bible, our relationship is likened to a marriage."[65]

Psalms reveal the Hebrew conviction that wisdom is prayer:

> Capturing the sentiments of both the individual and the collective soul of its people, the Hebrew Psalter reflects Israel's faith, her longing for God, her identity as God's own people. The Psalter constitutes a whole "school of prayer," so to speak, not in the sense merely of a collection of prayers to be said but, rather, as a *lesson*

60. Ibid., 115–17.

61. Carney and Long, "Job," 723–24.

62. Bowe, *Biblical Foundations of Spirituality*, 118.

63. Ibid., 119.

64. Ibid., 120.

65. Longman III, "Song of Solomon," 965.

> *in how to pray*, as an illustration of the many motifs, aspirations, fears, and hopes that can be employed by a community of faith. A full spectrum of the human condition is covered in these prayers.[66]

Psalms are the "mirror" of life. They are the analogy of human experience. They let us gauge our own emotions and reactions through comparison with those of the psalmist and foster a more direct encounter with God.[67]

> [R]eading, hearing, meditating on, and praying with these texts enables people to clarify their own thoughts, feelings, and desires, and to learn how we may lay bare our desires before God, who desires life and not death. When we see our own hearts reflected in the cursing psalms, a process of genuine repentance and renewal can begin.[68]

Psalmists reveal every human emotion so honestly in the form of prayer that readers get shocked. Human meanness, spite, vengeance, and violence are the indications of both intensity of prayer and human sinfulness.[69] In this way, psalms help people articulate their own experiences and move toward deeper self-knowledge in relationship with God.[70] This is called "expressive function of the psalms."[71] Brueggemann discusses lament psalms that complain against articulate religious problems:

> The lament makes an assertion about God: that this dangerous, available God matters in *every dimension of life*. Where God's dangerous availability is lost because we fail to carry on our part of the difficult conversation, where God's vulnerability and passion are removed from our speech, we are consigned to anxiety and despair, and the world as we now have it becomes absolutized. . . . A God who must always be praised and never assaulted correlates with a development of "False Self" and an uncritical status quo. But a God who is available in assault correlates with the emergence of genuine self and the development of serious justice.[72]

The perspectives of psalms are both human-centered and Christ-centered. Many early Christians understood Christ's life through reflection on

66. Bowe, *Biblical Foundations of Spirituality*, 122.

67. Endres, "Psalms and Spirituality," 149–50.

68. Ibid., 152.

69. Bowe, *Biblical Foundations of Spirituality*, 122–23.

70. Endres, "Psalms and Spirituality," 151.

71. Nasuti, "The Sacramental Function of the Psalms," 80–81.

72. Brueggemann, *The Psalms*, 108.

particular psalms, and the Gospel writers found significant religious patterns in such psalms as Psalms 22, 31, and 69 and considered them as prophetic pointers to Jesus' life and ministry. These Christ-centered approaches to psalms "allow the language of a mediator to stand as analog, Jesus Christ, who prays a psalm or is 'prophesied' in a psalm," while human-centered approaches "establish suggestive connections between language addressed to God and our experience."[73]

Biblical wisdom is a gift from God, and it begins with the fear of God. There is also a deep humility associated with biblical wisdom, the kind Job experienced in the presence of the creator God. If we are truly wise, we get to know who we are before God. The wisdom tradition brings us to life fully lived and leads us to find God right in its midst.[74]

New Testament Spirituality

As was the case with the Old Testament spirituality, there is no single New Testament spirituality. Nevertheless, there is one central undeniable theme that runs through the whole New Testament: the incarnate, crucified, resurrected, and ascended Jesus. The New Testament spirituality can be defined as "what the early Christians did to put into practice what they believed. . . . It was what they did to respond to a world filled with the presence of God and the risen Christ."[75] The life, death, and resurrection of Jesus required responses, and the New Testament spirituality is the people's responses to what God was doing in Jesus the Christ.[76] In this sense, New Testament spirituality is decisively *Christological.*[77]

Another important characteristic of New Testament spirituality is its *communal* character, carrying on from the Old Testament: "Early Christian spirituality was conceived, nurtured, and realized within the body of Christ."[78] The Spirit was given to edify the body of Christ: "When the Spirit blows the result is never to create good individual Christians but members

---

73. Endres, "Psalms and Spirituality," 152–54.

74. Bowe, *Biblical Foundations of Spirituality*, 124–25.

75. Thurston, *Spiritual Life in the Early Church*, 3.

76. Thurston, "The New Testament in Christian Spirituality," 58.

77. Saunders, "'Learning Christ,'" 155.

78. Ibid., 158.

of a community. This became fundamental for Christian spirituality in the New Testament and was in direct line with the Old Testament mentality."[79]

The third crucial characteristic of New Testament spirituality is the *eschatological* perspective:

> Eschatological materials and perspectives pervade the New Testament. The authors articulate the sense that they are living in the last days, when God breaks into the world to inaugurate a "new creation," in order to cultivate within their audiences alternative ways of seeing reality-transformed imagination. Whether it be Jesus' proclamation of the reign of God, miracles and healings, Paul's talk of Spirit and new creation, expectations of Jesus' parousia, reports of resurrection, the anticipation of a last judgment, or the claim that God's power has come to definitive expression in the cross of Jesus, we are dealing with eschatological imagination. . . . The eschatological dimensions of spiritual formation in the New Testament . . . provided Christians with the means to resist the particular worldviews and practices of the cultures in which they lived. By envisioning the end of all that is taken for granted and presumed stable, the eschatological perspectives at work in New Testament spirituality served to "undermine the cultural system that masquerades as common sense."[80]

Gospels

There is one Jesus and four gospels, which are testimonies of faith in Christ. The Gospels are remembrances and imaginative expressions of profound encounters with the Son of God to establish him as the basis for faith, repentance, and new life. The main element of gospel spirituality is testimony of divine revelation in time, space, and person. This testimony is conveyed through the experience of the first followers of Jesus in the form of compelling gospel narratives.[81]

As the first of the New Testament books, Matthew is fundamentally biblical and traditional in shape and texture. Old Testament spiritualities continue in Matthew in regard to divine presence, covenantal morality, wholehearted devotion to the one true God, love of neighbor, coming of God in judgment to reward the righteous and to punish the disobedient,

---

79. Zizioulas, "The Early Christian Community," 27.

80. Saunders, "Learning Christ," 158–59.

81. Barton, "Synoptic Gospels," 608.

etc. The Old Testament and Judaism pervade the book of Matthew. However, there is discontinuity with the tradition no matter how precious it is. In Matthew, Jesus is the Son of God in whom the promise of God to Israel has been fulfilled and completed. The life of Jesus fulfils the Scripture (Matt 1:23; 2:6, 15, 18, 23), and the death of Jesus for the forgiveness of sins ushers in a new covenant (Matt 26:28). Matthean spirituality is Christocentric and eschatological as well; following Jesus, doing his commandments, responding to God's presence in Jesus, and living the life of the kingdom of heaven as Christ's disciple in the church characterize Matthean spirituality.[82]

The Gospel of Mark consists of "the death of Jesus."[83] "Marcan spirituality is *a dark, strenuous spirituality*. It is a story of passion from beginning to end."[84] For the first eight chapters, Jesus is alive and does mighty acts of God: healing, working miracles, casting out demons, and challenging religious leaders. However, in the middle of the eighth chapter the tone changes:

> In the middle of section the reader sees that this illusion is to be shattered. The figure of power is to be handed over to people who kill him. Yet, even this illusion is to be shattered, for the brokenness of the cross is itself broken by the message, "He is risen." And yet the final illusion is shattered. "Risen" does not mean a return in power and presence to the community. The community must continue to struggle with illusions (with false christs, false messiahs) until they finally "see" him (13:26; 16:7).[85]

In Mark 8:27—10:52, three passion predictions (Mark 8:31–33; 9:30–32; 10:32–34) appear interspersed with Jesus' teaching about "taking up the cross" (Mark 8:34), "true greatness" (Mark 9:34), and the "cost of discipleship" (Mark 10:35–45). These three chapters are the turning point in the book of Mark.[86] The second half of Mark is dominated by talk of death. As Jesus heads straight for Jerusalem, urgency, gravity and destination characterize the narrative. "No incident in his life is told with this much detail. There can hardly be any question about the intent of St. Mark: the plot and emphasis and meaning of Jesus is his death."[87] Christian spirituality

82. Barton, *The Spirituality of the Gospels*, 33–34.

83. Peterson, "Saint Mark," 331.

84. Barton, *The Spirituality of the Gospels*, 63.

85. Donahue, "Jesus as the Parable of God," 385.

86. Bowe, *Biblical Foundations of Spirituality*, 134.

87. Peterson, "Saint Mark," 332.

is, for Mark, *cruciform*: "If anyone wishes to come after Me, let him deny himself, and take up his cross, and follow Me. For whoever wishes to save his life shall lose it; but whoever loses his life for My sake and the gospel's shall save it" (Mark 8:34–35). "This is *the* most important aspect of Marcan spirituality."[88]

The two-volume work of Luke-Acts is the story of Jesus and Christian origin rooted in Israel for the salvation of the world. Lucan spirituality is characterized from beginning to end by the overshadowing presence of the Spirit with powerful manifestations. God is present in the person of his Son Jesus and is present in power at the end of the age as the Holy Spirit.[89]

One of the most prominent features of Lucan spirituality is joy. "It is St Luke's Gospel that is *par excellence* 'the Gospel of Joy.'"[90] "Lucan spirituality is about the joyful acknowledgment of the universal salvation made possible by the dawning of the age of the eschatological Spirit with the coming of the Messiah."[91] Repentance and conversion are also distinct characteristics of Lucan spirituality: "For Luke, 'repentance and forgiveness' together sum up the Christian good news."[92]

Jesus left with these words "that repentance for forgiveness of sins should be proclaimed in his name to all nations" (Luke 24:47), and in the book of Acts the call to repentance for forgiveness of sins is a constant refrain (Acts 2:38; 3:19; 5:31; 8:22). Besides repentance, the conversion theme is also prominent in Luke-Acts. The only occurrence of *epistrophe* (conversion) comes in Acts 15:13, but the majority of uses of *epistrepsein* (to convert, to turn around) appear in Luke-Acts. The summons to "turn around" is typically dominant in Acts.[93] Repentance and conversion indicate a change of heart and life oriented to Jesus and the kingdom of God.[94]

Lucan spirituality is also public in that the grace of God is unrestricted. It reaches out to the Gentiles, to the uttermost part of the earth (Acts 13:47; 26:17–18). The gospel is not only for all the people of Israel (Luke 2:10; 3:18, 21; 6:17; 7:1, 29; 8:47; 9:13; 18:43; 19:47–48) but also for the Gentiles (Acts 2:5–12; 8:26–40; 10:1–48). The gospel requires believers to

88. Barton, *The Spirituality of the Gospels*, 49.

89. Ibid., 71–73.

90. Morrice, *Joy in the New Testament*, 91.

91. Barton, "Synoptic Gospels," 610.

92. Beck, *Christian Character in the Gospel of Luke*, 11.

93. Barton, *The Spirituality of the Gospels*, 78.

94. Barton, "Synoptic Gospels," 610.

set the captives free, to heal the blind, and to rescue the oppressed (Luke 4:18). Believers are not to hoard wealth but to share it with the poor (Luke 6:24–26; 12:13; 16:19–31). Hospitality should be extended to neighbors (Luke 10:29–37) and even to sinners and tax collectors (15:1–2).[95]

In the Gospel of John, Jesus is presented as the word of God who was made flesh, the fully adequate expression of God.[96] Here it is made crystal clear what they have said differently and sometimes hesitantly about Jesus in the previous three synoptic gospels: Jesus as God incarnate who reveals God, and the way to God uniquely. Thus Johannine spirituality is *thoroughly Christocentric.*[97] In John, "salvation is presented not in terms of expiatory or substitutionary sacrifice but in terms of revelation. . . . [T]he death of Jesus is not kenosis but a glorification, the absolute manifestation of the very being of God as love."[98] Barton states:

> Fundamentally, there is revelation of the divine glory, a call to believe, a way to go which leads to God, the offer of deliverance from darkness into light and from death to life, and a basis for assurance. In other words, John's gospel provides clear and authoritative answers to questions about God, the world, life and death, truth and goodness, and salvation and judgment.[99]

All of Jesus' words and actions reveal something about the mystery and the glory of God.[100]

Persons in their relationship with God and with one another set the tone for the Fourth Gospel. The revelation comes in a personal, incarnate form (1:14, 18), and it requires a personal, incarnated response. As the Son, Jesus comes from the Father, abides in the Father, and seeks to do the work of the Father. The relationship between the Son and the Father is unique in its intensity and reciprocity. This unique relationship brings persons into the relationship with God as children of God (1:12) and heirs of eternal life (3:16). In John there are narratives of personal encounters with Jesus: Jesus and Nicodemus (ch 3), Jesus and the Samaritan woman (ch 4), Jesus and the lame man (ch 5), Jesus and the blind man (ch 9), Jesus and his own (chs 13–17), and Jesus and Pilate (18:28—19:16). These personal encounters

95. Barton, *The Spirituality of the Gospels,* 97–102.
96. Schneiders, "Johannine Spirituality," 386.
97. Barton, *The Spirituality of the Gospels,* 113, 118.
98. Schneiders, "Johannine Spirituality," 386.
99. Barton, *The Spirituality of the Gospels,* 114.
100. Bowe, *Biblical Foundations of Spirituality,* 145.

strongly convey the sense that "believing Jesus is an inescapably personal matter requiring individual decision for or against him."[101]

James Dunn says the following about the personal characteristic of Johannine spirituality: "John seems to understand Christianity as much more an individual affair, the immediacy of the disciple's relationship with Christ through the Spirit who constitutes Christ's continuing presence in the believer (John 14:15–20; 1 John 3:24)."[102] Johannine spirituality is mystical spirituality in which presence, mutual indwelling, and union predominate, rather than dogma or ethics. "Union with Jesus is the source of intimate knowledge of God and strength to live as the body of Jesus in the world."[103] Jesus is the fulfillment of our spiritual longing as bread of life (6:35, 51), light of the world (8:12; 9:5), gate for the sheep (10:7, 9), the good shepherd (10:11, 14), the resurrection and the life (11:25), the way, the truth, and the life (14:6), and the true vine (15:1, 5).[104]

Pauline Spirituality

Pauline spirituality is strongly pneumatological. "The Spirit's activities so widely permeated the apostle's thought that there is hardly any aspect of Christian experience outside of the sphere of the Spirit."[105] The basic assumption of Paul's theology is that all believers are possessors of the Spirit and that "no one can respond to the claims of Christ without being activated and indwelt by the Holy Spirit."[106] Persons are regenerated through the work of the Holy Spirit and they cry out "Abba Father" (Rom 8:14–17). Guidance and illumination comes from the Spirit, who leads them to the deepest understanding of God (1 Cor 2:13). Renewal of the mind (Rom 12:2) is achieved through the Spirit, and he causes the believer to walk in the Spirit in opposition to the sinful nature of the flesh (Rom 8:4). Spiritual indwelling is encouraged (Eph 5:18), manifested by bearing the Spirit's fruits (Gal 5:22–23). The Spirit is utterly indispensable for Christian living.[107]

---

101. Barton, *The Spirituality of the Gospels*, 114–16.

102. Dunn, "Models of Christian Community," 13.

103. Schneiders, "Johannine Spirituality," 387.

104. Bowe, *Biblical Foundations of Spirituality*, 146.

105. Dockery, "An Outline of Paul's View," 340.

106. Guthrie, *New Testament Theology*, 551.

107. Dockery, "An Outline of Paul's View," 342.

The Spirit is also given to and for the community for the common good (1 Cor 12:7). "To drink of one Spirit" (1 Cor 12:13) denotes the baptism of the Spirit and shows the basic solidarity of all Christians in the Spirit.[108] "It is the Spirit who binds Christians together and enables them to be of the same mind."[109] About the corporate nature of Pauline spirituality, Barbara Bowe states:

> Christian identity is a corporate identity and there is no such thing as "an *individual Christian*." . . . To be a Christian is to be a member of the body of Christ. Paul's insistence on the corporate character of the body and his exhortations to communal living are key to his preaching of the gospel and to the way he responded to almost every pastoral question.[110]

"Paul's spirituality has its context in the community of believers and was never individualistic."[111] He demonstrates how individual believers must exercise their freedom in Christ with love for the community (1 Cor 13:1–13). Paul does not condone asceticism (Col 2:20–23), but presents an ascetic approach to the Christian life as worldly since it appeals to human pride and achievement rather than trusting in Christ and dependence on the Spirit. Paul sees his asceticism in sexual matters as a gift to enhance the gospel—not for great personal spiritual achievement.

Another important aspect of Pauline spirituality is Christ crucified and risen. The risen Christ is precisely the crucified one. Paul does not make a distinction between his experience of crucified and risen Christ and his experience of the Spirit. The risen Christ is the life-giving Spirit.[112] All who are baptized into Christ are baptized into his death and buried with him (Rom 6:4). Then the risen Christ empowers them to walk in newness of life, and they are alive to God in Christ Jesus (Rom 6:5–11). Death, resurrection, and exaltation are the examples to follow not only for Paul, but for all Christians (Phil 3:7–17). When the believer dies to Christ, he or she also becomes a slave to Christ and is freed from the power of sin and law by the life-giving Spirit (Rom 8:1–2). Paul's enigmatic phrase "in Christ" refers

---

108. Guthrie, *New Testament Theology*, 563.

109. Ibid., 562.

110. Bowe, *Biblical Foundations of Spirituality*, 158.

111. Deidun, "Pauline Spirituality," 480,

112. Ibid.

to the field of his divine power, which permeates and governs the lives of believers.[113]

In Pauline epistles there are tensions which make spiritual life balanced and vibrant: visionaries vs. pragmatists; already vs. not yet; freedom vs. responsibility. These tensions were already exemplified by two groups of people in Israel's postexilic community:

> On the one hand, there were the prophetic visionaries, such as Third Isaiah and Zechariah, whose creative religious imagination envisioned a future time of God's inclusive blessings poured out on all. And on the other hand were so-called pragmatists, the scribal leaders such as Ezra and Nehemiah who saw the future of the people linked to their strict living of Torah, their avoidance of intermarriage, and their more restrictive policies of Jewish communal solidarity in the midst of alien world.[114]

This distinction between the visionary and the pragmatic tendencies also existed in the late New Testament period. The letter to Colossians demonstrates the visionary tendency in chapter 1 by praising the cosmic Christ (Col 1:15–16, 19–20). The letter to Ephesians also reveals this cosmic nature of God's plan of salvation (Eph 1:3–4, 5–6, 9–10). On the other hand, the pragmatic perspective shows in the Pastoral Epistles where the "household codes" of appropriate behaviors of wives, children, and slaves, and the regulations and qualifications for Christian ministers are laid down. There is a creative tension "between the voices of pragmatism, boundary maintenance, and social order on the one hand, and the voices of prophetic visionaries, boundary breakers, and imaginative risk takers, on the other."[115]

Spiritual life is characterized by the polarities of the already/not yet and indicative/imperative tensions. While living in the Spirit as a new creation in Christ, believers still suffer consciousness of their old selves in Adam. Their struggle with indwelling sin continues (Rom 7:14–25), and the flesh continues to wage war against the Spirit (Gal 5:16–21). The kingdom of God of the gospel is already in their midst, but not yet realized.[116] Pauline spirituality is eschatological spirituality based on the present life in Christ. The believer's perspective is futuristic, looking ahead to the blessed future (1 Cor 7:29–31; 1 Thess 4:13–18), yet is firmly grounded in the present where

113. Ibid.

114. Bowe, *Biblical Foundations of Spirituality*, 166.

115. Ibid., 166–69.

116. Dockery, "An Outline of Paul's View," 346–47.

there is a Christian obligation to live a godly life. The future consummation is balanced with a missionary task (1 Thess 4:17; 1 Cor 9:23).

Summary

The biblical accounts of Christian spirituality lay a foundation in our search of authentic spirituality, relevant to our time. The biblical themes of creation, covenant, community, and the presence of God that pervade the Old Testament are the bedrocks of Christian spirituality. Creation as an act of the triune God for his glory is the basis of the Old Testament spirituality. In the creation narrative, the essential relationship between God and man is revealed. Bonding, closeness, and intimacy are the hallmarks of covenant, and it is justice and righteousness that maintain the covenant. There is no sound spirituality without community as well. From creation through the covenant relationships, God was present in Israelite community.

God's presence is evident in the Law, prophets, and wisdom tradition, that is, in the whole Old Testament. Prophets are those who, in love with God, experienced the divine pathos. They lived not only their own lives but also the life of God. They were aflame for justice and righteousness, which involve right and duty in a relational context. As opposed to the saving tradition, the blessing tradition is fascinated with the pursuit of wisdom as a central emphasis. This biblical wisdom leads us to find God in our midst and live our life to the fullest.

The spirituality of the New Testament is fundamentally Christological. It is people's responses to what God was doing in Jesus Christ. Early Christian spirituality was conceived, nurtured, and formed within the body of Christ. The church is a new community to make disciples of all nations. The Spirit was given to believers for the edification of the church. The eschatological dimension of the New Testament provided early Christians with the means to resist the particular worldviews and practices of the cultures in which they lived.

As the continuation of the Old Testament spiritualities and Judaism, Matthean spirituality manifests divine presence in Jesus: Jesus is *Immanuel* (God with us). Markan spirituality is *cruciform* spirituality which emphasizes the dark, strenuous spirituality of Jesus' death. Lucan spirituality is characterized by overshadowing presence and the powerful manifestations of the Holy Spirit. In Luke the joyous mood frames the whole gospel with repentance, forgiveness, and conversion, summing up the Christian good news in Luke-Acts: the gospel is not only for Jews but also for the Gentiles. Johannine spirituality is thoroughly Christocentric. As revelation of the divine glory, Jesus encountered individuals and proclaimed the good news to Jews, Samaritans, and Greeks. Taking an ambivalent attitude toward the world, John's Gospel takes on mystical and charismatic characters as well.

Pauline spirituality is strongly pneumatological. There is hardly any aspect of Christian experience outside the realm of the Spirit. It is also corporate spirituality in that the Spirit was given to the body of Christ for common good. Paul's spirituality is also strongly eschatological, while based on the present life in Christ. In Christian life, according to Paul, there is a creative tension between visionaries and pragmatists, already and not yet, and freedom and responsibility.

3

Patristic and Medieval Spirituality

"Christian spirituality is necessarily related to the Christian tradition."[1] Besides the Scriptures, the history of Christianity is another constitutive discipline that provides the resources, norms, and hermeneutical context of Christian spirituality.[2] Again, it is an impossible task to examine 2000 years of Christian spirituality here, so it would suffice to examine five major historical spiritualities in this book: the patristic, medieval West, Eastern Orthodox, Protestant, and Anglican. We will first discuss the patristic, medieval West, and Eastern Orthodox spiritualities.

The Patristic Period (100–c. 451 or 600)

The patristic period was the formative time for the fundamentals of Christian doctrine. Although there is disagreement, the Protestant tradition has tended to regard the Council of Chalcedon in AD 451 as an approximate end.[3] Alternatively, this era can cover AD 100–600, the era of the Roman Empire.[4]

During this period, the early church first faced the challenge of explaining its relationship with Judaism from which Christianity originated. Biblical interpretation, especially that Jesus fulfilled the prophecy of the Scriptures, was an important issue. Christians claimed that Jesus was the

---

1. Downey, *Understanding Christian Spirituality*, 54.
2. Schneiders, "The Study of Christian Spirituality," 3.
3. Sheldrake, *Spirituality & History*, 45.
4. Stewart, "Christian Spirituality during the Roman Empire," 73.

awaited Messiah of the Old Testament and that the history of Israel culminated in the incarnation of God in Jesus.

The formation of Christian canon was another critical issue. The precise contents of a Christian Bible were debated and finalized through various church councils. The Hellenistic Jewish version of the Bible, called Septuagint, was the basis of the Christian Old Testament, and apostolicity was the main criterion of the New Testament.[5] Regarding the Old Testament canon, the early church received from its Jewish heritage the concept of sacred Scriptures that it believed were the revelation of God and the prediction of Christ to come.[6] Concerning New Testament canonization, Lee McDonald states:

> Ultimately, it appears that the writings that were accorded scriptural status were the ones that best conveyed the earliest Christian proclamation and that also best met the growing needs of local churches in the third and fourth centuries. . . . The significance of the NT writings to the churches is shown by their widespread use in the life, teaching, and worship of those churches, and such use also contributed to their canonization.[7]

Patristic Theology

The doctrinal polemics of the early centuries were the general atmosphere of this period as the early Christian church worked out the central characteristics of its understanding of God, Christ, and redemption.[8]

Monotheism, the Trinity, Christology

Monotheism and the Trinitarian concept of God were developed early. The early "Logos Christology" of Justin Martyr (c. 100–c. 165), developed further by Origen (c. 185–c. 254), preserved monotheism, that God the Father has the primacy as the one who speaks the Word (*Logos*), the Son of God, who became flesh in Jesus Christ. Outlining a "grammar" of Christian prayer of a Trinitarian nature, Origen taught that prayer should always be addressed *to* God the Father, *through* the Son, and *in* the Holy Spirit. Basil of

5. Ibid., 73–74.

6. McDonald, *The Biblical Canon*, 208–9.

7. Ibid., 421.

8. Sheldrake, *Spirituality & History*, 47.

Caesarea (c. 330–379) and his friend Gregory of Nazianzus (c. 329–c. 390), two great Cappadocian theologians, expanded the Trinitarian questioning further. Gregory based distinction among the persons of the Trinity upon their relationships to each other, rather than upon any essential difference between them, and protected the unity of the Trinity (one God, indivisible) and the distinction of Father, Son, and Spirit within the Godhead (three persons, unconfused).[9]

The Arian controversy of the fourth century focused attention on the relationship between God the Father and God the Son. Against the more cautious Christology of Arius, the Council of Nicea (325) adopted the bolder assertion of Athanasius of the Son's full and equal divinity in the doctrine of the *homoousion*—the claim that the Son is of the same "being" (*ousios*) as the Father. In the fifth century, theological debate focused on the relationship between the divine and human natures in Christ. From this context, Marion devotion arose as some attributed to Mary the title "Mother of God" (*Theotokos*). To supporters of *Theotokos*, like Bishop of Alexandria Cyril (c. 378–444), it suggested the fundamental unity of the human and divine nature in Christ. In "Alexandrian" Christology, Christ became a single person *from* two natures. It was the Council of Chalcedon (451) that affirmed Christ is "one person *in* two natures" that are united "without confusion, without change, without division, without separation."[10]

Biblical and Pastoral Theology

The unifying features of the era were the Bible and biblical theology, that is, an exegetically based interpretation of the Scriptures to produce a fuller understanding of Christian faith and a deepening of the Christian life. They viewed the Bible from the context of Christian life. Theology was entwined with the life of the church, and preaching was regarded as the action of the living Word of God in the congregation. Thus, the theology of early fathers was primarily pastoral.[11]

Regarding the episcopate, Ignatius of Antioch taught that the church is a community of believers gathered around a single local bishop (mono-episcopate), who is helped in his ministry by presbyters and deacons. Soon his threefold ministry model of bishop, presbyter (later "priest"), and

9. Stewart, "Christian Spirituality during the Roman Empire," 75.

10. Ibid., 75–76.

11. Sheldrake, *Spirituality & History*, 45–46.

deacon became the norm for the Christian church and was extended in the next century to encompass a communion of bishops who all claimed their continuity with the teaching of the apostles. Apostolicity was used not only to validate writings as Scripture but also to make bishops legitimate and authoritative interpreters of the tradition.[12]

Liturgical Celebration

Baptism and Eucharist were considered as the means of initiation into the community and nurturing of faith respectively. Baptism allowed believers to participate in the Eucharist, which was celebrated weekly in obedience to Jesus' command at the Last Supper (Luke 22:19). The Eucharist became the typical form of Christian communal worship and soon became a distinct rite consisting of biblical readings, a kiss of peace, prayers, and the sharing of blessed bread and wine. Early Christians considered the Eucharist as a genuine reception of the body and blood of Jesus Christ in the form of bread and wine.[13] For example, Justin Martyr stated in his *First Apology*:

> For we do not receive these things as common bread nor common drink; but in like manner as Jesus Christ our Savior having been incarnate by God's logos took both flesh and blood for our salvation, so also we have been taught that the food eucharistized through the word of prayer that is from Him . . . is the flesh and blood of that Jesus who became incarnate.[14]

By the third and fourth centuries, the standard texts for the anaphora, the central Eucharistic prayer, was characterized by Jewish prayer of thanksgiving, blessing, and petition, but gradually replaced by sacrificial language and symbolism of Christ's death and resurrection.[15] "Throughout the latter half of the fourth century, the liturgy came to be regarded, like meditation on the Scriptures, as a privileged means of contemplative exercise and ascent."[16]

---

12. Stewart, "Christian Spirituality during the Roman Empire," 74–75.

13. Ibid., 77.

14. Justin Martyr, *The First and Second Apologies*, 66.2.

15. Stewart, "Christian Spirituality during the Roman Empire," 79.

16. For instance, the mystagogical and catechetical homilies of Cyril of Jerusalem (AD 315–86) and Ambrose of Milan (AD 339–97) presented liturgy as both a means of Christian catechesis and a spiritual exercise through which the soul perceives God and is transformed mysteriously. Thus the liturgical celebrations of the sacraments of baptism,

Mysticism

The patristic period is characteristic of mystical theology, mystical exegesis, mystical prayer, and mystical contemplation. Sheldrake states:

> The patristic period, in the limited sense of the early Christian centuries, was a formative time both for the fundamentals of doctrine and for what has been called "mystical theology." . . . Mystical theology aimed to provide a context for the direct apprehension of God who is revealed in Christ and within us as the Spirit. . . . When we talk about the "mystical theology" of this period, we must be careful not to confuse it with the later medieval fascination in the West with subjective experience or with the development of a detailed itinerary for the spiritual journey. Patristic "mysticism" is neither abstract nor systematic. It refers to the personal life of the Christian who knows God as revealed in Christ by belonging to the fellowship of the "mystery." This means the mystery of Christ as expressed in the Bible and the liturgy as well as in personal Christian living.[17]

For Origen, "mysticism was an experience of the inner person and the spiritual senses, a deeper realization of the mind's capacities rather than an ecstatic surpassing of them." He also encouraged personal and spiritual readings of the Bible. Following Origen, Evagrius of Pontus (345–399), emphasized identifying distracting thoughts and taught pure or imageless prayer. He stressed the rational mind's self-realization in prayer. However, Pseudo-Macarius, from the late fourth century, emphasized the heart rather than mind and was emotionally *warm* compared to Evagrius. These two figures were progenitors of later spiritual theologies. John Cassian's (c. 360–c. 432) prayer, however, was both pure and imageless and marked by tears, a combination of Evagrius and Pseudo-Macarius. The synthesis of these two approaches to prayer proved to be of great importance for later development of prayer and spiritual experience.[18]

Dionysius the Aereopagite, from the early sixth century, known as Pseudo-Dionysius, also wrote liturgical prayer which celebrated the apophatic divine darkness (mystical theology) and the radiantly kataphatic

---

the Eucharist, and ordination came to be regarded as unique occasions of *theosis* (deification). Dysinger, "Early Christian Spirituality," 258.

17. Sheldrake, *Spirituality & History*, 46.

18. Stewart, "Christian Spirituality during the Roman Empire," 80–81.

creation (the celestial and ecclesiastical hierarchies).[19] To him the liturgy was fundamental and central and was a means of drawing believers back to union with God. His symbolic interpretation of the liturgy began a significant tradition of liturgical commentary in the Byzantine world.[20]

Augustine of Hippo (354–430) was perhaps the most important person in Western theology during the patristic period and on through the next thousand years. A major influence on Augustine and his spiritual life was Neoplatonism, in which he found a doctrine of the soul—through purification and contemplation it can rise to God—and also man's frailty and his need for some kind of assistance in search for God. The mystical ascent of the soul is a "movement of withdrawal from the world and into oneself, a movement that involves purification and the acquiring of the virtues, leading to contemplation of God"[21] Augustine's spiritual theology was formed by two principle themes: the primacy of charity (love), both divine and human, and the insights into God's nature and the human search for God. To Augustine, God's presence is spiritual and can be sought by the rational mind, which is also immaterial and spiritual.[22] Andrew Louth says about the significance of love in Augustine's theology, "Augustine sees the importance of love as preventing us from being 'content with the world's darkness which through habit has become pleasant.'"[23] For Augustine, the dynamism of the Trinity is analogous to the intellectual faculties of recollection, contemplation, and love.[24] As seen in Augustine's writings, in the patristic period mystical contemplation was combined with reason and exegesis. Sheldrake argues, "In patristic theology biblical exegesis, speculative reasoning, and mystical contemplation are fused into a synthesis."[25] Biblical exegesis tended to be mystical.[26]

---

19. Dysinger, "Early Christian Spirituality," 258.

20. Stewart, "Christian Spirituality during the Roman Empire," 82.

21. Louth, "Augustine," 136.

22. Stewart, "Christian Spirituality during the Roman Empire," 83.

23. Louth, "Augustine," 140.

24. Stewart, "Christian Spirituality during the Roman Empire," 83.

25. Sheldrake, *Spirituality & History*, 46.

26. Irenaeus of Lyons (AD 200), Clement of Alexandria (AD 215), and Origen (AD 185) applied middle and Neoplatonic notions of ethical purification (*katharsis*), contemplative vision (*theōria*), and mystical exegesis (*allegoria*) to the Christian Scriptures and to spiritual theology, and yielded methods of biblical interpretation and models of spiritual progress. Dysinger, "Early Christian Spirituality," 257.

Martyrdom

After the elements of the New Testament, no other factor has had more lasting importance in constituting Christian spirituality than martyrdom. Up to the period of Constantine, the church was illegal. Adherence to the church meant the acceptance of the ban of ordinary society to the extent of direct threat to life and confiscation of possessions. The literature of martyrdom abounds. The Acts of the Martyrs are the simple verbal records of official judgments. *Acts of St. Justin and his companions, Acts of the Martyrs of Scillium in Africa,* and *Preconsular Acts of St. Cyprian* are some examples. There are other theological writings inspired by martyrdom such as *The Epistles of St. Ignatius of Antioch* and *The Exhortations to Martyrdom.*[27] The spiritual writings of early Christians that mention prayer, the vision of God, and spiritual progress are also strongly colored by the threat of persecution and possible martyrdom.[28] Stewart states of martyrs' faith:

> Their [martyrs'] commitment was to more than a lifestyle or philosophy. The Acts of ordinary men and women demonstrate that it was the courage of faith, not theological sophistication, that gave martyrs the strength to choose death rather than apostasy. . . . A devotional consequence of persecution was the cult of the martyrs, which began in the form of honouring them in their burial places. In this practice lay the beginning of Christian veneration of saints.[29]

The following document expresses the desire for martyrdom expressed powerfully in the *Epistle to the Romans*:

> I am writing to all the Churches and state emphatically to all that I die willingly for God, provided you do not interfere. I beg you, do not show me unseasonable kindness. Suffer me to be the food of wild beasts, which are the means of my making way to God. God's wheat I am, and by the teeth of wild beasts I am to be ground that I may prove Christ's pure bread. Better still, coax the wild beasts to become my tomb and to leave no part of my person behind: once I have fallen asleep, I do not wish to be a burden to anyone. Then only shall I be a genuine disciple of Jesus Christ when the world will not see even my body. Petition Christ in my behalf that through these instruments I may prove God's sacrifice. . . . At last

27. Bouyer, *The Spirituality of the New Testament and the Fathers,* 190–92.

28. Dysinger, "Early Christian Spirituality," 256–57.

29. Stewart, "Christian Spirituality during the Roman Empire," 84.

I am well on the way to being a disciple. May nothing *seen or unseen,* fascinate me, so that I may happily make my way to Jesus Christ! Fire, cross, struggles with wild beasts, wrenching of bones, mangling of limbs, crunching of the whole body, cruel tortures inflicted by the devil—let them come upon me, provided only I make my way to Jesus Christ. . . . Do not have Jesus Christ on your lips, and the world in your hearts. Give envy no place among you. And should I upon arrival plead for your intervention, do not listen to me. Rather, give heed to what I write to you. . . . My Love [eros] has been crucified, and I am not on fire with the love of earthly things. But there is in me a *Living Water,* which is eloquent and within me says: "Come to the Father." I have no taste for corruptible food or for the delight of this life. *Bread of God* is what I desire; that is, the Flesh of Jesus Christ, *who was of the seed of David;* and for my drink I desire His blood, that is, incorruptible love [*agape*].[30]

It is not death itself that martyrs sought, but it is Jesus Christ with whom they suffered.[31]

Asceticism

Martyrdom inspired other forms of Christian devotion. Asceticism is the sustained practice of physical and spiritual disciplines. It was a part of early Christian practice reflecting the ascetical orientation of some Jewish groups. It was not always clear to distinguish between unusual piety and elitist sectarianism. The latter were groups or individuals who separated themselves from the larger church, claiming perfection or true Christianity. They emphasized strict fasts, mandatory celibacy, and charismatic leadership. Such were Tatian's *Encratites* (from *enkrateia* or discipline) or the prophecy-oriented Montanists, and they made themselves an alternative church rather than a movement within the church. Ecclesial asceticism can be found in the *Sons and Daughters of the Covenant* of Syriac Christianity, who practiced celibacy in service to the church. In the fourth century, asceticism was formally integrated into the larger church through the emergence of monasticism and episcopal consecration of virgins. The apocryphal *Acts* and *Gospels* shed light on early Christian asceticism and

---

30. Ignatius, *Epistle to the Romans*, Ign. 4–7.

31. Bouyer, *The Spirituality of the New Testament and the Fathers*, 199.

illustrated the affinities between asceticism and martyrdom, the formative themes of monasticism.[32]

Monasticism

The phenomenal success of monasticism in the fourth century was partly due to a popular desire to preserve the spirituality of the church of martyrs. Asceticism within and outside the church also provided a ground for monasticism. Both monks and nuns were new models of spiritual heroism, and their spiritual practices coupled with geographical remoteness reflected their rejection of worldly culture. It was the monasteries, where methods of liturgical and private prayers were formalized, that used both kataphatic (image-filled) psalmody and silent apophatic (imageless) self-offering.[33] Antony (251–356), the "founder" and model of monasticism, is described as follows:

> Antony becomes the prototypical monk, renouncing an ordinary relationship with the world for the sake of another kind of relationship, and setting the normal issues of human existence against the backdrop of eternity and the vastness of the desert. Antony withdraws both geographically and psychologically, his ever-greater physical withdrawal echoing his deeper and deeper confrontation with himself and the "demons" that oppress him. Antony's teaching on the psychodynamics of temptation echoes the tradition of discernment of spirits found as early as the *Shepherd of Hermas* and developed by Origen in book 3 of *On First Principles*.[34]

The desert school of spirituality in fourth century Egypt emphasized rigorous self-examination in order to focus on God past the internal and external forces of subversion. This tradition was systematized by Evagrius and passed on to John Cassian and to Pope St. Gregory the Great (540–604). The goal of the monastic movement was not so much moral regulation as freedom from emotional and psychological disturbances for unceasing prayer and love of God and neighbor. Unlike Antony, Pachomius (292–346) abandoned solitude to form a community of monks that prayed, worked, and ate together in a very ordered and cloistered ascetic community. The two models of monasticism, solitary (anchoritic) and communal (cenobitic),

32. Stewart, "Christian Spirituality during the Roman Empire," 84–85.
33. Dysinger, "Early Christian Spirituality," 257.
34. Stewart, "Christian Spirituality during the Roman Empire," 86.

found many adherents, and monasticism became "typical Christianity" in the East, dominating spiritual theology and liturgical development. It appeared in the West later.[35]

When the persecutions and martyrdom ceased, it was monasticism that condensed the development of Christian spirituality. However, it should be remembered that the whole church did not become monastic. As much as monasticism was nurtured in the church, monasticism left with the church its legacy and teachings, which became the common possessions of the whole church.[36]

The Medieval West (600–1450)

Medieval spirituality was formed in a social environment shaped by deep divisions in social rank, gender status, and wealth, with a concentration of power and knowledge on a few. Holiness found its expression in a disciplined life of prayer, asceticism, loyalty to ecclesiastical authority, pastoral care of others, and the thorough keeping of liturgical hours. Medieval spirituality was in general public and communal, being tied to a wider range of issues than personal growth. The medieval millennium can be divided into three developmental phases: early medieval (sixth through eleventh centuries); the second phase (eleventh to thirteenth centuries); and late medieval (mid-thirteenth through early fifteenth centuries).[37]

Early Medieval Spirituality (Sixth to Eleventh Centuries)

During this period, the patristic synthesis from the previous era—biblical exegesis, speculative reasoning, and mystical contemplation—continued to dominate.[38] At the same time, the Roman church's adaptation of Roman administrative structures and the steady influx of indigenous practices to Christian spirituality brought forth Western monasticism and the Roman Catholic Church. Two religious leaders of the sixth century epitomize the medieval spirituality of this period: St. Benedict of Nursia (c. 480–547), the founder of Benedictine monasticism and mysticism, and St. Gregory the Great, a prolific writer, gifted administrator, and pastoral counselor. Both

---

35. Ibid., 86–87.

36. Bouyer, *The Spirituality of the New Testament and the Fathers*, 523–24.

37. Wiethaus, "Christian Spirituality in the Medieval West," 106–10.

38. Sheldrake, *Spirituality & History*, 48.

men integrated Roman and local indigenous traditions and laid the foundation for the growth of medieval spirituality.[39]

Benedictine Spirituality

Benedict lived a monastic life and wrote his *Rule* to a fellow Christian who is seeking God in the context of monasticism. The Rule was written in the sixth-century monastery at Monte Cassino, which was a lay institution where Christians came to live a consecrated life without aspiring to sacred orders. It was only centuries later that the clerical element in Benedictine monasteries became dominant.

One of the major themes of the Rule is *lectio divina,* a daily reading of the Scriptures with meditation and prayer. *Lectio* means "careful, reflective, frequent reading of Scripture so that its meaning and application to our individual lives might penetrate to the heart and become a living, transforming reality in shaping our inner lives."[40] Daily reading of the Scripture is balanced with daily manual labor. "Idleness is the enemy of the soul. Therefore, all the community must be occupied at definite times in manual labor and at other times in *lectio divina.*"[41] Obedience is another key theme in the Rule. Actually, it permeates the whole of the Rule. The prologue to the Rule says the following:

> It is not easy to accept and persevere in obedience, but it is the way to return to Christ, when you have strayed through the laxity and carelessness of disobedience. My words are addressed to you especially, whoever you may be, whatever your circumstances, who turn from the pursuit of your own self will and ask to enlist under Christ, who is Lord of all, by following him through taking to yourself that strong and blessed armor of *obedience* [emphasis mine] which he made his own on coming into our world.[42]

An order from a superior must be obeyed without delaying for a moment, as though it came from God himself. Obedience is also rewarding if it is carried out in a way that is not fearful, nor slow, nor halfhearted, nor marred by murmuring.[43] Placid Spearritt says, "It is a hard saying to

39. Wiethaus, "Christian Spirituality in the Medieval West," 110–11.

40. Benedict, *Saint Benedict's Rule,* 1.13.

41. Ibid., 48.1.

42. Ibid., Prologue.1.

43. Ibid., 5.1–5.4.

many modern ears, but there can be no doubt that total obedience is of the essence of Benedictine spirituality."[44] "They cannot count even their bodies and their wills as their own."[45]

Humility is another core of St. Benedict's teachings contained in the *Twelve Steps of Humility* in the seventh chapter of the Rule. Ulrike Wiethaus explains the twelve steps:

> Geared toward the harmonious cooperation of the monastic community and the liberation of the human spirit from the infantilising push and pull of human "sins and vices" . . . the twelve steps of humility paradoxically invert the image of a fierce warrior in stressing absolute mastery over the self and its passions. The steps include fear of God, doing Gods' will at all times, obeying the abbot (as long as the abbot fulfils his responsibilities), patient endurance of suffering, regular confession, ungrudging acceptance of menial work, regarding oneself as lesser than all other monks, following the rule with attentiveness, embracing silence, avoiding laughter, and speaking only with gentleness; in short, conducting oneself with humility at all times.[46]

This following of Christ in humility and obedience is not an ascetical imposition for monks and nuns, but it is the only way for the sinful creation to achieve the joy and fulfillment of Christ.[47] St. Benedictine valued silence and recommended it. Silence is an expression of humility, and by definition a monk is a disciple and should want to listen more than to speak. Silence characterizes the monastery at all times, but especially at night and in all places.[48]

St. Gregory

Wiethaus contends, "If St. Benedict created the stable foundation of medieval monasteries, St. Gregory the Great must be credited with bridging biblical and European cultures and forging the parameters of the multicultural encounter that defined early medieval spirituality."[49] His structured

---

44. Spearritt, "Benedict," 153.

45. Benedict, *Saint Benedict's Rule*, 33.1.

46. Wiethaus, "Christian Spirituality in the Medieval West," 112.

47. Benedict, *Saint Benedict's Rule*, 26.

48. Spearritt, "Benedict," 154.

49. Wiethaus, "Christian Spirituality in the Medieval West," 113.

reflection on Christian life and doctrine in a dialectic of presence and absence, faith and knowledge, dark and light, bridges the gap between the patristic world and the Middle Ages. Almost all the later vocabulary of the West regarding the spiritual life has its origin in Gregory's integration of the vocabulary of Cassian and Augustine.[50]

Becoming a model for later hagiography, *The Dialogues of St. Gregory* attempted to demonstrate that the Italy of his own era was a second Holy Land filled with amazing wonder workers evoking the patriarchs and prophets of the Bible. All four books of the *Dialogue* present paradigmatic Christian encounters with indigenous religious practices in narrative form and were widely read during the medieval times.[51] For example, in the *Life and Miracles of St. Benedict,* the second book of the *Dialogue,* Gregory describes Benedict at prayer:

> Long before the night office began, the man of God was standing at his window, where he watched and prayed while the rest were still asleep. In the dead of night he suddenly beheld a flood of light shining down from above more brilliant than the sun, and with it every trace of darkness cleared away. Another remarkable sight followed. . . . [T]he whole world was gathered up before his eyes in what appeared to be a single ray of light.[52]

St. Gregory also describes the active life and contemplative life as follows:

> The active life consists in giving bread to the hungry, in teaching wisdom to him who knows it not, in bringing the wanderer back to the right way, in recalling one's neighbour to the path of humility from that of pride, in giving to each what he needs, in providing for those who are committed to our care. In the contemplative life, however, while maintaining with his whole heart the love of God and his neighbour, a man is at rest (*quiescere*) from exterior works, cleaving by desire to his Maker alone, so that, having no wish for action and treading underfoot all preoccupations, his soul is on fire with longing to see the face of his creator.[53]

Jean Leclercq, Francois Vandenbroucke, and Louis Bouyer explain that although the impression that St. Gregory gives is that the active life is for

50. Ward, "Gregory the Great," 278.

51. Wiethaus, "Christian Spirituality in the Medieval West," 113.

52. Gregory the Great, *Dialogue*, 2.35.

53. Leclercq et al., *The Spirituality of the Middle Ages*, 10.

the salvation of others by our labors and the contemplative life for our own salvation through the work of prayer, the two lives are two kinds of complementary activity, asceticism and prayer, and both activities have their place in each life. In reality, the two lives are only two forms of the same charity. That is, both are our means of union with God. [54] Referring to the two lives, Wiethaus states:

> Mirroring his own active life, St. Gregory stressed the complementary function of action and contemplation. He taught that prayer and the meditative reading of Scripture eventually allow the soul to experience divine presence, which in turn prepares and strengthens the soul for the active life.[55]

According to Benedicta Ward, St. Gregory presented one of the main themes of Western spirituality: the continual conversion of the soul throughout life. The whole life of a believer is gradually freed from the bonds of earth and gets to see all things in the light of God in perspective, but the full union with him is fulfilled after death.[56]

> The soul illumined by the light of God, sees its own weakness and what is contrary to God in itself and continues more ardently the process of repentance, in a dialectic of self-knowledge and the knowledge of God by love. The teaching permeated the monastic Middle Ages in the West, giving both theology and vocabulary to barbarian Christians for them to use and to develop.[57]

High Middle Ages (Eleventh to Thirteenth Centuries)

The High Middle Ages is characteristic of contemplative textual spirituality and the mendicant movement, and was also the period of the twelfth-century renaissance. An increasingly urban-educated population created a demand for literacy and instruction, coupled with concerns for Christian unity and integrity.[58] This led to an enormously analytical attentiveness to processes of contemplative reading, writing, and textual exegesis.

---

54. Ibid., 10–11.
55. Wiethaus, "Christian Spirituality in the Medieval West," 113.
56. Ward, "Gregory the Great," 279.
57. Ibid., 280.
58. Wiethaus, "Christian Spirituality in the Medieval West," 114.

Contemplative Textual Spirituality

The distinctiveness of this era is a monasticization of spirituality throughout the church in which ascetic spirituality of the monks became the norm for the devout Christians, especially for the clergy. Poverty, solitude, silence, fasting, and manual work without many of the established structures of monastic houses characterize this reform movement. The movement took two forms: hermits living in solitude, and groups of monks living together in corporate solitude. The most successful group was the Cistercians who wished to follow the *Rule of St. Benedict* to the last dot. St. Bernard of Clairvaux[59] was the dominant spiritual influence in Europe at this time.[60] Ward summarizes this period as follows:

> The changes in monastic spirituality in this period were of profound importance for the devotional life of Europe. Many of those concerned with reform in the Church in this period were also monks of the new orders or under their influence, and saw monastic life as the ideal Christian way. This led to the monasticisation of Christian spirituality. . . . The contact of monastic spirituality with a wider circle than the monks themselves . . . led to a greater vigour in the art of prayer, and produced some of the most beautiful devotional works of the Middle Ages.[61]

Twelfth-Century Renaissance

The twelfth-century intellectual renaissance was different from the Renaissance of three centuries later. While the Renaissance was to break with the genius of the Middle Ages in almost every sphere, the twelfth-century renaissance was to carry on the monastic and patristic culture. In the eleventh century, the monasteries were the only centers of Christian thought. As it is said, "the abbeys remained the repositories of the great Christian ideas."[62] However, in the twelfth century, although the monasteries were still strong in intellectual life, theologians and thinkers began to appear

---

59. Bernard's central theme was his specific concern with the analysis of the soul in its relationship with God. His mystical theology of love and knowledge established a school of spirituality of lasting influence. The main emphasis of Bernard is action as the fruit and overflow of the intimacy of the soul with God.

60. Ward, "The New Orders," 285–87.

61. Ibid., 291.

62. Leclercq quoted from Leclercq et al., *The Spirituality of the Middle Ages*, 224.

outside of them, criticizing the monks as mere classifiers and copiers. These new scholars read and studied the Scriptures with the view of the mind rather than the heart. They aimed at theological interpretation and literal exegesis. This renaissance foreshadowed the Renaissance that destroyed the Church's monopoly of intellectual life a few centuries later.[63]

During this period, textual spirituality expanded beyond the monasteries to cathedral schools and newly founded universities. The so-called Victorine School of contemplative thought made efforts to systematize and classify religious experiences in light of the Bible with divine and human love at the center of creation. Some representatives of this academic and textual spirituality are Hugh of St. Victor (c. 1096–1141), his student, Richard of St. Victor (c. 1123–1173), Peter Abelard (1079–1142), and his highly educated wife Heloise (1102–1164).[64] Leclercq et al. claim that the scholastic method of theological research was a new one and augured the divorce between theology (now definitely science) and mysticism (spiritual life).[65]

Mendicant Movement

At the beginning of the thirteenth century, the sources of Christianity—the Bible and the Fathers—were being read anew due to the system and techniques developed in the previous century. There were also passionate efforts toward the pure ideal of the gospel.[66] In such an atmosphere, the mendicant movement was an attempt to break free from the dominance of the monastic elite in spirituality. It was a move from the stability and separation of the cloister into an itinerant way of life of crusade and preaching.[67] The Franciscan Order founded by St. Francis of Assisi (c. 1181–1226), and the Dominican Order of St. Dominic de Guzman (c. 1170–1221) are seen as attempts to channel within the institutional church the evangelistic aspirations which were driven underground in the previous century.[68] Unlike other contemporary "heretic" spiritual movements, the mendicant

---

63. Leclercq et al., *The Spirituality of the Middle Ages*, 223–25.

64. Wiethaus, "Christian Spirituality in the Medieval West," 115.

65. Leclercq et al., *The Spirituality of the Middle Ages*, 242.

66. Ibid., 283.

67. Sheldrake, *Spirituality & History*, 66.

68. Tugwell, "The Mendicants," 295.

movement was accepted by the church through the formal recognition of the way of the life of the friars.[69]

From the beginning, Dominican spirituality was dominated by a concern to be useful to the souls of the neighbor. The primacy of the apostolic job of preaching relativized the normal conventional practices of piety such as prayer, reading, liturgy, and sacraments. In the apostolic life, poverty was adopted as an essential ingredient. Dominic himself urged his brethren to make even their convents mendicant too. The Dominican Order taught their friars to trust in God rather than to earn their living since large estates or regular paid work would interfere with their work.

Perhaps the most important element of the Dominican Order was study. For example, Dominic himself took his first followers to theology classes in Toulouse and sent them to universities in Paris and Bologna. During the thirteenth century, study replaced the traditional practice of manual labor of the monks. The Dominicans also had a pragmatic attitude to piety. Poverty, chastity, and obedience were not values in their own right, but means to an end, perfect charity.[70]

Modeling an uncompromising return to apostolic simplicity and devotion, St. Francis lived a life of extreme poverty and strict obedience to the words of Christ. He went around the world preaching the gospel, tending lepers, writing the rule of living, and always praying. To Francis the sufferings of Christ were ever present with him.[71] His prayer on La Verna reveals his longing for the passion of Christ. He prayed in this way:

> "My Lord Jesus Christ, I pray You to grant me two graces before I die: the first is that during life I may feel in my soul and in my body, as much as possible, that pain which You, dear Jesus, sustained in the hour of Your most bitter Passion. The second is that I may feel in my heart, as much as possible, that excessive love with which You, O Son of God, were inflamed in willingly enduring such suffering for us sinners." And remaining for a long time in that prayer, he understood that God would grant it to him, and that it would soon be conceded to him to feel those things as much as is possible for a mere creature.[72]

---

69. Sheldrake, *Spirituality & History*, 74.

70. Tugwell, "The Dominicans," 296–98.

71. Moorman, "The Franciscans," 302–3.

72. Habig, ed., *St. Francis of Assisi*, 1448.

Francis' spirituality can be summed up as his total obedience to Christ, his prayer at all times, his desire to suffer with Christ, and his love of nature. Thomas of Celano says of his prayer habit:

> [H]is safest haven was prayer; not prayer of a single moment, or idle or presumptuous prayer, but prayer of long duration, full of devotion, serene in humility. If he began late, he would scarcely finish before morning. Walking, sitting, eating, or drinking, he was always intent upon prayer. He would go alone to pray at night in churches abandoned and located in deserted places, where under the protection of divine grace, he overcame many fears and many disturbances of mind.[73]

St. Francis worked closely with a female companion, St. Clare of Assisi (1194–1253). Clare founded the female branch of the order called the Poor Ladies or Poor Clares. The friars looked after the needs of fellow sisters, both temporal and spiritual. The Order grew rapidly, and by 1300 there were about 400 houses.[74] For Clare, poverty was the door to contemplation of Jesus since he himself was poor and served the poor. She resisted the continuous pressure to loosen the poverty of the Order.[75] The human Christ, the Word made flesh, the attachment of Christ to earthly things, and the sharing in the sufferings and joy of Christ are the characteristics of Franciscan spirituality.[76]

The Franciscan third order called *Apostoli* was added to Franciscan spirituality and became a powerful stimulus for those not called to the life of religious orders. This lay spirituality—not connected with monks and friars—spread and seriously contributed to Franciscan mysticism.[77] This lay movement produced extraordinary teachers who gave oral and written instructions. It flourished either as an attachment to the ecclesiastical network or independently around charismatic teachers and miracle workers.

The proliferation of this autonomous spiritual movement was curbed by the church authority beginning with the Fourth Lateran Council in 1215. The church also implemented clerical reform, improved education, and put a stronger emphasis on church rites, especially the Eucharist, in an effort to create a unified Christian spirituality. Social problems also

73. Ibid., 288.

74. Moorman, "The Franciscans," 303–4.

75. Holt, *Thirsty for God*, 90.

76. Moorman, "The Franciscans," 308.

77. Ibid., 307.

prompted the establishment of Christian lay organizations taking care of orphans, the destitute, chronically ill, and prostitutes. Women's groups, such as the Beguines, actively cared for the sick and the dying. "Beguine" is a loosely defined term designating religious lay communities of women in Northern Europe who shared their income and adhered to a common rule of life without supervision of an established order.[78]

Late Middle Ages (Thirteenth to Fifteenth Centuries)

The late Middle Ages was an era of penitential and apocalyptic themes. Devastating plagues, climatic changes and famines, the Hundred Years War, and a deep institutional crisis of the papacy challenged Christians so much that they reacted with either extremity or calmness. The flagellant movement, the most extreme form of mortification of one's own flesh by whipping it with various instruments, originated in Umbria in the 1260s because of a sense of imminent social and economic doom. Flagellants led violence against Jewish communities, condemning them for the plague epidemic. After the second outbreak of the flagellant movement, it was declared heretical by the church. Artistic expressions were also dismal, depicting hyperrealistic images of a tortured Christ on the cross and the reenactments of the so-called Dance of Death, in which the skeleton, Death, leads a group of victims from all walks of life in a round dance. In England, Christian communities also produced liturgical plays with a focus on Christ's suffering and the Last Judgment.[79]

Medieval Mysticism

The late Middle Ages saw the continuous development and systematization of mysticism that diverged into two streams: intellectual and philosophical on one hand, and affective on the other hand. It was also a division between university-trained scholars and lay people. The Dominican theologian, Meister Eckhart (c. 1260–c. 1328), was a scholar, administrator, preacher, and director of souls. He represents intellectual mysticism. Cyprian Smith and Oliver Davies say about Eckhart:

> Eckhart's doctrine is essentially mystical, concerned with the possible union between the human soul and God. Eckhart knew that

78. Wiethaus, "Christian Spirituality in the Medieval West," 117.

79. Ibid., 118.

this possibility rests upon the grace of God, freely given; but he maintained that it also rests upon something within the soul itself, its intrinsic similarity or analogical likeness to God. He sometimes stressed this likeness so much that he seemed to obliterate the distinction between creature and Creator. . . . The soul, which can be satisfied only by the transcendent God, mirrors his transcendence by never resting in any finite object.[80]

Jan van Ruysbroeck (1293–1381) drew together the two major strands of mysticism, the affective and the intellectual.[81] Holiness in unity, for him, meant the discarding of multiplicity or all things opposed to union with the One. It was approaching God with a bare mind. It also meant abandoning one's will to God's will and aligning all of one's affection to God without clinging to anything in the world. Finally, it meant dying to oneself, "melting" and flowing into God.[82]

A considerable amount of mystical writings from the years 1000 to 1500 survive. Four are outstanding: Richard Rolle, Walter Hilton, Julian of Norwich, and the anonymous author of *The Cloud of Unknowing*. All of them wrote with directness and purpose to help their readers with basic spirituality. Their writing also reflects rich personal testimony and experiential religion, and gives a sound introduction to the devotional life.[83]

Devotio Moderna

The *Devotio Moderna* was a movement that eschewed their concern with contemplation and speculative theology and stressed simple piety and asceticism.[84] Originating from Gerard Groote (1340–84), the movement developed through collaboration between lay people and clergy.[85] The frequent unfaithfulness of the monks and other religious to their vocation, the

80. Smith and Davies, "The Rhineland Mystics," 317–18.

81. Holt, *Thirsty for God*, 93; Davies, "Ruysbroeck, à Kempis and the *Theologia Deutsch*," 322. In his main work, *The Spiritual Espousals*, Ruysbroeck divides the spiritual path into three stages: the active life of virtue and obedience to the Church; the life of yearning for God or interior life; and the life of contemplation of God. According to him, the true union with God already occurs in the second stage, though intermittently. In this second stage, the inward person may know God without mediation.

82. Holt, *Thirsty for God*, 94.

83. Wolters, "The English Mystics," 329–30.

84. Davies, "Ruysbroeck, à Kempis and the *Theologia Deutsch*," 324.

85. Wiethaus, "Christian Spirituality in the Medieval West," 119.

greediness and unrestrained lives of the clergy, and false mystics tinged with pantheism led Groote to a realistic conception of spiritual life: conversion of heart, virtue, endurance of trials, the apostolate, and eternal salvation.[86] Groote's apostolate, the "Brethren of the Common Life," were practical mystics who strove for personal union with God, accompanied by efforts to reform the church through educating young people and instructing the laity in the essentials of the Christian faith. After Groote's death, his followers established the congregation of Windesheim, which became a center for monastic reform.[87] For Groote, contemplation was not an intellectual aspect but a practice with the perfection of charity. In practicing virtues, there was no other way than the imitation of the humanity of Christ.[88]

Among the most representative of the *Devotio Moderna* is Thomas à Kempis' (c. 1379–1471) *Imitation of Christ*. Composed of four books, the *Imitation* stresses the interior life and the Eucharist. After the extreme speculation and intellectualism of the era, the church needed to return to the absolute primacy of love, to a simple conformity to Christ, and to more realistic views and demands of Christian life. According to Thomas, learning is not enough. An uncompromising renunciation of the world is needed. At the center is the uplifting power of love.[89] Thomas says:

> If you would understand Christ's words fully and taste them truly, you must strive to form your whole life after His pattern. . . . If you knew the whole Bible by heart, and the sayings of all the philosophers, what would all that profit you without the love of God and His grace?[90]

> Nothing is sweeter than love, nothing stronger, nothing higher, nothing wider, nothing more pleasant, nothing fuller or better in heaven or in earth; for love is born of God, and cannot rest but in God, above all created things. . . . Love is submissive and obedient to superiors; in its own eyes mean and contemptible, towards God

---

86. Leclercq et al., *The Spirituality of the Middle Ages*, 429–30. The apostolate is a community of people, mainly laymen and some clergy members, for a ministry in the Catholic Church.

87. "Devotio Moderna: The Brethren of the Common Life," Retrieved 1/25/12 from http://www.eldrbarry.net/heidel/bcl.htm.

88. Leclercq et al., *The Spirituality of the Middle Ages*, 430.

89. Davies, "Ruysbroeck, à Kempis and the *Theologia Deutsch*," 324; Leclercq et al., *The Spirituality of the Middle Ages*, 439.

90. Thomas à Kempis, *Imitation of Christ*, 1.1.

devout and thankful; always trusting and hoping in Him, even when it does not taste the savour of God's sweetness; for there is no living in love without some sorrow. Whosoever is not ready to suffer all things, and to stand resigned to the will of his Beloved, he is not worthy to be called a lover. A lover must willingly embrace all that is hard and bitter for the sake of his Beloved, and never suffer himself to be turned away from Him by any obstacle whatsoever.[91]

Eastern Orthodoxy

Based on the traditions of Greek theology and the ecumenical councils up to 787, the Eastern Church developed distinctive emphases that differed from those of the West. Its basic theology was strongly Trinitarian based on the early councils. According to Eastern Orthodoxy, "God is not a monad, but a triad, a mystery of communion in which each Self or hypostasis of the Trinity remains itself even as it exists wholly in the Other."[92]

Theosis

The nature and aim of Eastern Orthodox spirituality can be summed up as in the patristic principle that God became human without ceasing to be God so that humanity might become God without ceasing to be human. The term *theosis* or *deification* summarizes the second half of the principle—God became human that humanity might become God—and signifies the soteriological consequence of the incarnation for humanity. This union with God (John 17:21) is possible to obtain when one learns to die in the mystery of Christ, and it is the goal of *theosis*. The *theosis* heals the separation from God, unites believers with God, and liberates them from death through the work of the Spirit of Christ. *Theosis* is a nuptial mystery in which God and humanity become one as bridegroom and bride.[93]

91. Ibid., 3.5.

92. Wesche, "Eastern Orthodox Spirituality," 41.

93. Ibid., 29–32.

Jesus Prayer

The "Jesus Prayer" emerged between the fifth and the eighth centuries deeply influencing the Christian East.[94] It is the remembrance or invocation of the name of Jesus with frequent repetition. The standard form is "Lord Jesus Christ, Son of God, have mercy on me" with many other variations. The four main elements of the Jesus Prayer are as follows:

1. Devotion to the Holy name "Jesus," which is felt to act in a semi-sacramental way as a source of power and grace.

2. The appeal for divine mercy, accompanied by a keen sense of compunction and inward grief (*penthos*).

3. The discipline of frequent repetition.

4. The quest for inner silence or stillness (*hēsuchia*), that is to say, for imageless, non-discursive prayer.[95]

The invocation of Jesus reaches out beyond language into silence and intuitive awareness, and it also leads to a feeling of warmth in the heart. Between the fifth and the eighth centuries, the Jesus Prayer came to be recognized as a spiritual way, and by the fourteenth century it became frequent in the Byzantine and Slav world.[96]

Icons

From 726 until 843, the Eastern Church struggled with the Iconoclast controversy. The use of icons in the church's worship was formally endorsed in 787 (the seventh ecumenical council), but the definitive restoration of icons to the church was not until 843. The dispute was about the legitimacy and the veneration of icons. Iconoclasts (icon smashers) argued that worship should be restricted to the mind alone, whereas iconodules (icon venerators) claimed that the making of icons is in some way a divine work.[97]

94. In the second half of the fifth century, St. Diadochus, Bishop of Photice in northern Greece, was a decisive catalyst of the Jesus Prayer. He was influenced both by Evagrius and by Macarian Homilies: understanding of prayer as the putting away of thoughts from Evagrius and an affective emphasis upon the spiritual senses, feelings, and conscious experiences from the Homilies.

95. Ware, "The Origins of the Jesus Prayer," 176.

96. Ibid., 177–84.

97. Ware, "The spirituality of the Icon," 196.

To the Eastern Orthodox the icon is not a mere piece of decoration, but a part of liturgy. It is a channel of grace, a point of meeting, and a means of communion. Through the icons of the Mother of God (*theotokos*), the angels, and the saints, the church walls become windows to eternity. The Orthodox home also becomes "heaven on earth" when lamps are lit, incense is offered, and the family prayers are said before an icon corner or shelf. Through the liturgical function of the icon, Orthodox Christians experience God not only as truth and love, but also as beauty.[98]

Apophatic and Kataphatic

Two different spiritual paths were identified in believers' approaches to God: apophatic and kataphatic. Apophatic stresses silence, darkness, passivity, and the absence of imagery, whereas kataphatic emphasizes images and the positive evaluation of creation or human relationships as contexts for the self-revelation of God. Thus kataphatic theology is interested in God's movement outward or self-manifestation in the cosmos, Scripture, and liturgy, and apophatic theology is concerned with the inward movements to God in the process of denial. These two ways are not mutually exclusive, but intricately linked.[99]

In regards to methods of prayer, the apophatic way is understood as still, imageless, or even truly contemplative prayer, and the kataphatic way attempts to imagine God using one's imagination and emotions.[100] In the Eastern Orthodox tradition, kataphatic prayer employed the imagination, poetry, music, symbols, and ritual gestures. Praying to the holy icons was a kataphatic way of prayer. On the other hand, apophatic prayer, expressed in the practice of the Jesus Prayer, transcended images and discursive thoughts as commended by Gregory of Nyssa, Evarius, Dionysius, and Maximus.[101] These two different approaches were used in the West as well.

Synergy

The word "synergy" (cooperation) was coined by Clement of Alexandria to express the workings of two energies: grace and human will. Synergy

98. Ibid., 197–98.

99. Sheldrake, *Spirituality & History*, 199–206.

100. Holt, *Thirsty for God*, 75.

101. Ware, "The Spirituality of the Icon," 198.

has represented the doctrine of the Orthodox Church in these matters. It is first expressed in asceticism and mysticism. The ascetical life is a life in which virtues resulting from human effort prevail, although accompanied by grace, whereas the mystical life is a life in which the gifts of the Holy Spirit dominate over human efforts. In other words, in mysticism, infused virtues lead acquired ones. The Greek Fathers distinguished between the "acting" of man and "acted upon." Generally, the spiritual life is a synthesis of the ascetical and mystical life with love as perfection.[102]

Contemplation is the state believers reach as a result of quieting their souls and the "prayer of simplicity." It is both acquired through human efforts and infused by divine grace. Infused contemplation leads to the mystical life, the culmination of contemplation. Thus contemplation and mystical union are identified with Christian perfection, which is love.[103] Eastern theologian Gregory Palamas (1296–1359), a defender of *hēsuchia* (stillness), stated that union with God is primarily by God's grace, but that the vision of God cannot be attained in this life without hard work. There should be synergy, cooperation between divine grace and human will.[104]

The Holy Mysteries of God

The "mystery" *(mystērion)* of the Orthodox Church is the "sacrament" of the Latin Church. The mystery, as means of grace, has such an important place in the Orthodox Church that it may be called a "mystic" Church. The Orthodox Church fears familiarity and wants a mystery to remain as a mystery. The three essential mysteries that lead to God—baptism, chrisma (confirmation by unction), and Eucharist, in ascending order—are signs. But the baptismal, Pentecostal, and Paschal graces are the realties beyond the signs and the very texture of spiritual life. Christians must go beyond the mere celebration of these signs of sacraments.[105] Kenneth Paul Wesche states:

> The call to baptism is the invitation of Christ . . . to the Eucharistic wedding feast. This is a call to be united to the death of Christ (see

102. A Monk of the Eastern Church, "The Essentials of Orthodox Spirituality," 109–11.

103. Ibid., 111–14.

104. Holt, *Thirsty for God*, 83–4.

105. A Monk of the Eastern Church, "The Essentials of Orthodox Spirituality," 114–120.

Rom 6:3) and so to pass over to the eschatological marriage feast, the eucharist. In the eschaton, that is, on the shores lying on the other side of the waters of death, one partakes of the divine nature (2 Pet 1:4), this is the body and blood of Christ, in a never ending celebration of life in the Spirit of Christ. . . . As one becomes ever more mindful of the movement from baptism to eucharist taking place in one's own interior depths, and as one becomes ever more adept at separating one's true self from the snares of egoism and worldly attachments, one learns how to overcome the world in Christ, and to live the life of Christ's eschatological heavenly kingdom in the world. . . . In the transformation of the Eucharistic gifts, the Logos becomes one with the communicants, deifies them, and sends them out into the world—this is the mystery of Pentecost—to be the salt of the earth, bearing witness, in the process of their own transformation in the way of the cross, to the mystery of Christ as the mystery of *theosis*: union with God in divine love.[106]

Summary

Central characteristics of its understanding of God, Christ, and redemption were worked out by the early Christian church, along with development of monotheism, the Trinity, and Christology. The unifying feature of the era was the Bible. Its theology was an exegetically based interpretation of the Scriptures for fuller Christian faith and life. Theology was also pastoral involving the life of the Church. The patristic period was characterized by the mystical—mystical theology, mystical exegesis, mystical prayer, and mystical contemplation. In this period, the threat of persecution and possible martyrdom, and asceticism as the sustained practice of physical and spiritual disciplines, provided the formative themes of monasticism.

In the medieval West, monastic spirituality dominated the church. Priorities of clergy over lay and majority over minority were characteristic of this time. The mendicant movement, however, found acceptance through the formal recognition of the lifestyle of the friars, especially the Franciscans. The monastic-contemplative approach to spirituality with its effort to transcend time and place also marked the early and middle medieval times. In the twelfth-century renaissance, new intellectual and textual content of spirituality was also developed, dividing spirituality from theology. Growth

106. Wesche, "Eastern Orthodox spirituality," 36–43.

of mystical, devotional spirituality was the most significant development of the late medieval time with its emphasis on the popular need for the specific—sacred places and objects. In the late medieval time, mysticism saw a shift from the objective mystery of Christ in the earlier patristic era to the subjective, experiential, and mystical experience. Radical spirituality—dissent and marginalization—was also characteristic of the late medieval spirituality.

Eastern Orthodox spirituality developed separately from Western spirituality. The aim of Eastern Orthodox spirituality is *theosis*—God became human so that humanity might become God. Having emerged between the fifth and the eighth centuries, Jesus Prayer also deeply influenced the Christian East. To the Eastern Orthodox the icon is not a mere piece of decoration but a part of liturgy. It is a channel of grace, a point of meeting, and a means of communion. Through the liturgical function of the icon, Orthodox Christians experience God not only as truth and love but also as beauty. For the Eastern Orthodox, the spiritual life is a synthesis of the ascetical (human effort) and mystical (gifts of the Holy Spirit) life with love as perfection. The mystery, as means of grace, has such an important place in the Orthodox Church that it may be called a "mystic" church.

4

Protestant Spirituality

IT IS NECESSARY TO distinguish Protestant spirituality from Catholic spirituality. It is hard to define Protestant and Catholic spirituality in single-dimension terms since these two traditions have developed since the Reformation, and both of them appreciate the plurality of the interpretation and practices of both traditions. Nonetheless, the following can be said as distinct, but not exclusive, characteristics of Protestant and Catholic spirituality.

Primarily, the Protestant spirituality emphasizes sole dependence on God, God's word, and eschatological hope. Images or ritual forms that get in the way of the Word of God are questioned, and the expounding of the Scripture and meditation on the Word requires a response of faith. The central task of the Christian is to receive the Word, and ethical purity replaces ritual purity. Catholic spirituality, however, involves concrete, sacramental instruments as mediation of the gospel message. Rituals actualize our relationship with God, and the sacraments fulfill the proclamation of the Word. Both ethical and ritual purity are the expressions of the presence of God. Second, Catholic spirituality emphasizes the unity of the community, images, and mysticism. If the Middle Ages were more concerned with a system of mediation through the church, sacraments, and the intercession of saints, the Protestant Reformation adopted the immediacy of communion with God. Third, while Catholic spirituality maintained a double standard by which the highest kind of spirituality is found in religious communities with a total focus on God and a detachment from worldly concerns,

Protestantism favored a single standard of holiness based on justification by faith, rejecting what they saw as the "works righteousness" of monasticism.[1]

Reformation Spirituality

The fundamental mark of Reformation spirituality was the principle of divine monergism, that it is *God* who initiates and accomplishes everything in the work of salvation.[2] The two vital elements of the Reformation spirituality were the depravity of human will and the unconditional love of God.[3] Sheldrake continues:

> In light of God's sovereign initiative, the theological bases for Reformation spirituality, as opposed to traditional Catholic spirituality, may be reduced to four classical slogans: *grace alone, faith alone, Christ alone and Scripture alone* [emphasis mine]. These, it has been argued, are stronger than merely alternative emphases because the Reformers believed that humans were quite incapable through sin of even *desiring* to be reconciled. God, therefore, completely overrides corrupt human will in order to redeem. . . . The "God emphasis" of the Reformers therefore completely reverses the conventional ideas of spirituality whereby the soul seeks God, ascends to the spiritual plane and the sinner can and must strive to come to God. On the contrary, God alone seeks, strives and descends to us.[4]

The following were the determinatives of Reformation spirituality: the view of individual salvation as the prime purpose of the Incarnation; an all-pervasive sense of personal and corporate sin; and a terrible urgency in the awareness of moral responsibility, especially in association with a preoccupation with personal eschatology. All these elements were based on the humanity of Jesus, specifically his sufferings. Martin Luther's (1483–1546) emphasis on justification and John Calvin's (1509–64) intensive treatment of sanctification were also two hallmarks of Reformation spirituality.[5] It was the absence of justification as a theological category in pre-Reformation spirituality that made Reformers react against Catholic spirituality. Luther

1. Sheldrake, *Spirituality and History*, 206–10.

2. The term, "Reformation spirituality," designates the spirituality of the Protestant Reformation inclusively and is used in comparison with traditional Catholic spirituality.

3. Sheldrake, *Spirituality and History*, 210.

4. Ibid., 210–11.

5. Tripp, "The Protestant Reformation," 342.

felt that the spirituality of all Catholics was affected by this justification gap since they believed they were justified in the process of being sanctified. They were unaware of the imputed righteousness of Christ.[6]

Lutheran Spirituality

In 1517, Martin Luther, an Augustinian monk, posted ninety-five theses for debate at the University of Wittenberg. He taught that grace is free and cannot be earned by works or merits since Jesus Christ merited all the grace needed for justification on the cross. Thus, Christians can only trust in God's promise of justification and respond to God in gratitude.[7]

The Word

For Luther, the scriptural Word was both outward and inward, an external sign and inner experience. The *Logos* is the inner Word, God himself, but for us to understand and absorb it, the Word must assume concrete shape and come in flesh. That concrete external Word is Christ. Christ is God's external Word to man.[8] When a sinner trusts in Christ, "the absorption of the Word makes the soul a sharer in everything that belongs to the Word."[9] Only the Word communicates the Spirit, and only through the Holy Spirit can God's Word open up to a person.[10] Luther emphasized preaching on the Scripture, putting the liturgy in the vernacular and translating the entire Bible into German as ways to enhance an encounter with the Word of God.[11]

Mystical Christ

Luther used such expressions as "the mystical Christ," "mystical incarnation," "mystical theology," and "mystical eyes" when he depicted life in God. He quoted Bernard of Clairvaux that "mystical theology" is "experimental

6. Lovelace, "Evangelical Spirituality," 215–17.

7. Raitt, "European Reformations," 124.

8. Hoffman, "Lutheran Spirituality," 128.

9. Luther quoted in Tripp, "Luther," 345.

10. Hoffman, "Lutheran Spirituality," 128–29.

11. Hanson, "Lutheran Spirituality," 415–17.

and experiential."[12] For Luther, mystical theology was experience of God.[13] Hoffman continues to say of the mystical theology of Luther:

> It is the inner, spiritual side of Christian faith. It is what prayer leads to. It is the awesome and joyful knowledge, beyond purely rational knowledge, that God is present. It is heart rather than head, but never the one without the other. . . . Luther's frequent use of the adjective "invisible" points to his trusting knowledge that faith always moves into dimensions not approachable by reason and logic but available to inner experience. Like the mystics, he assumes the reality of a supernatural or supernormal realm. . . . [M]ystical knowledge *was* part of Luther's spirituality, but it was not free-floating; it was rooted in the justifying *kerygma* of Scripture.[14]

Faith was also an "experiential knowledge" for Luther since "faith causes the heart to be carried away to dwell in things that are invisible." Christ is historical in that he walked on the earth, but this historical Jesus is at the same time mystical Christ as the cosmic Lord and mystical Presence. This double understanding of Christ being both historical and mystical has another important dimension in relation to believers. While orthodox Lutheran dogmaticians speak of the Christ-*for*-us as the basis of faith, Lutheran pietists emphasize Christ-*in*-us. These two sides of the gospel proclamation are both found in Luther. Luther advocated both the justifying for-you and the sanctifying in-you in his theology. Faith as both historical and inner realities are interlocked for Luther and should never be separated.[15]

Sacraments

The saving power of God in Christ is present in the church, not only through the Word, but also through the sacraments. Luther recognized only two sacraments, baptism and the Lord's Supper, although he taught that private confession should continue. He emphasized that baptism is significant lifelong since the Christian is to die to sin and rise to new life daily. Weekly Lord's Supper was the norm in Wittenberg, and in the Lord's Supper

---

12. Hoffman, "Lutheran Spirituality," 127.

13. Ibid.

14. Ibid., 127–28.

15. Ibid., 123–31.

Christ's body and blood were believed to be present in, with, and under the bread and wine.[16] "In Luther's spirituality the word is never separated from the sacraments but is embodied in baptism and the Lord's Supper."[17]

Alternative Model to Ascent

Luther had serious reservations about monasticism and the ascent model of the Christian life, such as Moses' ascent up Mount Sinai to meet God face to face. For Luther, there was no purgatory, pilgrimages, shrines, and relics evincing works righteousness. The grace of God was viewed as primarily forgiveness, utter dependence on God for salvation, and the equal holiness of service, all of which were basically shaped by Paul's imagery of dying and rising with Christ daily.[18]

Priesthood of All Believers and Vocations

Luther taught that the function of priests is to go to God, pray for others, and teach them about God. Every believer has such priestly responsibilities, although ordained pastors should preside over the public worship service of the church. Against the notion of vocation as the call to a holier life as a priest or member of a religious order, Luther said God calls people to serve others through their constructive social roles as family members, workers, or civil leaders. The service of a simple farmer is as holy as that of a priest. Luther thus undercut some of the traditional rationale for a special religious life and elevated the significance of ordinary daily life.[19] For Luther, celibacy is a work and contrary to God's command to increase and multiply. Luther himself married a former nun and urged other religious people to follow his example.[20]

16. Hanson, "Lutheran Spirituality," 415–17.

17. Luther, *Luther's Spirituality*, 183.

18. Hanson, "Lutheran Spirituality," 415–17; Raitt, "European Reformations of Christian Spirituality," 125.

19. Hanson, "Lutheran Spirituality," 415–17.

20. Raitt, "European Reformations," 124.

Moral Life

Luther connected the ethical and the spiritual. For Luther, the moral life was rooted in the mysterious presence of the Cosmic Lord. This inner union of believers with Christ—the mystical element in justification by faith—is the foundation of moral life. The spiritual communion with Christ brings forth active service in life and the doing of justice. In the world, true Christians play a central moral role since Christ is always present with believers in invisible, but real and powerful ways.[21] Luther says about the moral role of believers through prayers:

> This is a paradox: Christians look like "poor beggars," but . . . it is because of Christians and their prayers and actions that "power, honor and goods" exist among people. The unrepenting world does not understand this and "thanks the Christians poorly for it." When "the Christians' words and wonders cease . . . God will end it all; it will all be consumed by fire." Until that happens, those who are spiritually "glued" to the Lord are called to "suffer the stench" from those who do not know the Christ, "in the same manner as the legs carry the paunch and the reeking belly."[22]

Prayer

In prayer, Luther recommended the petitions of the Our Father (the Lord's Prayer) and the use of the Psalms for petition, praise, and thanksgiving. Prayer should not be offered to the Virgin Mary since she is unable to answer prayer. Saints cannot respond to prayer, nor is mass or prayer efficacious for the dead. Christ is the sole mediator of prayer.[23] For Luther prayer was the act of faith *par excellence*, and the powers of darkness attack prayer most sharply. His doctrine about prayer is "without the Word of God the enemy is too strong for us. But he cannot endure prayer and the Word of God."[24] In prayer sinful persons rise so far above themselves that they give the primacy to the honor of God's name, the triumph of God's

---

21. Hoffman, "Lutheran Spirituality," 133.
22. Ibid., 133–34.
23. Raitt, "European Reformations," 124–25.
24. Luther quoted in Tripp, "Luther," 345.

kingdom, and fulfillment of God's will over the matters of our own safety and deliverance.[25]

Reformed Spirituality

The heart of the Christian life is the deeply confident affirmation of experiential faith in God and response to his gracious initiative in both the private relationship with him and corporate expressions of faith. This belief of the Reformed spirituality can be traced back to the Swiss Reformation in the sixteenth century led by Huldrych Zwingli (1484–1531) in Zurich and by Calvin in Geneva. The Protestant denominations are generally called *Reformed* if they originated on the European continent and *Presbyterian* if they started in the British Isles.[26]

The Spirituality of Zwingli

The primary figure in the Reformed tradition, Zwingli's reform efforts resembled those of Luther, but Zwingli went further.

The Supremacy of the Scripture

While Luther allowed whatever is not forbidden by the Scripture, Zwingli taught that only what the Scripture permits is allowed. The piety of Zwinglian Protestantism thus was extremely "biblical." The Word of God was the only source and sustainer of the new life in Christ. Zwingli instituted a weekday service called the *prophesying* to promote familiarity with the Word, and the weekday service was as important as the Sunday liturgy. It was a sort of adult Bible study where the participants shared their understanding of the Word with each other. Zwingli insisted on the scriptural knowledge which is the source of the right knowledge and would cast out ignorance.[27]

In Zwingli's theology and spirituality, prayer is direct from the heart and needs no intermediary. Since Christ is the sole mediator, there is no need of the intercession of the Blessed Virgin Mary or of the saints.

---

25. Tripp, "Luther," 345–46.

26. Rice, *Reformed Spirituality*, 8–9.

27. Hageman, "Reformed Spirituality," 139–40; Raitt, "European Reformations of Christian Spirituality," 125.

Desiderius Erasmus (1466–1536) may have influenced him to oppose the cult of saints. Furthermore, many words are not necessary in prayer, ostentation is hypocritical, and the best prayer is a silent prayer for both the individual and the congregation.[28] He also dispensed with all forms of church music, including choirs and organs, reduced public prayer to bare minimum, and relegated the Eucharist to a quarterly celebration to remind the believers of the atoning death of Christ, all to emphasize the supremacy of the Word.[29]

Predominant Pneumatology

For Zwingli, the Spirit opens up the heart of the believer, and true religion is totally dependent on the inbreathing of the Spirit, without which man turns to idolatry. The Scriptures themselves, therefore, must be approached through the work of the Spirit. There is no conflict between these two.[30] For Zwingli, this inward work of the Spirit is essential and even precedes the work of the Scriptures:

> If you want to speak on any matter, or learn of it, you must first think like this: Before I say anything or listen to the teaching of man, I will first consult the mind of the Spirit of God: "I will hear what God the Lord will speak." Then you should reverently ask God for his grace, that he may give you his mind and Spirit, so that you will not lay hold of your own opinion but of his. And have a firm trust that he will teach you a right understanding, for all wisdom is of God the Lord. And then go to the written word of the Gospel.[31]

Theocentric Emphasis

For Zwingli, believers are those who have the Spirit of God, know that Christ is their salvation, and rely on the Word. They do not sin, and unbelief is the only mortal sin. This theocentric emphasis is applied not only to the individual believer and the community of the elect, but also to the whole life in society: political, social, and even military life. Christian teaching

28. Dent, "Zwingli," 348–49.
29. Hageman, "Reformed Spirituality," 139.
30. Dent, "Zwingli," 347.
31. Zwingli, "Of the Clarity and Certainty of the Word of God," 88–89.

and moral expectations reach into all aspects of life.[32] This fundamental theocentric emphasis of Zwingli is well expressed as follows:

> Only the eternal and infinite and uncreated God is the basis of faith. Hence the collapse of all that foolish confidence with which some rely upon most sacred things or the most holy sacraments. For it is in God that we must put our firm and sure trust. If we were to trust in the creature, the creature would have to be the Creator. If we were to trust in the sacraments, the sacraments would have to be God. . . . For true piety is the same everywhere and in all men, having its source in one and the self-same Spirit.[33]

The Spirituality of Calvin

Calvin read deeply in the fathers of the church. He was also influenced by a Lutheran pastor named Martin Bucer (1491–1551), and it is quite possible that Zwinglian spirituality of Geneva forced him to consider many new questions.

Union with Christ

Calvin's spirituality was based on gratitude for all God had done in Christ.[34] According to Wilhelm Niesel, one of the best modern interpreters of Calvin, the real center of Calvinism as a living faith is not predestination or the eternal decrees, but the union of Christ with believers. It is the basic reality upon which all other spiritual benefits rest. It is baptism that assures us that we are united with Christ and share in his blessings. The understanding of baptism as a sign of the decision of the convert has brought about consequences for different understanding of the church and sacraments.[35]

Faith as Inner and Outer Expressions

Calvin saw the life of faith as unity in both inner and outer expressions.[36] The assurance of the believer's union with Christ is to be expressed not

32. Dent, "Zwingli," 347; Raitt, "European Reformations," 126.
33. Zwingli, "An Exposition of the Faith (I)," 247.
34. Raitt, "European Reformations," 127.
35. Hageman, "Reformed Spirituality," 142.
36. Rice, *Reformed Spirituality*, 11.

only in inward feelings but also in outward lives. Ethical life is emphasized in Calvin's spirituality.[37] It also needs to be stressed that Calvin did not use the words *justification* and *sanctification* sequentially, as is often the case. He saw them as dual gifts coming from the relationship with Christ. From the time of baptism, the believer is not only made right with God through indwelling Christ but is also enabled to grow continually into the grace and likeness of Christ. The believer's union with Christ and his growth into Christ are closely intertwined.[38] The believer's relationship with God is summed up by prayer and a fusion of deep humility with complete confidence. "For Calvin (3.20.1–14), prayer is the chief exercise of faith and we receive God's benefits from it. The rules of prayer are (1) 'reverence'; (2) 'we pray from a sincere sense of want, and with penitence': (3) 'we yield all confidence in ourselves and humbly plead for pardon'; (4) 'we pray with confident hope.'"[39]

The Church as Our Mother

Chapter One of Book Four of the *Institutes* begins with the title "The true Church with which as Mother of all the godly we must keep unity." For Calvin, the church precedes the individual, and by baptism we are brought into the church. It is also in the context of the church that we grow up into Christ by the means of grace. The lonely individual striving alone to achieve sanctification has no place in Calvin's spirituality. It is in the church that Christian growth takes place, and that always as the gift of God in Christ, not as a result of human effort.[40] Within the church, the primary agent for spiritual growth is the preaching of the Word. For Calvin, reading and preaching of the Word is what Christ uses to share himself with believers, strengthening and deepening their commitment and assurance. For Reformed spirituality, the Word is the center of the life of the church and Christian growth. Calvin differs with Luther here in that for Calvin, the Word empowers the believer for a righteous life, but for Luther, the assurance of forgiveness is the final result of the real presence of Christ in the Word.[41]

37. Hageman, "Reformed Spirituality," 144.
38. Ibid., 144–45.
39. Tripp, "Calvin," 356.
40. Hageman, "Reformed Spirituality," 145–46.
41. Ibid., 146–48.

Importance of Liturgy

Calvin departs from Zwingli here by claiming that liturgy is more than preaching and includes prayer, praise, and the celebration of Eucharist. The real purpose of worship is to glorify God, and the real way of glorifying God is by obeying him. Liturgical activities thus enable believers to give God glory in their secular service. For Calvin, Eucharist is the *visible* form of the Word, whereas preaching is the *audible* form of the Word.[42] Brian Gerrish puts Calvin's thoughts well: "The very nature of its symbolism suggests to Calvin that the Lord's Supper is a matter of nourishing, sustaining and increasing a communion with Christ to which the Word and baptism have initiated us."[43]

Calvin's spirituality is well summarized by Howard Hageman:

> What was the spirituality of John Calvin? Once we have been received into God's new people by baptism, we are given everything that Jesus Christ is and has and are enabled to appropriate it in increasing measure by sharing Christ in the preaching of his Word, in the receiving of his Supper, in the liturgical life of his body, the Church. From the power and the strength which we receive in these ways, we are enabled and expected for obedient service to God in the world which is under his promise.[44]

Later Protestant Spirituality

Puritanism

The name "Puritan" was first applied to those who thought that the Elizabethan Settlement of 1559 did not go far enough to reform the English church.[45] They were not separatists, though not satisfied with the established church in England. Most Puritans were influenced by Calvinism, and they developed Calvin's emphasis on sanctification further. For Puritans, conversion was a necessity not achieved without agony or struggle,

42. Ibid., 148–50.

43. Gerrish, *The Old Protestantism and the New*, 111–12.

44. Hageman, "Reformed Spirituality," 151.

45. The spirituality of Calvin flourished in seventeenth-century Scotland among a group known as the Aberdeen Doctors and in Puritan New England. According to *The Practice of Piety* of Charles Hambrick-Stowe, Puritan piety, however, contains two contradictory strains, one anti-sacramental and the other Calvinistic. Hageman, "Reformed Spirituality," 152–53.

and assurance of salvation was crucial. Leaning toward ascetic legalism to create a distinctive Protestant spirituality against Counter-Reformation piety, Puritans sought to attach patristic and medieval spirituality to the Reformation spirituality of justification by faith. They wanted to rule out cheap grace. The goal of Puritanism was the power of godliness as opposed to a form of godliness that denies its power. They opposed lifeless traditionalism or heterodoxy.[46]

Following the tradition of Zwinglian reformation and the Reformed churches of the mid-sixteenth century, Christians are never without the church for one moment. God's covenant is with the church, which is formed by God's act in Christ, not by a mystical hierarchy of supposed succession from the first apostles. Infant baptism was accepted following Luther, Calvin, and the *Book of Common Prayer*, and the Lord's Supper was a permanent obligation for Christians. The Lord's Day was to be devoted wholly to the exercise of religion, and play and work were considered unlawful. At home, the whole household must assemble for worship twice a day, and inordinate affection between husband and wife and parents and children were feared for resulting in detachment in family relationships.[47]

For Puritans, meditation was central to prayer, and a sermon was also a meditation. The sacraments as visible words were a supreme medium of meditation. However, contemplation beyond meditation was suspected, and irrationalism was feared. The mind was a doorway to God. Spiritual guidance was provided not only through sermons but through private counseling as well.[48]

Pietism

Pietism was the great religious movement of revitalization between the Reformation and the Enlightenment within continental Protestantism. It stirred and renewed the Protestant church during the seventeenth and eighteenth centuries, both Lutheran and Reformed, in Germany first, then the Netherlands, France, Switzerland, Scandinavia, and even the new and distant United States. Pietism was the response of sincere Christians to the religious and moral lassitude in Germany after the devastating Thirty Years

---

46. Lovelace, "Evangelical Spirituality," 218–19; Wakefield, "The Puritans," 438–39.
47. Wakefield, "The Puritans," 440–43.
48. Ibid., 443–44.

War (1618–48). They criticized the government-controlled churches and called for the separation of church and state.

Pietism was also a reaction to the dry intellectualism of Lutheran and Reformed orthodoxy. Thus the Pietists emphasized pure life as opposed to pure doctrine, doing over knowing, and experiential knowledge of pastors to awaken their hearers. In Pietism, regeneration and conversion was a focus. Experiencing a breakthrough from sin to the new life of Christian perfection was identified with becoming partakers of the divine nature, and the goal of conversion was the real moral transformation of the believer, the evidence of which was works of love.[49]

The founder of German Pietism is Philipp Jakob Spencer (1635–1705), whose *Pia Desideria* (pious longing) became the seminal text for German Pietism. Then, A. H. Francke (1663–1727) made Halle a center of Pietism, and Count Nikolaus Zinzendorf (1700–1760) founded the Herrnhut Brotherhood in 1722 and welcomed Moravian refugees. Zinzendorf proclaimed a "religion of the heart" based on intimate fellowship with the Savior and gave a profound influence to John Wesley (1703–91). Pietism found its new expression in Wesleyan Methodism. Freidrich Schleiermacher (1768–1834), the father of modern Protestant theology, was also a Pietist influenced by Spencer.[50] About the contribution of Pietism, David Lotz says the following:

> While Pietism often encouraged and sometimes ended in subjectivism, separation, legalism, anti-intellectualism, and mystical-ascetic flight from the world, it must be given credit on the whole, and in its mainline representatives, for the rise of Protestant ecumenicity and mission-mindedness; for significant impulses to philanthropic and educational work; for renewal of the pastoral ministry and preaching office, as well as for a remarkable efflorescence of hymnody and devotional literature; and, not least, for restoring the emphasis on *personal* Christianity (faith as decision) in opposition to "nominal" Christianity, and for saving the institutional church (the *community* of the faithful) from dissolution by a radical religious individualism that might otherwise have won the day.[51]

---

49. Lotz, "Continental Pietism," 449–50.

50. Raitt, "European Reformations," 132; Lotz, "Continental Pietism," 450–51.

51. Lotz, "Continental Pietism," 452.

John Wesley and Methodism

Wesley was the most prominent figure of the eighteenth-century evangelical revival. He was influenced by both Anglicans and Pietists. Although he was a man of one book, the Bible, he read widely. Thomas à Kempis, Jeremy Taylor, and the *Christian Perfection* and *Serious Call* of William Law influenced him the most. The influence of the Moravians was also significant in the conversion of Wesley. The pious group he established was known as the Methodists or the Holy Club. After conversion, he preached the common doctrines of evangelical faith, such as salvation by faith and new birth through the Holy Spirit. He emphasized the Arminian doctrine of God's universal love, prevenient grace, present assurance through the Spirit, entire sanctification, and perfect love.[52] Since humans are able to resist the divine initiative with the freedom of prevenient grace, the path to perfection is a growth in obedience to the divine initiative. God permits a freedom of choice to humans, but because of sin it is not a freedom of choice between good and evil, but rather between resistance and submission to the divine initiative.[53]

Wesley put great emphasis on the means of grace for spiritual life and listed them. The instituted means are prayer (private, family, public), scriptural search (reading, meditating, hearing), the Lord's Supper, fasting, and Christian conference. The prudential means are the Society, Class and Band meetings of the Methodist system, watch nights, love feasts, and covenant services. Though he laid emphasis on the Spirit, his spirituality was not of a Pentecostal or enthusiastic type. Various holiness movements[54] are rooted in Methodism.[55] Although criticized for suggesting that a "second blessing" can provide some Christians with a higher kind of sanctification

52. George, "John Wesley," 455–57; Raitt, "European Reformations," 132.

53. Watson, "Methodist Spirituality," 178.

54. Included in the Holiness Movement were the "Tuesday Meeting" of Phoebe Palmer in New York, the urban revival of 1857–58, the Wesleyan Methodist and Free Methodist in the mid-nineteenth century, the Church of God, Indiana (1880), Church of Nazarene (1908), Pilgrim Holiness Church (1897—merged with the Wesleyan Methodists in 1968 to form the Wesleyan Church), the United Missionary Church (a Mennonite group), the Brethren in Christ, the Salvation Army, the Christian Missionary Alliance, Pentecostalism (as an offshoot of the Holiness movement), and the Church of the Nazarene. The Keswick movement, which originated in Britain in 1875, however, emphasized "deeper life" rather than holiness and rejected the Wesley-Arminian view of sanctification. Pierard, "Holiness Movement, American," 516–18.

55. George, "John Wesley," 457–58.

than that which flows from one's justification, "the Holiness movement contributed to a deepening of the spiritual life in a materialistic age, and it was a welcome contrast to the sterile intellectualism and dead orthodoxy that characterized so many churches at the time."[56] David Watson analyses Methodist spirituality as follows:

> For in the final analysis, Methodist spirituality is nothing if not a responsiveness to the divine initiative. And on this, Wesley's word remains definitive and timely: as we yearn for the Spirit to move in our lives and across the world, let us wait, "not in careless indifference, or indolent inactivity; but in vigorous, universal obedience, in a zealous keeping of all the commandments, in watchfulness and painfulness, in denying ourselves and taking up our cross daily, as well as in earnest prayer and fasting, and a close attendance on all the ordinances of God."[57]

Awakening Spirituality

Living in the eighteenth century, Jonathan Edwards (1703–58) embodied the rationalist ideal of the early modern period. He believed that humans could use reason to know about God and God's universe but must employ the affections to know God. The affections must be turned on by God's divine agency, and only when God instills the soul with a "divine and supernatural light" could the justified comprehend God's beauty and respond to it through growth in holiness. He connected the Calvinist doctrine of predestination and Enlightenment philosophical ideas with God's saving activity.[58] To Edwards, the divine and spiritual light was "a true sense of the divine and superlative excellency of God and Jesus Christ and of the work of redemption and the ways and works of God revealed in the gospel." He taught that this spiritual light is conveyed to the mind by the word of God, and the sense of the divine excellence of Christ is the work of the Holy Spirit.[59] Such preaching, his deep piety, and fervent devotion based on the Reformed and Calvinist traditions prepared the way for the Great Awakening in New England in which Edwards played a major role.[60]

---

56. Pierard, "Holiness Movement, American," 516–18.

57. Watson, "Methodist Spirituality," 207.

58. Bass and Stewart-Sicking, "Christian Spirituality," 143.

59. Faust and Johnson, *Jonathan Edwards*, 102–11.

60. Handy, "Some Patterns in American Protestantism," 474–75.

Awakening spirituality was not simply perfecting individual spirituality but waiting on God in corporate prayer for a Pentecostal outpouring of the Holy Spirit, invigorating the church to attack the kingdom of darkness. Awakening spirituality was also consciously ecumenical. Discernment of the Spirit as work across denominational boundaries of Calvinism, Lutheranism, and Arminianism was a mark of eighteenth- and nineteenth-century evangelicalism.[61] Diana Bass and Joseph Stewart-Sicking say about the development of evangelical Protestantism:

> Other eighteenth-century Protestants, notably John Wesley and George Whitefield, developed Edwards's insights and initiated a popular trans-continental revival movement which emphasized the emotive aspects of faith through a felt experience of being "born again." A Christian spirituality thus seated in the heart—rather than in the head—would eventually shape much of Anglo-American evangelical Protestantism.[62]

Anglican Spirituality

The Caroline age (1594–1728) forms the foundation and first flowering of the Anglican tradition, although Anglicanism traces its root to the New Testament and the Fathers.[63] Anglican spirituality is distinctively corporate, liturgical, and sacramental. Although the Bible is central to Anglican spirituality and is read regularly and extensively, the Bible itself is not the basis of Anglican spirituality. Its basis is the *Book of Common Prayer*, which is the means by which the corporate, liturgical, and sacramental life of the Anglican Church are participated in by both clergy and laity.[64] As an ascetical system in the line of the *Rule of St. Benedict* and liturgical composition, the prayer book is a symbol of domestic emphasis and provides spiritual stimulus, moral guidance, meditative material, and family prayer.[65] The Anglican Church is also pragmatic in that the basic thing Anglicans have in common is neither a doctrinal position nor a religious experience but participating in what the Church does as a church. They are concerned with (1) whether the sacraments are presided over by validly ordained ministers; (2) which vestments may be worn on occasions of public worship; (3) whether the

61. Lovelace, "Evangelical Spirituality," 221.

62. Bass and Stewart-Sicking, "Christian Spirituality," 143.

63. Thornton, "The Caroline Divines and the Cambridge Platonists," 432.

64. Guthrie, "Anglican Spirituality," 161–62.

65. Thornton, "The Caroline Divines and the Cambridge Platonists," 435.

persons proposing to vote in a parish meeting have been baptized, received communion at least three times during the past year, and supported the parish financially.[66]

In Anglican spirituality, personal devotion and meditation are not central. The center of the spiritual life is participation in the corporate, liturgical, and sacramental life of the Church. The Church itself in its entire life and liturgy is the principal spiritual director. There is no special class of believers who possess knowledge or techniques or status that common people do not have.[67] Thornton states, "The patristic doctrine of priesthood is also maintained but not the professional and sacerdotal clericalism of the Middle Ages. The emphasis is upon the *unity of the Church* with the lay intelligentsia playing a leading part. The Prayer Book is nether Missal, Breviary nor lay-manual but *common* Prayer for the whole Church."[68] The "true piety with sound learning" of the Caroline age, however, developed into the scholastic principle of synthesis between faith, reason, and revelation in the philosophical group called the Cambridge Platonists, and moved further towards learning against piety, reason against affective feeling, and transcendence against immanence.[69]

De-traditionalization

During the past few centuries, Christianity experienced enormous challenges in Europe and North America. Christian tradition became less acceptable in the face of philosophical, scientific, political, and social changes. Responding to these massive cultural changes, Western Christianity nevertheless retained its vital sense of the sacred against the forces of "secularization"—secular forces and social organization replacing religious belief and institutions.[70] Scholars of Christian spirituality such as Hans Urs von Balthasar and Louis Dupré trace the roots of modernity back to the fourteenth century nominalist philosophy that emphasized God's inscrutable otherness and argued that it is impossible to speak about God's reality through analogies from the natural world. Thus philosophy and science came to be regarded independent of theology and faith. When this

66. Guthrie, "Anglican Spirituality," 159–60.

67. Ibid., 166–68.

68. Thornton, "The Caroline Divines and the Cambridge Platonists," 433–34.

69. Ibid., 437.

70. Bass and Stewart-Sicking, "Christian Spirituality," 140.

nominalism combined with a rising humanistic thought that stressed human creativity, a new modern thought pattern emerged.[71]

The basis of modernity is separation of science and religion along with the rivalry of reason versus revelation. This separation is not necessarily a process of secularization, but is called by contemporary cultural theorists as "de-traditionalization"—a set of processes by which societies that were once shaped by univocal authority became multivocal cultures where authority shifts to individuals.[72] Bass & Stewart-Sicking continue, "Through the past three centuries, the displacement of external authorities has nurtured a profound sense of the self in relation to God, allowed for an enlarged vision of human community and creation, and prompted serious re-engagement, re-appropriation, and re-working of Christian traditions."[73] Christian spirituality in modernity is characteristic of the multitude of spirituality, a shift from univocality to multivocality.[74]

Summary

Protestant spirituality can be summarized as sole dependence on God, God's word, faith response to the Word, ethical purity, justification by faith, and eschatological hope. The four main characteristics of Reformation spirituality are *sola gratia, sola fide, solus Christus,* and *sola scriptura.* While Lutheran spirituality emphasizes Christ-centered faith (Christ-for-us and Christ-in-us), in Reformed spirituality the heart of the Christian life is the deeply confident affirmation of experiential faith in God and response to his gracious initiative, which can be traced to Zwingli and Calvin. For Zwingli, the Word is supreme. The Scriptures must be approached through the work of the Spirit, and only the eternal, infinite and uncreated God is the basis of faith. Calvin's spirituality is based on gratitude for all God has done in Christ, and union of believers with Christ is the real center of Calvinism.

For Puritans, conversion was a necessity, and assurance of salvation was crucial. Leaning toward ascetic legalism to create a distinctive Protestant spirituality against Counter-Reformation piety, Puritans sought to attach patristic and medieval spirituality to the Reformation spirituality of justification by faith. Pietism was revitalization between the Reformation

71. Ibid.
72. Ibid., 139–40.
73. Ibid., 141.
74. Ibid., 154.

and the Enlightenment within continental Protestantism. Pietists, reacting to the dry intellectualism of Lutheran and Reformed orthodoxy, emphasized experiential knowledge and pure life over pure doctrine. In Pietism, regeneration and conversion were the focus, and the goal of conversion was real moral transformation resulting in works of love. In Methodist spirituality, John Wesley emphasized the Arminian doctrine of God's universal love, the prevenient grace, present assurance through the Spirit, entire sanctification, and perfect love. Awakening spirituality was waiting on God in corporate prayer for Pentecostal outpouring of the Holy Spirit to invigorate the church to attack the kingdom of darkness. Awakening spirituality was also consciously ecumenical across denominational boundaries of Calvinism, Lutheranism, and Arminianism. The twentieth-century Pentecostal/charismatic renewal and its spirituality, which is a genuine part of Protestant spirituality, will be discussed in chapter 6.

In Part 1 of this book, the biblical and historical spiritual traditions have been examined. Truly, both biblical and historical spirituality are varied and diverse, deep and wide. A few observations are worthy to be mentioned. First of all, the spirituality of each era was developed distinctively by the needs of the time. Sheldrake's words ring true:

> Spiritual traditions are not merely accidental "instances of enduring truth," but arise and develop in accord with historical circumstances. . . . [A] theological as well as a historical truth for the realm of spiritual experience is not cut off from the concreteness of the world and history.[75]

Second, there have been healthy tensions between two opposing ideas such as intellectual vs. affectionate, kataphatic vs. apophatic, clergy vs. laity, and contemplative vs. active to name a few. These tensions provide a healthy balance to those who pursue spirituality. Third, the love of God has always been the final goal or objective of spiritual pursuit as Deut 6:4 says, "Love the Lord your God with all your heart and with all your soul and with all your strength."

---

75. Sheldrake, *Spirituality & History*, 218.

PART TWO

Development of Christianity in Kenya

5

Mission Christianity

Two THOUSAND YEARS OF Christian spirituality, though Western, provide invaluable insights into and resources for studying Christian spirituality in Africa. Now, Part Two will examine the historical development of Christianity in Kenya: mission Christianity, the Presbyterian Church of East Africa (PCEA) as a form of mission Christianity, the East Africa Revival Movement, and charismatic and Pentecostal movements. These studies will add essential dynamics to Christian spirituality in Kenya.

Early Catholic (1498–1889) and Protestant (1844–1890) Missions

Early Catholic missions started in 1498 with the arrival of Portuguese explorer Vasco da Gama and several Roman Catholic missionaries to the Kenyan coast. Subsequent attempts by the Catholics left some converts on the coast, but by the time Protestant missions began in the late nineteenth century, there were only a handful of Catholics left. Except for Fort Jesus and remnant church buildings erected by the Portuguese, there remain no significant traces of these early Catholic missions.[1]

Employed by the Church Missionary Society of London, German Lutheran preacher Johann Ludwig Krapf (1810–c. 1885) began the modern era of Christianity in East Africa when he landed in Mombasa in 1844. The main source of this Protestant missionary movement in Britain was the Evangelical Revival in the Church of England, which had resulted from the work of John and Charles Wesley (1707–88) and George Whitefield

---

1. Barrett et al., *Kenya Churches Handbook*, 29–30.

(1714–70) in the eighteenth century. Their work challenged the churches to reach out to the people of the world who had never heard the gospel of Jesus Christ. Although the mainstream churches were reluctant to accept the challenge, those who accepted the challenge formed missionary societies within their membership, and the Church Missionary Society was one of those.[2]

Krapf's main contribution was the translation of the whole New Testament into Kiswahili and the compilation of a grammar and Kiswahili dictionary in two years. In June 1846, he was joined by another Lutheran pastor from Germany, Johannes Rebmann (1820–76).[3] Being optimistic, Krapf explored the interior and thought that the mission could flourish there under healthier conditions, but Rebmann opposed this plan. Krapf left the Church Missionary Society in 1853 and returned to Europe.[4]

Although Krapf left active missionary work in 1853, his influence was still felt broadly in East Africa. He wrote about his experiences in a book, *Travels, Researches and Missionary Labours in East Africa,* published in 1860. This book impacted the United Methodist Free Churches in England, and he persuaded the Methodists to start a mission in East Africa.[5] Krapf returned to Mombasa in 1862 in order to help Thomas Wakefield (1836–1901), the first missionary of the United Methodist Free Church, to establish a mission station at Ribe.[6] The mission among the coastal Mijikenda tribe was considered "as the first link in an equatorial chain of missions which would stretch right across the African continent from east to west."[7]

Then Sir Bartle Frere (1815–84), governor of Bombay, India and a convinced evangelical, brought a new vision of missionary work to Kenya. When visiting Kenya to sign a treaty ending the slave trade, Frere recommended that missions should take an active part in its abolition.[8] Frere objected to the merely "evangelical" mission of the Church Missionary Society and Methodists. He wanted more emphasis placed on the civilizing effects of Christianity. "I regard," he wrote, "the spread of Christianity as practically the same thing as the extinction of both slave-trade and slavery." Frere

2. Wilkinson, *The Story of Chogoria*, 1.

3. Ibid., 2.

4. Nthamburi, "The Beginning and Development of Christianity," 8.

5. Anderson, *The Church in East Africa*, 6.

6. Nthamburi, "The Beginning and Development of Christianity," 8–9.

7. Wilkinson, *The Story of Chogoria*, 3.

8. Barrett, *Kenya Churches Handbook*, 30–31.

did not object to preaching the gospel, but he wanted it in conjunction with "civilizing."[9] Kenya's first schools were established in Freretown and other ex-slave communities, producing the first African teachers and evangelists, and in 1885, Kenya witnessed its first ordained ministers. By 1890, there were about 2,000 baptized Anglicans and a few Methodists—Kenya's first form of organized and enduring Christianity.[10]

The Proliferation of Protestant Missions (1890–1940)

Although the beginning of the colonial era did not immediately bring a large number of missions to Kenya, it changed the missionary movement in Kenya radically, especially when the new Uganda railway came through Nairobi and reached Lake Victoria in 1901.[11] Missionary societies also tended to follow their national flags for the sake of protection after the Berlin Conference (1885) partitioned African countries into British and German spheres.[12]

One prominent characteristic of the Protestant missions in Kenya was that they were denominational missions. The Methodists represented the Methodist Church of Britain. The Church of Scotland Mission was the official mission of the Church of Scotland. The Church Missionary Society started with the evangelical wing of the Church of England. Evangelical Friends in the United States organized the Friends Africa Mission. Missionaries from the Church of God also came from the United States to western Kenya in 1905. The Pentecostal Assemblies of Canada and the Salvation Army both became active in Kenya in 1921. The Southern Baptists started much later in 1956 but spread quickly to many areas due to their large number of missionaries.[13]

At the same time, a number of independent "faith" missions arrived, the major ones being the Africa Inland Mission, the Gospel Missionary

---

9. Anderson, *The Church in East Africa*, 9.

10. Barrett, *Kenya Churches Handbook*, 31.

11. Anderson, *The Church in East Africa*, 62; Barrett, *Kenya Churches Handbook*, 33.

12. Barrett, *Kenya Churches Handbook*, 22; Nthamburi, "The Beginning and Development of Christianity," 10.

13. Anderson, *The Church in East Africa*, 63; Nthamburi, "The Beginning and Development of Christianity," 11–13.

Society (Pentecostal wing of the Africa Inland Mission) among the Kikuyu, World Gospel Mission at Kericho, and the Pentecostal missions.[14]

As for the Catholic Church's reignition, the Holy Ghost Fathers reached Mombasa in 1890. By 1899 they established headquarters at St. Austin near Nairobi, which became a center for industrial training. The Mt. Kenya area, however, was assigned to the Italian Consolata Fathers. In western Kenya, Mill Hill Fathers came in from Uganda.[15]

From early on, Protestant missions divided Kenya into different mission areas with an informal comity. When their aims changed slightly as different missions found they had similar perspectives and purposes, they decided to organize and establish a united, self-governing, self-supporting, and self-extending native church. Coming up with the idea of a "Federation of Missions," each mission would be responsible for its own area but fully recognize the Christians from other areas. The coalition would be comprised of the Church of Scotland Mission, Africa Inland Mission, Gospel Missionary Society, Church Missionary Society, and Methodists. However, doctrinal and ecclesial issues frustrated the creation of the federation, and in 1918 the Alliance of Protestant Missions was formed instead. The Alliance sought to start an Alliance Medical Training Centre, Alliance High School, and Alliance Theological College. It was desirable that the missions should cooperate in the areas of theological training, education, medical work, and general evangelistic outreach.[16] The prominent Alliance High School (established 1926) and St. Paul's United Theological College (founded 1954) are the products of this accord.[17] However, as William Anderson points out, "One obvious defect of alliance effort was that in the whole quest for unity in Kenya, at the conference of 1913 and 1918, no single African Christian attended."[18]

Missionary Methods

From the beginning, missionaries were involved in many activities besides simply preaching the gospel. Roman Catholics believed in the mission of

14. Anderson, *The Church in East Africa*, 63–64.

15. Ibid., 63.

16. Anderson, *The Church in East Africa*, 72; Nthamburi, "The Beginning and Development of Christianity," 22.

17. Barrett, *Kenya Churches Handbook*, 24, 26.

18. Anderson, *The Church in East Africa*, 72.

the church as the source of all true civilizations. They saw the "mission of civilization" as a necessary part of the preaching of the gospel. Presbyterians believed, perhaps even more intensely, in creating Christian communities which were economically self-supporting. They tried to instill in their members the spiritual values of skilled and honest labor of the hands.[19] F. B. Welbourn states with a decisive tone, "The Christian mission must . . . be directed towards the whole man *in his total environment*."[20] It is a well-known fact that "Christians made a unique contribution to education and medicine,"[21] and "both these fields of public service in the name of Christ, [that is] education and medicine were early mainstays of the Christian Council of Kenya."[22]

During the period between 1920 and 1945, a distinctive form of Christianity called *kusoma* (to read) Christianity was developed in Kenya, in which literacy was considered as the cornerstone. Christians used to say *kusoma* when they went to church rather than *kusali* (to pray). Missionaries also helped to shape Christianity in the areas of prayer, worship, biblical translation, and music through the introduction of hymns. The *kusoma* Christianity spread through the pattern of school-dispensary-church. The impact of the *kusoma* Christianity was such that when independent churches broke away from the missionary churches, they used the same pattern of *kusoma* Christianity.[23]

Except in the relatively small areas of Muslim influence, Christianity in Kenya became the religion associated with respectability. Boys and girls tended to accept that it accorded them with superior status as literates. Indeed, it became a common practice, even for those who had not been baptized, to adopt a "Christian" name or to seek baptism for no other purpose than to acquire one.[24] Although many were persuaded by the goodness of the Christian religion, there were always a few nominal Christians

19. Welbourn, *East African Christian*, 80.

20. Ibid., 79.

21. Anderson, *The Church in East Africa*, 87

22. Beetham, "Co-operation between the Churches," 150. The Kenya Missionary Council, originally formed in 1924, which comprised all Protestant missions, changed its name to the Christian Council of Kenya in 1943. Barrett, *Kenya Churches Handbook*, 24–25.

23. Anderson, *The Church in East Africa*, 111.

24. Welbourn, *East African Christian*, 89.

who did not approve or believe in it at heart. For them, it was the "password to learning the arts of reading and writing."[25]

Missionary Attitudes toward African Culture

The first missionaries came to a society that condoned the slave trade. Even Africans were making good profit out of selling their fellow Africans to the Arabs. The society in which missionaries found themselves was polygamous by conviction. Bride price, commonly known as dowry, determined the stability of marriage; women's status was generally low, although they were practically valued as much as men. Women not only looked after their children but also did all the cooking and almost all the cultivation, while men devoted themselves to hunting and to war. A man's importance was measured by the number of wives he had as well as the number of cattle he owned. The institution of marriage was not an individual, but family and community matter.

Dances were an essential part of tribal life but were viewed by missionaries as potentially leading to sexual promiscuity to let out the stress of being bound by rigid social rules. Missionaries found that in some tribes, male circumcision, with all its accompanying pagan rituals, was the only way of entry into adult tribal membership. At the same time, female circumcision, also known as clitoridectomy, was practiced in varying degrees to signify entrance into adulthood.[26]

It is not surprising that the missionaries disapproved of what they saw since, according to Welbourn, "The first Protestant missionaries had been reared in the strictly puritanical surroundings of nineteenth century English middle-class society. . . . They have tended to identify Christian morality with the accepted behaviour of their particular section of western society. Anything African, which conflicted with that behaviour, was by definition, of the devil."[27] John Mbiti states, "The Protestant and Roman Catholic forms of Christianity have meant separating Africans from their society and putting them on the side of Europeans—evidenced by taking European names, joining mission Churches, receiving literary education and hoping for promotion in the mission . . ."[28]

25. Leakey, *Mau Mau and the Kikuyu*, 59–60.

26. Welbourn, *East African Christian*, 104.

27. Ibid.

28. Mbiti, *African Religions and Philosophy*, 237.

Since Christianity came to Africa clothed in the cultural values of missionaries, conflict with African religion and culture was unavoidable. But the Roman Catholics were less disturbed and High Anglicans less rigid than other Christians.[29] The missionaries of the Church of Scotland Mission were negative toward traditional customs, and they made little attempt to understand the significance of African customs, let alone preserve it.[30] For example, the Presbyterian missionaries could accept polygamy before conversion, and did not immediately consider it as a barrier to membership of the Christian community—but reversion to polygamy after conversion led to automatic expulsion. Over time, the practice of tribal dances faded out. In case of circumcision, traditional circumcision rites for boys decreased as Western education gained popularity, and circumcision in hospital became an acceptable substitute. In the case of female circumcision, however, there continues to be a strong resistance to its elimination.[31]

Missionaries tended to beautify or legitimize what they did to African culture, although they claimed that they accepted blame where necessary. Compared to missionaries' writing, the perception of Africans is quite different. According to David Githii, former moderator of the Presbyterian Church of East Africa, missionaries totally rejected Kikuyu religion and culture, and thought "The African customs were a real obstacle to evangelization."[32] Githii continues:

> They [missionaries] thought the "superior" Western culture could be used to civilise the "inferior" African cultures. They therefore endeavoured to rescue the depraved African souls from eternal fire by uprooting the African from his culture by shattering his traditions and trampling on his institutions. . . . Missionaries like Scott and Arthur of the Scottish Presbyterian Church and others of their time believed that Africans could not be redeemed unless evils within their social systems were first destroyed. . . . They did not even take the initiative of trying to understand why the African way of life was the way it was and what the Western way of life could contribute to it. Thus, the missionary told the polygamist to give up all his wives apart from one so that he could become a Christian. Wives and children were to be driven away. This was totally confusing to an African who looked upon motherhood as

29. Welbourn, *East African Christian*, 106.

30. Macpherson, *The Presbyterian Church in Kenya*, 105.

31. Ibid., 105.

32. Githii, "The East African Revival Movement," 16–17.

a religious duty and the children as owned by the clan. Where was the love that the missionary preached to them? How could one love God and one's neighbour and drive away wives and children who had become part of one's life? This made the Africans despise the Gospel, making evangelisation even more difficult.[33]

African theologian J. N. K. Mugambi asks rhetorically, "The identification of the Christian missionary enterprise with imperialism was the evidence of its betrayal of the Gospel! How could God who liberates peoples condone imperialism, alienation of land by foreign settlers; and cultural indoctrination to make people hate their own history and culture?"[34]

Mission Church and Colonial Government

The missionaries who brought Christianity to Kenya were of the same race, and in many instances of the same nationality, as the colonizers. However, missionaries preceded colonialists and, thus, were the first Europeans to come into contact with Africans. The missionaries in some instances greatly helped the colonization process at its initial stage as administrators when there were no government agents. In fact, the missionaries in the nineteenth century believed that European powers were the benefactors of Africa. They did not fully realize what the colonial movement, which they welcomed, would become. Domination by European settlers, forced labor, a color bar, and assault on the African culture were coming.[35]

For a long time, missionaries represented Africans in the Legislative Council of the colonial government. They also depended on government aid for their schools. Missionaries were considered as the intermediary between the Africans and the government, and consequently enjoyed a position of prestige as well. Given their relatively comfortable position, missionaries were unlikely to speak out on social change.[36] The missions' alliance with the colonial governments overshadowed any conflict of interest with the moral problems of imperialism. Missionary styles of life and work became more colonial as well.[37] S. G. Kibicho says along the same line, "The fact that the missionaries belonged to the invader-colonizing race had

33. Ibid., 17–29.

34. Mugambi, "Evangelistic and Charismatic Initiatives," 113.

35. Nthamburi, "The Beginning and Development of Christianity," 27.

36. Ibid., 28.

37. Anderson, *The Church in East Africa*, 88.

an inhibiting effect on their perception and evaluation of African humanity and religion, on the one hand, and of their own Western humanity and religion, on the other."[38] When the Mau Mau Revolt erupted (explained in chapter 7), missionaries condemned it vehemently. At the time, most Europeans, including missionaries, were not prepared to admit that the fierce and prolonged struggle of the Kikuyu that led to the Mau Mau Revolt was due to deep embitterment of Kikuyu peasants who were desperately short of land. By attacking the Mau Mau Revolt, the church established its position as desiring to maintain the status quo.[39]

Even by 1930, long before the Mau Mau Revolt, many Kikuyu considered most missions to be anti-African.[40] In the 1930s, distrust of Europeans and missionaries had grown so intense that the Kikuyu made a proverb of it:

> They [missionaries and white settlers] both needed the land. The missionary approached the chief humbly holding the Bible with one hand and asking for a small piece of land to which to build the mission station. Sooner or later, an agreement was made between the chief and the British governor who became his protector and friend. This was later followed by a treaty whereby the chief agreed to the seizure of a large piece of land that belonged to the tribe. This is why it is a common saying among the Africans that "Gutiri mubea na muthungu" (there is no difference between a missionary and a settler).[41]

There was a time when the agenda of a priest and settler were quite distinct, but this saying implies that the Kikuyu changed their attitudes to missions and that both missionaries and settlers took land from the Kikuyu. Nevertheless, the presence, influence, and activity of missionaries was a stabilizing factor in the colonial period through their access to African opinions and aspirations on one hand, and their access to the Colonial Office via their overseas parent churches and the International Missionary Council on the other.[42] Anderson argues against the suggestion that missionaries were part of a conspiracy to take away African land and limit the natives' freedom by saying, "It is much more accurate to say that while

38. Kibicho, "The Kikuyu Conception of God," 135.

39. Nthamburi, "The Beginning and Development of Christianity," 28.

40. Barrett, *Kenya Churches Handbook*, 35.

41. Githii, "The East African Revival Movement," 29.

42. Macpherson, *The Presbyterian Church in Kenya*, 56–57.

Africans became progressively more critical and rebellious over colonial rule, missions became less critical and more comfortable in it."[43]

Despite the argument presented above that casts missionary activity in a negative light, missions consistently and openly advocated the rights of Africans on any question of exploitation of African labor or ignorance during the early stages of Kenya's colonial history. In 1913, Arthur Barlow (1888–1965) of the Church of Scotland Mission wrote in the *Kikuyu News*, "We believe that the moral and spiritual development of the children of the soil is of as much importance as the financial prosperity of their conquerors."[44]

When colonialism became oppressive in Kenya after World War I, the settlers pressed for a policy of forced labor to obtain it cheaply and abundantly. When Governor Edward Northey (1868–1953) promulgated a policy of forced labor in 1919, the Alliance of Protestant Missions criticized it as being cruel to the Africans. Conference of British Missionary Societies Secretary Dr. J. H. Oldham (1874–1969) also protested to the British government on behalf of Africans in Kenya, resulting in the issuance of the Devonshire White Paper in 1923, which declared that the interests of the Africans must be considered paramount.[45]

Dr. John Arthur (1881–1952), the senior missionary of the Church of Scotland, in that same year entered the Legislative Council to represent African interests. On November 17, 1922, Dr. Arthur had written to Kenya's Chief Native Commissioner about the feelings of Africans against British rule. Arthur asserted that Africans needed to know the laws, to have their interests safeguarded by laws, to receive much more education, and have more tax money spent on their welfare. In short, he said, they needed "a right native policy." He explained, "This naturally embraces steps to be taken towards self-government and control of their own affairs under central authority, increasing with their sense of responsibility." In the Council, Dr. Arthur was an effective spokesman who secured the first large government support for African education.[46]

43. Anderson, *The Church in East Africa*, 104.

44. Ibid., 105.

45. Nthamburi, "The Beginning and Development of Christianity," 27.

46. Ibid., 107.

Missionary Contributions

The following descriptions are the missionary legacy among the Kikuyu, but these statements are also true of other Kenyan tribes.

Demise of Traditional Structure

The most far-reaching condition imposed on the Kikuyu by the Westerners was the halting of Kikuyu expansion into virgin forests, making the old economy useless by creating tension and insecurity about existing land. The failure to provide land to every family member, prohibiting the setting up of new family groups, subsequently weakened family bonds and undermined the very foundation of Kikuyu life. At the same time, large-scale farming and industrial enterprise by the newcomers demanded a good supply of labor and an efficient economic system, including a monetary system and tax collection for public administration. These economic factors and urbanization took men and women away from their traditional settings, weakening further the already jeopardized traditional structure.[47] Robert Macpherson states, "The part of the missionaries in the economic changes brought about by the European occupation was negligible, but in producing conditions which undermined the social and religious foundations of Kikuyu society, they had a leading role."[48] The effect of European settlement in Kenya, including missions, was to gradually obliterate the traditional way of life by forcefully setting Western cultural examples and imposing living conditions that made the ancient tribal practices and sanctions insignificant and obsolete.

Introduction of Western Education and Medicine

It was the systematic Western schooling of children that caused Kikuyu society to be profoundly altered. The Western education that missionaries introduced to the Kikuyu was incompatible with the traditional education system. Based on prolonged exposure of the young to the pressures of family and group life, the traditional process culminated in circumcision and initiation, incorporating the initiates into an age-group and recognizing them as members of the whole tribal society. Western education's replacement

47. Macpherson, *The Presbyterian Church in Kenya*, 94.
48. Ibid., 95–96.

of tribal education created social and economic class stratification. In addition, the very education the missionaries placed in the hands of Africans provided them with means of resistance to colonial rule. When educated, they began to argue with their foreign rulers on equal terms, formed political parties and trade boycotts, and were able to take their case to the United Nations.[49] Missionaries also spread scientific causation to the Kikuyu by introducing Western medicine and hygiene through the building of hospitals and dispensaries. Ancestral spirits and ritual contamination as the main causes of disease were devalued as a result, and tribal sanctions became ineffective.

Introduction of New Religious Ideas

Missionaries brought in new religious ideas. "By their teaching on the nature of God and his relationship to men, they drove a wedge into Kikuyu life at the very grass-roots of religious belief and thereby turned the Kikuyu world upside-down."[50] According to Kikuyu traditional religion, *Ngai* (God) was a remote, transcendent being, and was only accessible by the whole group on occasions of emergency. However, the missionaries taught that God is accessible through prayer individually, anytime, anywhere through Christ. In traditional religion, the after-life was a shadowy existence fading into an unending past, *zamani*[51] in Mbiti's term. Missionaries gave a new meaning to life, a future fulfillment contrary to the habitual focus on the present life as sanctioned by customary law.

New morality was also introduced. Since God is a loving God and is concerned with the welfare of every individual, each individual was now faced with a choice of either reciprocating his love and living properly according to his expectation or not reciprocating his love and being held personally responsible for his or her decision. This personal divine-human relationship was totally new to the Kikuyu. However, Christian Kikuyu claim that missionaries did not bring God to them, but explained him more fully to them!

49. Welbourn, *East African Christian*, 154.
50. Macpherson, *The Presbyterian Church in Kenya*, 96.
51. Kiswahili word meaning "time, age, or past."

A New Status of Woman

Missions raised the status of women. Traditionally, men were hunters and warriors, and women took care of household matters. In the past, more wives meant the possibility of more land. They were considered as assets. However, with increasing shortage of land and introduction of a cash economy, multiple wives and children became an economic liability. The status of women was also seriously but implicitly questioned by the female circumcision issue. Traditionally, women did not have a voice even in matters directly related to them. Although their value as the source of life was acknowledged, their status in the traditional Kikuyu society was low. Women's status as well as their roles changed as a result of the introduction of Christianity. Through education, women were viewed as partners of men and were able to find employment, mainly as teachers and nurses, which made them economically independent.[52]

Regarding gender roles, research participants[53] were asked the question of men going into the kitchen. Two young male participants were not afraid of going into the kitchen to help their wives even though it was considered shameful for a man to enter the kitchen in the traditional Kikuyu culture. It seemed that these men did not follow traditional gender roles. A female research participant said that the traditional gender role had been replaced by the Christian virtue of the husband-wife team helping each other and sharing the burden of family work. Her mother used to say that all work was for everybody. In her own family, her husband was also willing to help her with housework, even with cooking sometimes, although she did not insist that he help. However, another female participant said that the Kikuyu society is still patriarchal, and that a woman is subordinate to her husband. She seemed to follow the traditional Kikuyu culture in regard to gender roles, and she apparently enjoyed the patriarchal nature of Kikuyu home. These examples imply that the research participants live within a changing Kikuyu society.

52. Welbourn, *East African Christian*, 123–28.

53. This research was narrative research done in Nairobi in 2005 on five Kikuyu pastors, listening to their life stories. Thus, the result is not comprehensive but reveals some valuable insights.

Denominational Christianity

Missionaries brought in denominationalism to Kenya. Every major Christian tradition is represented in Kenya, including Roman Catholics, Anglicans, Orthodox, Presbyterians, Lutherans, Methodists, Baptists, Quakers, Seventh-day Adventists, and independents. Mbiti criticizes the legacy of denominationalism as follows:

> Denominationalism and its proliferation . . . are the product of human selfishness and weakness. Our church leaders in Kenya, present and past, African and expatriate, have made a mess of the church through inheriting and agreeing to accept divisions, through multiplying divisions, and through perpetuating divisions. . . . [However,] [t]he essentials of the Christian faith have remained intact, so that the causes and the fact of denominational division are fundamentally peripheral to, and not an essential of, the Christian faith which otherwise is grounded on Jesus Christ who Himself is unchangeable and indivisible. Perhaps Kenya is learning to live above denominationalism and to reap the benefits of the Christian faith in spite of the divided churches on its soil; yet the nettle's sting of denominationalism remains, and as long as it is there no Christian can rest comfortably.[54]

Protestant missions proliferated from the early stage. They even made a comity, divided up the land, and assigned a certain portion to a certain denomination. That is why one denomination is more prevalent in one area and less popular in another. For example, the Pentecostal Assemblies of God (PAG) spread among the Luo and Luhya; Quakers are strong among the Luhya; Seventh-Day Adventists are more prominent among the Luo; and the Presbyterian Church of East Africa is predominantly Kikuyu.

The Presbyterian Church of East Africa (PCEA)

The PCEA is a denomination established by Scottish Presbyterian and American Baptist missionaries.[55] It is presented here as an example of mission Christianity.

---

54. Mbiti, "Diversity, Divisions and Denominationalism," 147.

55. Macpherson, *The Presbyterian Church in Kenya*, 21.

Early History

Sir William Mackinnon (1823–93), chairman of the Imperial British East Africa Company, was a staunch member of the Free Church of Scotland, a body which had separated from the Church of Scotland in 1843 on the issue of state interference in church affairs. Mackinnon formed a small committee of directors for their own independent mission called the East African Scottish Mission. In 1891, they approached the Free Church of Scotland to request the service of Rev. Dr. James Stewart (1831–1905), the principal of the Lovedale Missionary Institution in South Africa. Their request was granted, and Stewart launched a pioneer missionary expedition to Kenya on September 19, 1891. They arrived in Kibwezi in Ukambani, about 200 miles inland from Mombasa. The area turned out to be unhealthy with a sparse population, so it became clear that Kibwezi could not be the permanent site of the mission.

Thomas Watson (d. 1900) moved the mission to Dagoretti, and finally to Thogoto, which became better known as Kikuyu after the name of the people living there. Upon the death of Watson, the directors of the East African Scottish Mission approached the Church of Scotland to request the takeover of the mission. In May 1901, the General Assembly of the Church of Scotland agreed to accept this request, and, on January 1, 1903, the Church of Scotland Foreign Mission Committee assumed responsibility for the Kikuyu mission. The Church of Scotland Mission followed the direction set by the missionaries at Lovedale, South Africa, and Livingstonia and Blantyre, Malawi, that is, the combination of religious, educational, medical, and industrial activity.[56]

As of 1920, the Church of Scotland Mission introduced African church governance by ordaining the first seventeen native elders at Tumutumu, constituting the Tumutumu Kirk Session, the first African Kirk Session. In 1926, the first three African pastors were ordained at Kikuyu.[57]

The Gospel Missionary Society was a product of the Dwight Moody (1837–99) and Ira Sankey (1840–1908) revival campaigns in the United States in the 1870s and '80s. The revival was to reclaim men from the power of evil by faith in Christ through evangelistic preaching and gospel hymn singing. They drew support from Baptist congregations and revivalist groups in the States, especially from the north. The society began its

---

56. Wilkinson, *The Story of Chogoria*, 4–8.

57. *Presbyterian Church of East Africa: Centinnial Celebrations*, 11–13.

work in Kenya in 1895 with the arrival of a group of missionaries from the United States, which included Peter Scott (1867–96), the founder of the Africa Inland Mission, and Rev. and Mrs. Frederick and Bertha Kreiger, who represented the Gospel Missionary Society. They maintained a close link with the Africa Inland Mission working under its general direction until they were able to become independent sometime between 1911 and 1913. In 1899, the Kreigers were joined by Rev. and Mrs. W. P. and Myrtle Knapp.[58]

Macpherson explains the reasons for the success of the Gospel Missionary Society in Kenya, which lay partly in the character and quality of their missionaries, such as the Knapps, and the open attitude of the leading families of central Kiambu. As a missionary, Knapp's conviction was that his role was secondary only to the power of the gospel itself, and Mrs. Knapp's hospitality was appreciated by the Kikuyu. Despite weakness in education and informal organization structure as a missionary society, Knapp was an excellent evangelist and advisor. At the same time, Kikuyu leaders in Kiambu were unusually progressive and open to new ideas, especially after six years of natural disasters had swept through their region.[59]

The Kambui mission station of the Presbyterian Church of East Africa began under the Gospel Missionary Society. They remained in close contact with the Presbyterians despite differences in doctrine. In 1943, the Synod of the Presbyterian Church of East Africa was formed with the Kikuyu and Tumutumu Presbyteries, and the PCEA was declared by the Church of Scotland to be autonomous. Shortly after, in 1946, the Gospel Missionary Society was united with the Presbyterian Church of East Africa to form a third presbytery, the Presbytery of Chania. The Overseas Presbytery of the Church of Scotland, Kenya and the Synod of the Presbyterian Church of East Africa were amalgamated to form the General Assembly of the Presbyterian Church of East Africa in 1956, and it was the new beginning of the PCEA as a new Protestant denomination in East Africa.[60]

The Issue of Female Circumcision and Schism

Female circumcision is an age-old custom practiced by the Kikuyu, symbolically similar to male circumcision. The ritual initiates Kikuyu girls into

58. Macpherson, *The Presbyterian Church in Kenya*, 84–85.

59. Ibid., 88–89.

60. Muita, *Hewn from the Quarry*, 13, 126–28, 133.

full membership of the tribe. Without circumcision, a girl was considered as a child regardless of her age. Missionaries were shocked by this practice, and one missionary in Kikuyu called it "sexual mutilation." The official term of this practice by the World Health Organization (2000) is "female genital mutilation." It comprises all procedures involving the partial or total removal of the external female genitalia or other injury to the female genital organs—whether for cultural, religious, or other non-therapeutic reasons. The causes of female genital mutilation comprise a mix of cultural, religious and social factors within families and communities.[61] In the case of the Kikuyu, the purpose of female circumcision is sociological, that is, for identification with the cultural tradition, initiation of girls into adulthood, social integration, and the maintenance of social cohesion.

The Church of Scotland Mission in Kikuyu had doctors and hospital facilities and were conscious of the serious medical risks of this practice. They started teaching girls and their parents about the risks of female circumcision even before 1910. Over the next twenty years, there were many debates and discussions between missionaries and African Christians of different missions. Discussion was also among African Christians themselves of both sexes, the majority of which was against the practice. For example, a group of African Christians from Kiambu declared, "We find it our duty to take up our stand on the matter and show that it is not the Europeans that make the law against circumcision of women but we Kikuyu ourselves."[62] However, in September 1926, Kiambu Native Council adopted a resolution that the operation may be performed by skilled women authorized by the Council, and that it should be minimal. The Church of Scotland Mission Memorandum reveals the ethos of the Kikuyu in those days:

> Great importance is attached to it by conservative natives and it will take many years to get native public opinion to view the practice with the disfavour with which Europeans regard it. Its devotees firmly believe that it is a serious disgrace for an uncircumcised girl to give birth to a child, and the operation is thus in their eyes an essential precedent to marriage, and the girls in most cases insistently demand it.[63]

In 1920, the Church of Scotland Mission made it a rule that baptized church members undergoing the operation or allowing their daughters to

61. World Health Organization 2000, "Fact Sheet No 241."

62. Wilkinson, *The Story of Chogoria*, 67.

63. Githii, "The Introduction and Development," 139.

undergo it ought to be disciplined by being suspended from church membership.[64] Thus, the campaign of the Church of Scotland Mission against female circumcision had built steadily until the young church had a head-on collision with the Kikuyu Central Association in 1929. In March 1929 in Tumutumu, a "United Native Conference" of African representatives from all the Protestant missions in Kikuyuland was held. They voted unanimously that female circumcision was "evil and should be abandoned by all Christians."[65] On September 28, 1929, at the Chogoria Church of Scotland mission station, Dr. Clive Irvine (1893–1974) and his leaders prepared a paper that contained the following promise for people to sign: "I promise to have done with everything connected with the circumcision of women, because it is not in agreement with the things of God, and to have done with the Kikuyu Central Association because it aims at destroying the Church of God." The "Chogoria Oath," as it was called, spread quickly through Kikuyuland.[66] Louis Leakey explains the response of the Kikuyu as follows:

> The majority of the Kikuyu took this to be a violent attack on an age-old custom which was considered essential to the welfare of the tribe, since, without initiation, girls could not become full members of the tribe, nor, by Kikuyu custom, were they eligible for marriage. A wave of fury swept through Kikuyu country and the K.C.A. [Kikuyu Central Association] were not slow to take advantage of this in order to point out how greatly the white man, and particularly the missionary, was an enemy of the people. They said, in effect, "First the land has been taken from us" . . . "and now they attack our most sacred customs; what will they do next?"[67]

Around this time, the dance song called *Muthirigu* also spread throughout Kikuyuland defaming missionaries, administrators, loyal church elders, and Kiambu chiefs.[68] It was used as a medium of resistance to combat all forms of foreign domination during the colonial period, even after the song was legally banned in 1929. The Kikuyu used the song to campaign against the colonial administration and missionaries' efforts to distort, erase, and change the Kikuyu way of life in order to make them

---

64. Strayer, *The Making of Mission Communities*, 137.

65. Ibid., 138.

66. Wilkinson, *The Story of Chogoria*, 71.

67. Leakey, *Mau Mau and the Kikuyu*, 89.

68. Strayer, *The Making of Mission Communities*, 139.

more effective servants of the white man.[69] Wanjiku Kabira and Karega Mutahi present three verses of the song:

> Agikuyu you are fools (x2)
>
> You abandoned your *gika* (the base wood) because of the match box
>
> *Gika* and *rurindi* (the stick used to rub against the base wood to make fire) (x2)
>
> Were passed on to us by *Iregi* generation (the rebel generation)

> An uncircumcised church girl is foolish.
>
> When sent to work in the garden she goes to climb the castor trees.

> An uncircumcised girl is foolish.
>
> You know, she is because when a child gets choked by bananas she bursts into laughter.
>
> *Rwenji* (the circumcising knife) and *ndangwa* (the wrapping cloth of the knife) were passed on to us by Iregi generation (x2).[70]

In the first verse the artist rebukes the people for their blind acceptance of the white man's ways while forsaking their own which were handed down by their ancestors. In the second verse the artist despises an uncircumcised girl by depicting her as a small child who is immature and irresponsible. The third verse emphasizes further the weakness of immature girls who do not know how to take care of a baby.

For most missionaries in Kikuyuland, female circumcision was simply abhorrent. For Kikuyu girls, the issue at stake was whether they had the right to refuse the brutal practice and other marriage-related rituals that were not morally acceptable to believers. But for the Kikuyu Central Association and the politically minded Kikuyu leaders, the issue was nothing less than the unity of the Kikuyu. They argued that if girls were allowed to refuse circumcision, it would divide the tribe at a time when the Kikuyu politicians needed to unite the people and demand redress of land, labor, and political grievances arising from European settlement in the Kenya Highlands.[71] Through the clash with the Kikuyu Central Association, the

---

69. Kabira and Mutahi, *Gikuyu Oral Literature*, 23–24.

70. Ibid.

71. Wilkinson, *The Story of Chogoria*, 69.

only African political party in existence at that time, the missionaries began to understand the anxiety felt by the Kikuyu about security of land tenure.[72] Missionaries had failed to see the deep cultural and religious values associated with the initiation ceremonies and circumcision rituals.[73] Through all this, the colonial government refused to support the missionaries in their campaign to suppress female circumcision.[74] R. W. Strayer writes:

> The noticeable reluctance of the government fully to support mission efforts for wholesale suppression of female circumcision was in large measure responsible for limiting the political impact of the crisis, though it opened up a considerable breach between the more conservative missions and colonial authorities.[75]

The importance of this episode was that it led to the start of many Kikuyu separatist churches and schools away from mission Christianity. The two main separatist churches were the Kikuyu Orthodox Church and the Kikuyu Independent Pentecostal Church, which came out of the Kikuyu Karing'a (tribal unity and purity) Schools Association and the Kikuyu Independent Schools Association respectively. These new churches and organizations were closely affiliated with the Kikuyu Central Association, and became more and more the training ground for nationalist and anti-white sentiments, even becoming the recruiting ground for hundreds of Mau Mau adherents later.[76] Githii also says the female circumcision issue led to the awakening of Kenyan nationalism among the Kikuyu.[77]

The Church of Scotland Mission experienced a temporary setback due to the crisis but regained the previous level of church and school attendance within a few years and continued to increase steadily throughout the colonial period. It was the mission communities that provided Kenyans with cultural and material benefits such as respectability, employment opportunities, and the most advanced education available in the colony.[78]

---

72. Macpherson, *The Presbyterian Church in Kenya*, 114.

73. Nthamburi, "The Beginning and Development of Christianity," 18.

74. Githii, "The Introduction and Development," 138.

75. Strayer, *The Making of Mission Communities*, 138.

76. Leakey, *Mau Mau and the Kikuyu*, 89–91; Nthamburi, "The Beginning and Development of Christianity," 18–19.

77. Githii, "The Introduction and Development," 169.

78. Strayer, *The Making of Mission Communities*, 157–58.

Developments

The Presbyterian Church of East Africa continued to grow. They had many church-sponsored schools, community projects, and the Kikuyu, Chogoria, and Tumutumu hospitals. With the achievement of independence in 1956 under a new constitution, the PCEA entered a new phase of its existence. All of its work fell under the authority of the individual General Assembly, which met every three years, with its General Administration Committee meeting annually in between years. The church put great emphasis on training its leaders because of increased membership after the end of the Mau Mau Revolt. In 1956, they joined the Anglican and Methodists to set up a joint theological college named St. Paul's United Theological College. Future ministers would be sent to this college for training before ordination. They also established the Lay Training Centre at Kikuyu in 1962 to provide training for elders and church members at large.[79]

Another important event in the growth of the Presbyterian Church was the establishment of the Church School. Although Sunday Schools existed from early on in the Church of Scotland Mission, it was not until 1964 that the first Church School Committee was formed in Chogoria Presbytery and found its secure place within the Church. With removal of primary school management from the Church by the Education Act of 1968, the importance of these Church Schools for religious education was recognized.[80] All of my research participants attended and were benefited by the Church School as they grew up. They are the living legacy of this great program.

In 1968, when the PCEA celebrated its 70th anniversary, it adopted a new emphasis on mission called *NENDENI* ("Go ye . . .") outside the normal boundary of the Presbytery. It was a clarion call for the PCEA. Muita explains:

> Up to this time, the PCEA had been basically a church for people around Mt. Kenya and the Agikuyu in the Rift Valley working on the white settlers' farms, although there was some work going on among the Maasai at Ngong. The language used in the programmes of outreach up to that time was largely Kikuyu. The church decided to extend its mission outreach beyond the Gikuyu-Meru borders in order to fulfil Christ's command in Matthew 28:19–20. . . .

79. Wilkinson, *The Story of Chogoria*, 140–41.

80. Ibid., 157.

> The General Assembly decided that the whole church should be involved in mission work as the primary objective of the calling from God.[81]

From this point on, the Presbyterian Church expanded its work to other tribal areas in Kenya and also into Uganda and Tanzania.

Another ministry worth mentioning is the Woman's Guild. This body was set up originally in 1887 in Scotland and became a national movement united in its service and support of the church. Kenya's Woman's Guild was begun in 1922 by Minnie Watson, widow of Thogoto Mission founder Thomas Watson, and has become an important part of the work and witness of the Presbyterian Church through fundraising, visiting the sick, distributing food and clothing, teaching hygiene to girls and women, and leading worship and prayer.[82] Isaiah Muita describes the activities of the Woman's Guild:

> The Guild continues to give life to the church in worship, fellowship and church development. Today, there are many women deacons and elders in the church who grew into leadership through the Guild. Woman's Guild members do significant charitable work in the country nationally, as well as in their local parishes. They also reach beyond the borders of Kenya.[83]

The PCEA first published the "Practice and Procedure Manual," in 1969, incorporating materials from the past manuals of 1935 and 1956 and from various acts and resolutions on procedural matters approved by the General Assemblies of 1958, 1961, 1964, and 1967. The current edition was published in 1998.[84] One research participant attributed the orderliness of the Presbyterian Church to the "Practice and Procedure Manual."

To encourage the search for self-identity and independence of the PCEA from Scottish influence, then Secretary General Rev. John Gatu issued a moratorium in 1971. The concept had surfaced the previous year in the World Council of Churches' debate, encouraging a "cessation of sending and receiving money and missionary personnel for a period to allow time for the review of the best use of persons and money in response

---

81. Muita, *Hewn from the Quarry*, 77.

82. Wilkinson, *The Story of Chogoria*, 178.

83. Muita, *Hewn from the Quarry*, 62.

84. Ibid., 74.

to God's mission and the churches' search for self-hood."[85] He argued that the "time has come for the withdrawal of foreign missionaries from many parts of the third world, that the churches of the third world must be allowed to find their own identity, and the continuation of the present missionary movement is a hindrance to this self-hood of the church."[86] Despite the misunderstanding of many missionaries, the Presbyterian Church of East Africa took up the challenge to do its ministry and mission work using local resources, and the concept of JITEGEMEA was adopted in 1971.[87] JITEGEMEA literally means "to stand on your own feet," but as a concept it means "movement toward self reliance."[88] In 1973 the JITEGEMEA motto became the working philosophy of the Presbyterian Church towards self-reliance and was included in the Church's logo. With this concept of self-support and self-determination, the Presbyterian Church moved forward, and every individual and congregation realized that the Church must now be financially supported by the local people.[89]

For almost thirty years, the logo of the Presbyterian Church had a cross with the word JITEGEMEA printed over the cross. With JITEGEMEA, the PCEA's mission was to transform formerly dependent people into competent individuals so that the church could become truly independent.[90] In 1991, the PCEA created the centennial logo with the JITEGEMEA cross still in the middle. In 2006, the PCEA's 18th General Assembly adopted the current logo, replacing the JITEGEMEA cross at the center with a plain cross (emblem of Christian faith), and included a dove (Holy Spirit), two torches (light of the gospel), a burning bush (burning but not consumed despite trials and tribulations) surrounding all, and the Bible and "faith," "hope," and "love" (pillars of the faith) on the foundation. Unlike the previous logos, this new logo seeks to express the theology of the Church's dependence on God and its interdependence with all Christian believers.[91]

---

85. Anderson quoted in Muita, *Hewn from the Quarry*, 81.

86. Muita, *Hewn from the Quarry*, 81.

87. Ibid.

88. Moffatt, *The Presbyterian Church of East Africa*, 1–2.

89. Muita, *Hewn from the Quarry*, 82.

90. Ibid.

91. Presybterian Church of East Africa, *New Logo*.

Occupying more than 60 percent of PCEA membership, women have been instrumental in strengthening the witness of the church. The ordination of women as elders was first discussed in 1962 and declared at the fifth General Assembly in 1967, with the restriction that their number chosen for ordination to the office of ruling elder would not exceed one-fifth of the total active membership of the kirk session. The restriction remained for a time, but it is no longer valid.[92] Two of my research participants are women, and they are the product of this resolution. Presently, within in the PCEA, female pastors are being appreciated, and are in more demand than male pastors because of their hard work and service. Furthermore, many women study theology at St. Paul's University with their own money. On the General Assembly level, people are more understanding of women pastors than in the past.

Despite frustration with the pace of implementation due to the many steps required of an issue to reach the General Assembly, the Presbyterian Church of East Africa continues to reform. Recent years have seen the denomination decentralize finances. For example, minister salaries since 2003 have been paid by the individual presbytery rather than from the head office. This can be a problem when there is monetary imbalance between the presbyteries. Worship is also being transformed. Many young people left the PCEA, feeling the inherited format was rigid or dull. Thus, "praise and worship" was introduced into the Sunday worship. The congregation is allowed to praise with freedom and pray aloud, even in tongues.

92. Muita, *Hewn from the Quarry*, 62, 73.

Officially, they also changed the language used in worship. Moving from the Kikuyu language of the majority, Kiswahili and English services have been implemented to accommodate people of other tribes. It has not been easy since many old people feel more comfortable with Kikuyu, even some of the ministers themselves.

As a predominantly Kikuyu denomination, they have an advantage of bringing the Kikuyu together and enhancing or retaining the culture. This cohesiveness is a real strength for their development. The disadvantages are tribalism and pride.

Summary

The interpretation of the effects of mission Christianity by missionaries is rather biased. Missionaries tended to amplify their successes while diminishing their failures. However, the interpretation by Africans is quite critical. Africans feel grateful to mission Christianity for its contribution to civilization, but they resent colonialism, which is almost inseparable from mission Christianity. Mission Christianity, both Catholic and Protestant, is still strong in Kenyan religious milieu, is well established in Kenyan society, and influences society and politics. However, it is just one of many forms and expressions of Kenyan Christianity, which includes the Orthodox, African Independent Church, and the charismatic and Pentecostal church. Mission Christianity brought to Africa the gospel, clothed in Western attire and under the colonial regime, and Africans did not have much choice but to follow the instructions and examples shown to them by their colonial masters. Perhaps it is time for leaders of mission churches to readjust their theology and practices to address the real needs and deep desires of Africans for meaningful existence in the African continent.

Scottish missionaries laid a foundation for the PCEA. It was combined with American evangelical missionaries, and the PCEA became an independent church in Kenya in 1956. Despite setbacks caused by cultural and political conflicts, the PCEA developed into one of well-established Protestant denominations in Kenya providing various services to Kenyans including education and medicine. The church's orderliness, development mindedness, and governance are considered its strengths, with Kikuyu tribalism viewed as disadvantageous. The PCEA has been trying to reform itself internally by bringing in new mission emphasis (*nendeni)*, self-reliance (*jitegemea*), stewardship practice (tithing over pledging), new transfer policies for pastors, and introduction of Kiswahili and English services to urban areas. The PCEA has suffered the loss of many of its youth to charismatic churches, and they are trying to cope with this challenge by renovating its worship services and ministry practices. There also have been struggles between staunch adherents of the Church of Scotland traditions and charismatic pastors within the denomination.

6

East Africa Revival Movement & Charismatic and Pentecostal Movements

East Africa Revival Movement

THE MISSION CHURCH OF East Africa experienced a setback and a chaos due to the controversial issue of female circumcision before the Rwanda revivalists came to Kenya. Confused and shaken up over the dispute, as well as the general disintegration of African traditional society and its culture, many Christians went back to their former way of life, church membership decreased, and spirituality and morality also declined.[1] In this context the spread of the East Africa Revival Movement to Kenya was essential and deeply comforting to the mission church.

History

The Ruanda (Rwanda) General and Medical Mission was an independent auxiliary of the Church Missionary Society in Rwanda.[2] Its first mission station was built in July 1925 at Gahini on the eastern shore of Lake Muhazi. At Gahini, medical work was begun early, and a hospital of seventy-five beds was finished in 1928. It was among the staff at this hospital that the East Africa Revival Movement began in December 1933.[3] It is said that

---

1. Githii, "The East African Revival Movement," 42.
2. The Church Missionary Society was founded by the Anglican Church in 1799.
3. Smith, *Road to Revival*, 57.

the movement was influenced by the Keswick Conventions of England[4] because of Joe Church, who arrived in Rwanda with a clear conviction of Keswick experience.[5] In 1937, the first team of Revival leaders from Ruanda travelled to Kenya and spoke at meetings in Nairobi, Kabete, Weithaga, and elsewhere. A small group of Christians, including a prominent Anglican clergyman, experienced salvation in a deep sense. Another Revival group visited Kenya in 1938 and held successful campaigns at the Pumwani Church of the Church Missionary Society in Nairobi. More Anglican clergy were among a number of Christians who experienced renewal, or were "saved," along with many other laymen who graduated from Kikuyu's prominent Alliance High School.[6]

The members of the Revival movement were called *balokole* (the saved ones) in the Luganda term. However, the members of the Revival called themselves "Brethren."[7] Although the Revival leadership began with European missionaries, soon African leadership took over the movement and it became truly indigenous.[8] The movement developed rapidly in Kenya following World War II and membership increased greatly, especially in the Anglican, Presbyterian, and Methodist churches, where its dynamic evangelistic influences gained confidence of those denominations.[9]

Organization

The organization of the Revival movement was quite different from the structures of mission churches. It had no officials, no executives, no salaried workers, no headquarters, no offices, no paperwork, no minutes, no budgets, no membership list, and no annual subscription fees.[10] Nevertheless,

4. Keswick Conventions of England was an annual summer gathering of evangelical Christians. The first Keswick convention, held in 1875, became the mother of similar conventions not only in England but also in many other countries throughout the world. It had a characteristic of spiritual clinic where defeated and ineffective Christians were restored to spiritual health. The convention also stressed the importance of missions and deeply influenced the missionary movement. Barabas, "Keswick convention," 603–4

5. Wanyoike, *An African Pastor*, 151; Ward, "'Ukutendereza Yesu' the Balokole Revival," 113.

6. Githii, "The East African Revival Movement," 42; Wilkinson, *The Story of Chogoria*, 100; Mambo, "The Revival Fellowship," 111.

7. Mambo, "The Revival Fellowship," 110.

8. Wilkinson, *The Story of Chogoria*, 100.

9. Mambo, "The Revival Fellowship," 112.

10. Ibid., 113.

the movement was not totally without structure. It had a main body called "team meeting," which is a loose framework of planning at various levels—national, provincial, district, and divisional. It was comprised of a representative group of brethren meeting regularly to discuss matters of mutual spiritual interest and to coordinate Revival activities throughout Kenya. At the provincial and national levels, teams organized conventions, while at the district and divisional levels, teams planned monthly or fortnightly fellowship gatherings or open-air evangelistic meetings. A unique feature of the team meeting was that all decisions were made unanimously; majority voting was not practiced.[11] The main team in Kenya of *wandugu wa mzigo* (those who carry the burden) was held in high esteem, like the elders in traditional society.[12]

Revival brethren met regularly. Small group meetings were held in private homes, under trees, and in church buildings every one or two weeks. These meetings were an important feature of the Revival since they provided opportunities for testimony, open confession of sins, mutual encouragement, prayer, Bible reading, and frequent singing of the Revival chorus *Tukutendereza* (We praise Thee, Jesus).[13] Besides these fellowships, provincial, national, or regional (East African) conventions were held, which played a significant role in raising African Christian leadership.

Conventions

Local conventions were held in Kenya from 1937, but it was in 1947 that the Revival made a breakthrough at Kahuhia convention in Kikuyuland. Up to Kahuhia convention, missionaries planned and organized large conventions, but Kahuhia saw African leadership take complete charge, which turned out to be crucial to the success of the Revival.[14] Anderson says about this convention:

> With missionary organizers only a few hundred could have attended. But Africans did not count beds—they cleared classrooms and laid down banana leaves, so that visitors could sleep wall-to-wall. They organized great kitchens, collected food and cooks, dug latrines, and took in three to four thousand people.

11. Ibid., 115.

12. Githii, "The East African Revival Movement," 47.

13. Wilkinson, *The Story of Chogoria*, 101; Mambo, "The Revival Fellowship," 112–13.

14. Anderson, *The Church in East Africa*, 128.

> The convention reached five to ten times as many people as a missionary-organized one could have reached.[15]

Following Kahuhia convention, there were three other powerful conventions from 1948 to 1950. The 1949 and 1950 Kabete and Thogoto (Kikuyu) conventions especially reached a climax to the spread of the Revival movement through Central Kenya. Besides these large conventions, smaller conventions in parishes and congregations spread the Revival to the Gospel Missionary Society churches.[16] The large-scale conventions must have been phenomenal. John Wilkinson quotes *Kikuyu News*:

> No one who has been to such a convention can forget it—the spontaneous praise, the joy, the orderly way in which physical needs are cared for, and the simplicity which is sufficient. Usually a short verse became a motto for the convention,[17] and a message to take back at its end.[18]

These major conventions contributed to the emergence of nation-wide African leadership. They also brought about great spiritual inspiration and awakening to both clergy and laypeople and challenged the mainstream churches to re-emphasize their evangelistic effort and missionary concern.[19] Githii further explains that during these conventions, a sense of universality was developed as members of different denominations were converted and joined the fellowship. Among those converted were a few Roman Catholics, illiterates, semi-Christianized drunkards, businessmen, and even Protestant ministers.[20]

Characteristics

The main characteristic of the Revival was that it was a movement within the major Anglican, Presbyterian, and Methodist mission churches. Nevertheless, the brethren preached certain distinct elements: the emphasis on repentance through open confession, the necessity of being born again, that

15. Ibid.

16. Ibid., 128–29.

17. For example, The theme of Kahuhia convention (1947) was "God wants all men to be saved" (1 Tim 2:3–4); Kabete convention (1949) "Come let us reason together" (Isa 1:18); Kikuyu convention (1950) "Jesus satisfies" (John 7:37).

18. Wilkinson, *The Story of Chogoria*, 101.

19. Mambo, The Revival Fellowship," 112.

20. Githii, "The East African Revival Movement," 57.

is, experiencing (accepting) Jesus as personal Lord and Savior, the breaking down of barriers of race, tribe or clan, and the awareness of a new equality between Europeans and Africans.[21]

With the prominent symbols of the crucifixion and shed blood of Jesus in mind,[22] the brethren desired a deep religious experience similar to St. Paul's conversion. Going beyond an initial salvation experience, the Revival emphasized what was known as "walking in the light" because the brethren needed to live in a continuous renewal process. This was a process of constant cleansing in the blood of Jesus through continuous confession of their sins to each other.[23] The individual transformation of the brethren was so dramatic that it invited opposition from some church members and leaders. Wilkinson writes:

> There was a greater honesty reflected in the restitution of stolen property. There was a greater faithfulness in daily work includ-ing a marked responsibility in the use of time. There was a greater readiness to admit to wrongdoing and a new sensitivity to the difference between right and wrong. There was an absence of any racial bitterness and a new feeling of fellowship between the races. Finally, there was a new keenness for Christian things; for Bible teaching, for the conversion of non-Christian, for fellowship with other Christians, and for responsible financial support of the church and Christian activities.[24]

The Revival also enforced strong community norms on its members in such areas as clothes, fashions, hairstyles, drinking, smoking, and rela-tions with the opposite sex. For example, ladies had to wear head scarves, and jeans were banned for boys. The Fellowship saw itself as a new clan. However, one research participant said she left the movement when they started acting like a new clan trying to take over her wedding. The Revival gave women a new status previously unseen in traditional society, thus al-lowing women to preach, testify, and hold important offices as men did. Al-though the Revivalists tended to follow the African community structure, with leaders and members making a sort of extended family, they avoided African traditional rituals. The movement generally encouraged education

---

21. Ward, "'Ukutendereza Yesu' the Balokole Revival," 116.

22. Mambo, The Revival Fellowship," 116.

23. Githii, "The East African Revival Movement," 49.

24. Wilkinson, *The Story of Chogoria*, 104–5.

and modern living, but discouraged involvement with politics to avoid being soiled by earthly dealings.[25]

Initial response of the missions and churches when the Revival reached Kenya was hostile. The tendency of the brethren to judge other people's spiritual condition and to separate themselves from normal church activities for the sake of Revival activities incurred criticism. The PCEA, for example, organized a committee to probe the situation when the movement caused a crisis within the church. Twenty-two criticisms of exclusiveness and subjectivism were listed by the committee of enquiry. Some of the criticisms included holding separate meetings after church, collecting funds for the Revival, emphasizing subjective experience over the Scriptures, and putting down the ordained ministry and church authorities. Positive aspects the committee found were the great zeal for the gospel, emphasis on the need for repentance, commitment to upright living, and ability to rouse the church.[26] The recommendation of the committee was that the church should not oppose the Revival. Committee Chairman Charles Kareri explained:

> Revival cannot survive except within the Church for its function is to revive the Church and that function cannot be fulfilled if it is outside the church. The church also stands in great need of the help which God gives it through revival. Our committee therefore urges that all our members, of whatever persuasion, should strive always to live together in peace and in charity towards all.[27]

Contribution and Spirituality of the Revival Movement

The first and foremost contribution of the East Africa Revival Movement to the Kenyan church is that it gave the church indigenous roots. The Revival put in the heart of East Africans a strong desire for East African forms of worship, discipline, and organization. Through the Revival Movement, African evangelists and ministers were produced, along with lay leadership, and they were proven effective.

The Revival brought a new and deeper grasp of Christian truth and revelation through direct spiritual encounter with Christ himself and a new

25. Nthamburi, "Mainline Christian Churches," 79.

26. Macpherson, *The Presbyterian Church in Kenya*, 127–28; Wilkinson, *The Story of Chogoria*, 105.

27. Macpherson, *The Presbyterian Church in Kenya*, 127.

sense of responsibility to holy and upright living. It is in this area that some research participants' spirituality was affected directly by the Revival.[28] One participant accepted Jesus Christ as his personal savior and started growing spiritually when he was a youth because of his benefactors who were involved in the Revival. Another research participant was taken care of spiritually by PCEA Revival people, who laid a spiritual foundation and nourished her. Still another participant heard the gospel and was saved at a church district prayer meeting. It was the Revivalists who led her to Christ. They nurtured her spiritually teaching her the word of God and Christian morals. She was a part of the movement until she got married. In the lives of these three people, the movement became a crucial element of their spirituality.

Perhaps the definition of spirituality by these three people—"whole *engagement with God*," "growing to be *godlier*," and "how you are *going with your God* throughout the life" [emphasis mine]—reflects the influence of the Revival upon their lives and the formation of their spirituality. The other two research participants were not directly involved in it but were well aware of the effects and contribution of the movement to the Presbyterian Church. They talked about the impact of the Revival movement in general terms.

The Revival also created a new ecumenical sense of fellowship that transcends family, tribal, national, racial, and denominational boundaries. For example, it was in line with the efforts of the missionary churches in Kikuyuland to form a united church that would foster the common welfare of the Kikuyu. One research participant said that at his fellowship, Anglicans, Methodists, and Presbyterians all gathered together, and people there did not care about that. He said it was good!

Finally, the Revival prepared the Kenyan church, especially in Kikuyuland, to face and withstand the attack of the 1950s Mau Mau movement.[29] The Mau Mau warriors attacked the church, missionaries, and national Christians, among others. It was a time of trial, and the church needed strength and faith to overcome the trial. The faith and boldness that the East Africa Revival Movement supplied to the church was timely, and the church turned out to be strong enough to defeat the Mau Mau attacks.

---

28. The research was narrative research done on five PCEA pastors. This research was mainly to listen to the stories of these five individuals. One of the themes that surfaced which affected their spirituality was East Africa Revival movement.

29. Wilkinson, Wilkinson, *The Story of Chogoria*, 121.

However, over time the Revivalists became too rigid and dogmatic, preventing the movement from passing to the next generation. Macpherson explained the effect of the movement as follows:

> The revival brought an entirely new possibility into the situation, that of direct spiritual encounter with Christ himself in a contemporary African setting. It was as if, up to that point, a grafting of Christianity had been made into African life but, although the graft had not been rejected, it had also not yet fully grown into the life of the African host. And the coming of the Revival was as if the graft had now fully "taken" and was able to derive full sustenance from truly African roots.[30]

Charismatic and Pentecostal Movements[31]

Pentecostal missionaries began their work in Kenya from as early as 1912. According to one record, Finnish missionary Emil Danielsson came to Kenya before any organized missions began. Then Otto and Marion Keller started their work at Nyang'ori near Kisumu on Lake Victoria in 1918. They built a church, school, and a workshop affiliated with the Pentecostal Assemblies of Canada. Other Pentecostal missionaries later arrived from Finland, Canada, Sweden, Norway, and the USA, forming local Pentecostal denominations such as Pentecostal Evangelistic Fellowship of Africa, the Full Gospel Churches of Kenya, the Free Pentecostal Fellowship in Kenya, the Kenya Assemblies of God, Elim Pentecostal Church of Kenya, and the New Testament Church of God. Later, with the breakup of the East African Federation (Kenya, Uganda, and Tanganyika), the Pentecostal Assemblies of Canada changed its name to the Pentecostal Assemblies of God.[32]

It is worthwhile to note differences between older Pentecostal denominations and the newer charismatic movement. Pentecostalism, which traces its root to an outbreak of tongue speaking in Topeka, Kansas in 1901 and the Azusa Street revival in downtown Los Angeles from 1906 to 1909, became a worldwide movement emphasizing a conscious experience of baptism in the Holy Spirit, the first sign of which is speaking in tongues. When "neo-Pentecostalism" appeared in American mainline churches in 1960 with distinctly Pentecostal blessings and phenomena, the

---

30. Macpherson, *The Presbyterian Church in Kenya*, 128.
31. Park, "Charismatic Spirituality," 1–17.
32. Garrard, "Kenya," 150–55.

word "charismatic" was introduced to make a distinction between the older Pentecostal denominations from these newer Pentecostals.[33] Later, the term "charismatic movement" was also applied to nondenominational churches experiencing the same Pentecostal phenomena.

Peter Hocken defines charismatic movement as "all manifestations of pentecostal-type Christianity that in some way differ from classical pentecostalism in affiliation and/or doctrine."[34] In Kenya, Pentecostals are based on denominations, and they are more established and structured than charismatics, who are more personality driven. New groups of charismatics continue to launch and are too numerous to know the exact number. Having said the differences between Pentecostals and charismatics, I would like to treat in this book both Pentecostal and charismatic spiritualities in the same category because of similar features, convictions, and expressions in regard to spirituality.

African Independent Churches

In discussing Kenyan Pentecostal and charismatic movements, it is almost impossible not to talk about the rise of African Independent (Initiated, Indigenous, Instituted) Churches (AIC), many of whom are Pentecostal and charismatic. These African Independent Churches are distinguished from mission churches and can be summarized into three distinct groups: (1) nationalist or secessionist churches; (2) spirit churches; (3) newer Pentecostal or charismatic churches.[35]

Nationalist/Secessionist Churches

Nationalist or secessionist churches are those who broke away from the established mission churches. The first of these is the African Independent Pentecostal Church, which began in 1929 over the issue of female circumcision. This church accepted polygamy and female circumcision but theologically did not greatly differ from the Anglican and Presbyterian Churches from which they came. Then the African Orthodox Church started in 1932 over the same issue. These two churches started as a result of dissatisfaction over the type of education at mission and government schools, anxiety

33. Synan, "Pentecostalism," 835–38.
34. Hocken, "Charismatic Movement," 477.
35. Mwaura, "African Instituted Churches," 103.

over land, and resentment of missionaries' attempts to change traditional customs. In 1945, the African Brotherhood Church came out of the Africa Inland Church in Kambaland, and African Christian Churches and Schools started in Kikuyuland from the same Africa Inland Church, mainly as a result of disputes over educational policy. The rise of these churches is related to African nationalism.[36]

Spirit Churches

"Spirit churches" were founded by prophets who also parted ways with mission churches for cultural and nationalistic reasons, but primarily due to the theology of manifestation of spiritual gifts such as prophecy, healing, speaking in tongues, etc.[37] According to Anderson, "The Roho (Spirit) movement was one of the earliest African Pentecostal movements that commenced in 1912 among the Luo people of western Kenya, at first as a popular Charismatic movement among young people within the Anglican church" and spread to neighboring Luhya people.[38]

Among the Kikuyu, these churches were known as *Akurinu, Aroti* (dreamers), *Anabii* (prophets), or *Andu a Iremba* (turban people). The colonial government called them *Watu wa Mungu* (People of God or Men of God) and persecuted them. Rejecting Western medicine, education, clothing, and other amenities, they sought guidance from the Bible and the Holy Spirit and mixed Christian tradition with African rituals and beliefs.[39] The Kikuyu *Akurinu* was formed with little or no contact with mission churches or other spirit churches, and its significance lies in their conscious attempt to establish an African form of Christianity.[40] Some examples of this type of church are Akorino churches in Central, Rift Valley, and Nairobi provinces, Africa Church of the Holy Spirit, Africa Divine Church, Roho Ruwe Church, Holy Spirit Church of East Africa, Nabii Christian Church of Kenya, True Pentecostal Church, and Jerusalem Church of Christ.[41]

There is still another church, similar to the Spirit churches, known as *Arata a Roho Mutheru* (Friends of the Holy Spirit). Springing up during

36. Ibid., 104; Murray, "Varieties of Kikuyu Independent Churches," 129–30.

37. Mwaura, "African Instituted Churches," 105–6.

38. Anderson, *An Introduction to Pentecostalism*, 112.

39. Murray, "Varieties of Kikuyu Independent Churches," 131–33.

40. Anderson, *An Introduction to Pentecostalism*, 113.

41. Mwaura, "African Instituted Churches," 105–6.

the East Africa Revival Movement in the 1940s because of Revivalists' rejection of charismatic gifts,[42] they emerged at different times in different circumstances but have similar characteristics. Perhaps the first of its kind in Kikuyuland is *Dini ya Kaggia*, named after nationalist Bildad Kaggia, who was one of its most-prominent leaders.

One common characteristic of these independent churches is that they were founded by concerned laymen who left their mother churches and thus naturally adopted a traditional African worldview. Prayer is central to the life of the church to confront spiritual powers with the power of Almighty God. Baptism by immersion, baptism of the Holy Spirit and charismatic gifts, and healing and prophecy are practiced, and dreams and visions are important to them. Another common characteristic is a vigorous community life. The church assumes the role of a kinship group, providing a sense of identity to her members where a traditional extended family system has broken down. Their worship service is lively and the role of women in the church is prominent. Interestingly, these churches have a deep devotion to Bible reading and study, although some rejected the Bible in their early years. They see the Bible providing similar worldviews to their own without theological complications.[43]

What these African Independent Churches desired to achieve was African expression of Christianity. It was brought forth by a clash of cultures between the African and the European. The ethos of the AIC is described by Nathaniel Ndiokwere as follows:

> It is a well-known fact that in religion the African feels God, experiences him, before reflecting meaningfully about him. He does not begin with contemplation or meditation. He rather responds to a religious impulse whose reality he has already experienced. That is why in his religion he likes to feel God, he likes to feel religion.[44]

Charismatic Churches

The third kind of African Independent Church is very different from the aforementioned churches and is the main discussion here. They are more affiliated with North and South American Pentecostals and charismatics

42. Murray, "Varieties of Kikuyu Independent Churches," 130–31.

43. Okite, "Politics of Africa's Independent Churches," 122.

44. Ndiokwere, *Prophecy and Revolution*, 275.

and are not related to the older Pentecostal churches planted in Kenya be-tween 1910–1920s. They also oppose the other AICs because of their "pa-gan" practices.[45] This third type of independent church and the charismatic movement introduced to Kenya in the 1970s is the one that has challenged the mission churches in recent decades.

Charismatic Movement in the 1970s

Vinson Synan describes the worldwide Holy Spirit renewal as follows:

> The 20th-century Pentecostal/charismatic renewal in the Holy Spirit has not entered the world scene on one single, sudden clear-cut occasion, nor even gradually over a hundred years. It has arrived in three distinct and separate surges or explosions sufficiently distinct and distinctive for us to label them the first wave (the Pentecostal renewal), the second wave (the charismatic renewal), and the third wave (the neo-charismatic renewal). All these waves share the same experience of the infilling power of the Holy Spirit, the Third person of the Triune God. The Spirit has entered and transformed the lives not simply of small numbers of heroic individuals and scattered communities, but of vast num-bers of millions of Christians across the world today.[46]

The first wave, the Pentecostal renewal, is the oldest in its history, ex-perience, and theology of Pentecostalism. The second wave, the charismatic renewal, is non-Pentecostal mainline churches experiencing Pentecostal phenomena. The third wave, a term coined by C. Peter Wagner in 1983, is unrelated or no longer related to the previous Pentecostals or charismatic renewals. Rejecting Pentecostal terminology, the third wave—considered as a global phenomena rather than simply a Western one—gathered mo-mentum in the 1960s to 1990s. Since this movement constitutes a major new revitalizing force, it is also called the neo-charismatic renewal; in-dependents and post-denominational churches belong to this category.[47] Stanley Burgess explains the third wave, neo-charismatics, as follows:

> The so-called third wave should be viewed as part of a broader category, "neocharismatics," which includes the vast numbers of independent and indigenous churches and groups that cannot be

45. Mwaura, "African Instituted Churches," 107.
46. Barrett, "The Worldwide Holy Spirit Renewal," 381.
47. Ibid., 388–404.

classified as either pentecostal or charismatic. These are Christian bodies with pentecostal-like experiences that have no traditional pentecostal or charismatic denominational connections. Their greatest concentrations of strength are in the prophetic African independent churches, in Asia—especially the house-church movement in China—and in Latin American countries, especially Brazil.[48]

The charismatic renewal that Africa experienced from the 1970s is an African extension of the neo-charismatics. According to Hocken,

> The new wave of charismatic-type churches that have sprung up in Africa since the 1970s often call themselves pentecostal, but many have no particular relationship with the Pentecostal movement and are in effect an African version of new charismatic churches. These new churches are different in theology, emphases and style from the African Independent Churches, more evangelical in their theology and less liturgical, and hostile to the perceived syncretism of many AICs [African Independent Churches]. Their similarities to Western Pentecostal-charismatic patterns can lead to an overlooking of their more African features. The new African charismatic churches give a major place to ministries of healing and deliverance, taking seriously the power of witch doctors and spiritism in a way that the missionary churches have not.[49]

What needs to be noted about the emergence of these charismatic independent churches in Kenya is a role played by the classic Pentecostals and the Spirit churches. In other words, the neo-charismatic wave in Kenya is not a totally isolated event.[50] Equally important, there was another factor from overseas. According to Mugambi, Kenya hosted itinerant evangelists such as Billy Graham, Oral Roberts, T. L. Osborn from the 1960s, and they were followed by other televangelists such as Reinhart Bonnke, Morris Cerullo, Harry Das, Benny Hinn, and Joyce Meyer. Generally, these evangelists were not affiliated with any specific denomination and claimed to have "spiritual gifts" and charismatic power of preaching and healing.[51] Thus, under the guidance from North America and Europe, dozens of new Pentecostal and charismatic churches have been formed since 1963. Some examples of these churches are: Gilbert Deya Ministries; Faith Evangelistic

48. Burgess, "Neocharismatics," 928.

49. Hocken, "Charismatic movement," 477–519.

50. Allan, *An Introduction to Pentecostalism*, 162.

51. Mugambi, "Evangelistic and Charismatic Initiatives," 121.

Ministries of Teresia Wairimu; Deliverance Church; God's Power Church; Redeemed Gospel Church; Jesus Celebration Centre; Chrisco-Fellowship; and Jesus is Alive Ministries.[52]

Pentecostal and Charismatic Spirituality

Pentecostal and charismatic spirituality is spreading powerfully, influencing even mainline mission churches in Africa. The charismatic movement appeals to African worldview more effectively than older mission churches. African Pentecostal spirituality is also liturgically free and spontaneous, and sympathetic to African culture and universal human needs.[53] According to Pentecostal theologian Amos Yong, Pentecostalism fosters:

> (1) [A] holistic understanding of human religiosity and that the Pentecostal and Charismatic experience "demands interpretation of the experiential dimension of spirituality over and against an emphasis on textuality in religious life." Pentecostal spiritualities reflect the conviction that Pentecostals experience God through the Spirit and are expressed in liturgies that are primarily oral, narrative and participatory. It is also (2) pneumatocentric spirituality, where the Spirit invades all human life.[54]

In African Pentecostal Churches, the power of the Holy Spirit is more than just "spiritual" significance. It means dignity, authority and power over all types of oppression. The power of the Holy Spirit gives believers liberation. This conscious experience of the Holy Spirit is a fundamental characteristic of Pentecostal and charismatic churches.[55] Pentecostalism also "affirmed their sense of personal worth and gave them control over their lives by sustaining the individual force to cope with the insecurities of change."[56]

The following are nine constant characteristics cited by Hocken as common at each stage of the charismatic and Pentecostal movement and in all of its different manifestations: (1) Focus on Jesus—"Renewal in the Spirit is everywhere marked by a focus on Jesus Christ"; (2) Praise—"Being filled with the Holy Spirit always issues in the praise of God and of his Son

52. Mwaura, "African Instituted Churches," 107.

53. Yong, quoted in Anderson, *An Introduction to Pentecostalism*, 201.

54. Ibid.

55. Ibid., 269, 284.

56. Peterson, *Not by Might nor by Power*, 31, 35.

Jesus Christ"; (3) Love of the Bible—"Charismatic renewal has been consistently marked by a great love and thirst for the Scriptures"; (4) God speaks today—"Renewal is characterized by the conviction that God speaks to his people, corporately and personally, as directly and as regularly as in the first Christian century"; (5) Evangelism—"Holy Spirit renewal regularly brings a heightened urgency for evangelism"; (6) Awareness of evil—"Conscious awareness of the Holy Spirit is typically followed by a new awareness of the reality of Satan and the powers of evil"; (7) Spiritual gifts—"The spiritual gifts listed in 1 Cor 12:8–10 were seen from the start as characteristic features of charismatic renewal"; (8) Eschatological expectation—"The coming of the Spirit is generally accompanied by an increased expectancy and longing for the return of Jesus"; (9) Spiritual power—"Holy Spirit renewal is everywhere concerned with spiritual impact and a concern to transform the condition of a powerless church."[57]

R. P. Spittler also lists five implicit values of the Pentecostal and charismatic movement: experience, orality, spontaneity, otherworldliness and biblical authority. He says, "The five implicit values . . . combine variously to yield a constellation of characteristic practices found in pentecostal and/ or charismatic spirituality."[58]

Contextual Spirituality

As noted earlier, charismatic spirituality is closely linked to African Independent Churches. These African Independent Churches comprise nationalist/secessionist, Spirit, and charismatic churches. The first two types of African Independent Churches desired to achieve African expression of Christianity as a result of a clash between African and European cultures. However, these churches tend to be traditional and engage in "pagan" practices. The spirituality of the third type, charismatic churches, can be considered contextualized spirituality in African Christianity.

Contextualization encompasses contextualization of biblical message, theology and/or ministry. It is a "hermeneutical bridge" into the real-life contexts of ordinary people.[59] It is also called "enculturation." In regards to the current African context, African worldviews and religious traditions are still supernatural, and socioeconomic-political subsystems are closely

57. Hocken, "Charismatic Movement," 477–519.

58. Spittler, "Spirituality, Pentecostal and Charismatic," 1099.

59. Kraft, *Christianity in Culture*, 112.

intertwined with religion. Religion affects the cultural subsystems and vice versa. In such a milieu, charismatic spirituality that holds supernatural religious orientation and expression provides adequate answers to issues and problems that Africans face on a daily basis. It is a viable option for contextual spirituality among many religious expressions such as African traditional, Orthodox, and mainline Christianity.

In Kenya, charismatic spirituality affected both urban and rural settings as contextual spirituality. Urbanization is still a process in Kenya. Urban life is not completely separated from rural life. For example, during the Christmas season urban centers are empty since almost everybody travels to their rural homes. People are still strongly rooted in a rural fabric of life as much as an urban life. However, different dynamics operate for urban and rural settings. Urban charismatic churches grow mainly due to the large influx of the younger generation that has migrated to urban centers. These young people prefer associating with charismatic/Pentecostal churches to old mission churches since the charismatic movement exhibits open attitudes toward modern music, uses the latest technology and English as media of communication, and provides a space for leadership for the younger generation.

Individualism in urban settings, as opposed to community spirit, is another factor that causes the growth of urban charismatic churches since they do not require strict accountability of members. Actually, rules for joining and retaining membership is almost absent in charismatic churches. Economy has also played a role in urban church growth. Poverty coupled with the preaching of prosperity gospel is still another contextual dynamic that has caused the growth of urban charismatic churches. In regards to church leadership, initially pastors of urban charismatic churches were not as well educated as those of mission churches. However, a high level of awareness of theological and leadership training and availability of resources in urban areas have contributed to the equipping of urban charismatic pastors for effective ministry and church growth. In urban centers, therefore, mega churches have come into being because of the factors mentioned above.

In rural settings, on the other hand, different dynamics are in operation. People live in closed societies where kinship is still strong and communal spirit impacts decision making. Conversion of an opinion leader means conversion of the whole family or a large portion of the village. Poverty and disease also make rural folks attracted to charismatic churches, which address these issues immediately. Kenya is the most developed among East African countries mainly because of English language,[60] through which Western culture and Christianity affected Kenya most. Relative peace has also been enjoyed in the last four decades since independence from Britain in 1963. This relative political stability has contributed to Kenya's church growth, including the wide spread of the charismatic movement.

Pentecostal and charismatic spirituality in Africa is a contextual spirituality since it provides for solutions to both spiritual and other human problems. Appealing to African worldviews—holistic perception of reality and spirit-centered universe—and providing more adequate explanations and answers to the problems of life, charismatic spirituality appears to be more contextualized than older mission churches or African Traditional Religion.[61] Referring to the charismatic movement in Africa, Kwame Bediako stated that the significance of the movement of the African Independent Church (including charismatic movements) is that it points to the directions in which African Christianity is moving and to the trends of the African response to the Christian faith in African terms.[62]

Hocken analyzed charismatic renewal of the 1970s: The new charismatic churches are different in theology, emphases, and style from the African Independent Churches; they are more evangelical in their theology and less liturgical, and hostile to the syncretism of many African Independent Churches. It was also stated before that the Pentecostal and charismatic experiences demand interpretation of the experiential dimension of spirituality over and against an emphasis on textuality in religious life, and that their experience of God is through the Spirit. The charismatic churches emphasize ministries of healing and deliverance, taking seriously the power of witch doctors and spiritism.[63] All the above elements of charismatic spirituality—oral, narrative, participatory, healing and deliverance, and experience—are genuine expressions of African religiosity.

60. In Kenya both English and Kiswahili are official languages. Both are used as a medium of communication. While English is preferred in urban settings, Kiswahili is more used in rural villages.

61. Anderson, *An Introduction to Pentecostalism*, 201–2.

62. Bediako, *Christianity in Africa*, 66.

63. Hocken, "Charismatic Movement," 477–519.

Contribution to African Spirituality

Traditional African culture did not separate religion and society. A religious leader was a leader in the society as a whole since the society was a religious society. When missionaries came to Africa, however, they presented the gospel that divided the "sacred" and the "secular." Missionaries brought a religion divorced from life.[64] African theologian Laurenti Magesa states that the charismatic movements "address the real needs of the people" and "strike a deep religious chord in the heart of African peoples."[65] Magoti claims that one of the main contributions of the charismatic and Pentecostal movements is the bestowal of pride in African culture back to Africans:

> Charismatic movements are not ashamed about belonging to a culture that believes in the existence of devils and evil spirits as active forces in the world. Even when they are accused as being primitive and unscientific, they do not abandon that belief. Furthermore, charismatics are not ashamed to belong to a culture that believes in the ancestors as mediators between human life and God, and they are certainly not ashamed to belong to a culture that cherishes the charismas of its members and values prayer as a free and communal expression of peoples' inner feelings or emotions. To be sure, they value all these elements and take pride in them.[66]

Another contribution is that charismatics provided Africans with a choice:

> For quite a long time the mainline churches have been claiming for themselves the right to authentic interpretation of the Christian message and how to live and express it. . . . In a very real sense, Charismatic movements reject this kind of cultural monism. They do not accept that Christian revelation can only be understood and interpreted from the perspective of only one culture. To many charismatics, cultural monism is not only an insult but also oppressive and dehumanising. They believe that there are various ways of expressing the Christian faith; their way is certainly one of them and should be taken seriously.[67]

Bediako argues for charismatic movements as follows:

64. Welbourn, *East African Christian*, 189.
65. Magesa, "Charismatic Movements," 38.
66. Magoti, "Charismatic Movement in the Context of Inculturation," 95.
67. Ibid., 96.

> The distinction between the historical churches, of missionary origins, and the independent or African instituted churches, have since become less meaningful, as features which were once thought to be characteristics of the latter have been found to be shared also by the former. The significance of the independents, therefore, has been that they pointed to the directions in which broad sections of African Christianity were moving, and so they testified to the existence of some generalised trends in the African response to the Christian faith in African terms.[68]

Charismatic renewal is somehow liberation for Africans who have been searching for authentic African Christianity in their milieu. The mainline mission churches have no choice but to adapt themselves to these changing situations of religious atmosphere and adopt charismatic elements in their ethos for the sake of survival and continual influence in their context.

Not all African scholars condone the charismatic movement. Mugambi criticizes the evangelistic and charismatic initiatives in post-colonial tropical Africa as having resulted in cultural alienation of the African proselytes and the fragmentation of Christian denominations. He argues that the recent new Pentecostal and charismatic movements held the assumption that the early missionary achievements were not "biblical" enough, and that the older mission churches found it difficult to match these evangelistic and charismatic initiatives.[69] As if the said assumption is true, young people started moving away from mission churches to charismatic churches from the 1990s.

The charismatic movement is not without problems. Some Christians lament a great deal of American cultural influence in charismatic churches such as imitation of American English and culture. Some charismatic churches, especially in urban settings, exhibit celebrity mentality, and the absence of a celebrity figure means the death of spirituality. The prosperity gospel preached in most Pentecostal and charismatic churches in Kenya also poses theological problems. Despite such criticisms, the relevance of the charismatic movement in Africa is that the charismatic spirituality acknowledges and takes seriously the spiritual world and power that seem real to Africans. The characteristics of the charismatic spirituality that contributes to African spirituality can be summarized as below:

---

68. Bediako, *Christianity in Africa*, 66.

69. Mugambi, "Evangelistic and Charismatic Initiatives," 123–27, 141.

Characteristics of Charismatic Spirituality in Africa
• Contextual spirituality (African expression of spirituality)
• Liberation from oppression
• Holistic understanding of human religiosity
• Pneumatocentric spirituality

Perspective from Biblical and Historical Spiritualities

Pauline spirituality is distinctly pneumatological. According to Paul, there is hardly any aspect of Christian experience outside the realm of the Spirit. Paul's enigmatic phrase "in Christ" also refers to the field of divine power of Christ that governs the lives of believers. Johannine spirituality also has a charismatic dimension. Jesus baptizes with the Holy Spirit; individuals are born of the Spirit; and the Spirit abides in the believer and reveals the truth to believers. The source of life is the Spirit rather than the observance of rules or the practice of rituals.[70]

Historical spirituality also includes a charismatic tradition. Richard Foster identifies the Charismatic Stream of Christian life and faith as a focus on the empowering charisms or gifts of the Spirit and the nurturing fruit of the Spirit.[71] The pneumatology of charismatic spirituality, however, focuses on spiritual gifts and power rather than the inward works of the Spirit.

Another element of charismatic spirituality is eschatological expectation. The New Testament has eschatological dimension which provided early Christians with the means to resist the worldviews and practices of the cultures they lived in. Paul's eschatology is strongly based on the present life in Christ. The eschatological element of charismatic spirituality must provide future hope for African Christians riddled with problems of the present life. It also counters the present-oriented, pragmatic African Traditional Religion.

70. Schneiders, "Johannine spirituality," 385–87.

71. Foster, *Streams of Living Water*, 99. Foster identified six major streams (traditions) of spirituality: the Contemplative tradition, the Holiness tradition, the Charismatic tradition, the Social Justice tradition, the Evangelical tradition, the Incarnational tradition.

Summary

The East Africa Revival Movement is the first major renewal movement within the mission churches. It was a movement within the church and renewed the church as purposed by God. Although the mission church was opposed to the Revival at first, it embraced the movement only to the benefit of further development and establishment. Its implications are both theological and sociological in that the Revival brought to the mission church not only the keen sense of the need for personal salvation experience and holiness, but also the idea of oneness and Christian community among brethren across tribal and denominational lines. Having experienced divisions afterwards because of the issues of financial organization and leadership struggles between the young and the old, and the stiffness and dogmatic stance of the old generation toward the younger generation, The Revival movement became stagnant and opened a loophole for the Pentecostal churches. The Revival was also reluctant to be open to the gifts of the Holy Spirit and did not emphasize or practice healing through prayers, unlike the independent or Pentecostal churches in Kenya.

The charismatic movement is one of the fastest growing Christian movements in Africa. The Pentecostal/charismatic influence on Africa, which started as early as mission Christianity in the late nineteen th century, has been growing in Africa since the 1970s through the planting of various types of AICs, including the newer charismatic churches. Not being related to the early Pentecostal movement in Kenya, these neo-charismatic churches also oppose other syncretistic AICs. In the present Kenyan socioeconomic-political milieu, charismatic spirituality meets the needs and yearnings of African people holistically by providing answers to both religious and human problems with sound biblical teaching, affirmation of African music, balanced approaches to the ministry of the Holy Spirit, and non-syncretistic methods in spiritual warfare and deliverance ministry.

PART THREE

African Culture and Religion

7

African Culture
(The Kikuyu)

RELIGION PERMEATES ALL AREAS of life in Africa, thus the socioeconomic and political arenas are all bound up together with their religion to form a comprehensive life experience.[1] Spirituality is a comprehensive study of the peoples' spiritual/religious experience including all the complexities of life. Cultural systems, therefore, are a relevant part of this study that deserves due consideration. We turn our attention to African culture as part of Christian spirituality in Africa (Kenya). Although it is difficult to describe African culture in a general term, some commonalities exist. Thus I will use the Kikuyu tribe, the largest tribal group in Kenya, as an example to describe African culture.

Traditional Socioeconomic-Political Structure

Social Organization

Traditionally, the Kikuyu tribe is organized under the three most important kinship systems: family, clan, and age-group. Family is made of grandparents, parents, and children, and is a basic societal unit. Clans are made of extended families and meet on such big occasions as marriage and initiation ceremonies. Age-groups are the solidifying factor of the whole tribe by acting harmoniously in the political, social, economic, and religious life of

---

1. Mbiti, *African Religions and Philosophy*, 1.

the tribe.[2] In a sense, the whole tribal relationship is a very closely interwoven framework.[3]

Leakey observed two distinct patterns in Kikuyu social organization, *mbari* and *rugongo*. Before explaining these two systems, it is worthwhile to mention Kikuyu family classification. There are three fundamental equations: (1) I and my grandfather are one; (2) I and my brother and my sister are one; (3) I and my wife are one. Thus, it follows that all the brothers, half-brothers, and male cousins on the patrilineal side are one person, who is yet many people. The head of family is one but many, although the headship rests on the senior living person.[4]

Mbari was an organization founded upon a patriarchal system in which the basic unit was the extended family. This organization, otherwise known as "sub-clan," was composed of extended family units, which consisted of the head of the family or father, his children, possibly grandchildren, and even great-grandchildren. This system, closely linked with land ownership, consisted of a thousand or more adults and was regarded as a social unit which was bound by complex rules and regulations. The head of a group was chosen by a unanimous decision, and all matters of the sub-clan members such as land, religion, law, etc., were the concern of *mbari*.[5]

The other social structure, *rugongo*, means a ridge. There are three main geographical divisions in Kikuyuland: Murang'a (or Fort Hall), Nyeri, and Kiambu. These areas are further divided into the smaller territorial units called *rugongo*, which is simply a territory that lies between two separating streams and extends for about 20 to 30 miles. For all tribal matters such as law, religious worship, warfare, and all else affecting members of the whole tribe irrespective of their sub-clan status, the *rugongo* was the most important administrative unit. Each ridge was controlled by a council of senior elders. Although the Kikuyu had no chief, the leading member of a council was known as chief, who in a real sense was "spokesman for the senior council." The spokesman was not a chief as the word implies but simply the chairman of the council of nine in whom authority lay. When there were disputes or religious matters that affected persons of more than one ridge, a special *ad hoc* council of nine would convene from all the ridges

---

2. Kenyatta, *Facing Mount Kenya*, 2–3.

3. Mugo, *Kikuyu People*, 5.

4. Leakey, *Mau Mau and the Kikuyu*, 28–36.

5. Ibid.

involved. This social organization of decentralized control was highly effective in traditional Kikuyu religious, judicial, and secular affairs.[6]

Initiation and Marriage

Initiation is the most important custom among the Kikuyu. It is regarded as imparting on a boy or girl the status of manhood or womanhood. Circumcision, as the core of initiation, symbolizes the unification of the whole tribe, and with it comes the right to participate in various governing groups in the tribal administration. The whole of circumcision ceremonies are also closely related to communion with ancestors. Through circumcision, children are born again not as the children of individual families but of the whole tribe. It should be noted, though, that what makes the initiation ceremony the most important custom is not the surgical operation itself, but the enormous educational, social, moral, psychological, and religious implications of it.[7]

Therefore, under traditional culture, no one in Kikuyu society could claim the benefits of adult status and full membership of the tribe and age-group unless he or she had gone through the initiation rites. Although the outward sign of the initiation ceremony was the circumcision of both the male and female, the whole ceremony was intended to extend the education of young people and prepare them for citizenship and responsible adult life. Among the Kikuyu, it was taboo to have sexual relations with someone who had not undergone this operation. But when the ceremonies were over, the boys and girls became full members of an age-group of their own and began to live a corporate life that transcended family and clan obligations and was linked with tribal responsibilities. The young men now had the duty of defending their own tribe and learning how to conduct tribal business, and the young girls were subjected to communal labor and began to seek their husbands. After initiation, men passed through different levels of status such as junior warrior, senior warrior, junior elder, and senior elder. Girls passed through the levels of status from girl to married woman, and reached another status at the birth of the first child.[8]

As noted earlier, the two primary governing principles of Kikuyu social relationships were the age-group that started with the circumcision

6. Ibid.
7. Kenyatta, *Facing Mt. Kenya*, 132–51.
8. Leakey, *Mau Mau and the Kikuyu*, 23–27.

rite, and the genealogical groups such as family or sub-clan.[9] Between these two, it was the age-group system that contributed significantly to the egalitarianism prevalent among the Kikuyu.[10] However, marriage was one of the most powerful means of maintaining the cohesion of Kikuyu society, without which kinship systems and tribal organization became impossible. Thus, marriage was not viewed as merely a personal matter, but a family matter. There were four stages that a boy and a girl must go through before the marriage ceremony. It is not necessary to elaborate on them here, but suffice it to say that Kikuyu marriage was based on mutual love and the gratification of sexual instinct between two individuals.[11]

Polygamy was also a nearly inviolable central tenet of traditional marriage. Kikuyu customary law provided that a man may have as many wives as he can support, and that the larger one's family, the better it was for him and the tribe. According to Jomo Kenyatta, "The Kikuyu were taught from childhood that to be a man is to be able to love and keep a homestead with as many wives as possible."[12] Kenyatta also asserts that African social structure is based on polygamy.[13]

The reasons for polygamy are explained in several ways. One of the strong contributing factors to polygamy was love of children. The Kikuyu believed that each individual is a channel for the transmission of life, and that it is wrong to interrupt that transmission. Therefore, in Kikuyuland one must not only be married, but also have children. From this concept came the ideas that a childless marriage is a failure and that polygamy should be enforced.[14] If a man died without a male child, his family group came to an end under the patrilineal system. That is what the Kikuyu feared dreadfully and was another reason for polygamous marriages.[15] Leakey, on the other hand, explains polygamous marriage in terms of simple numbers:

> There seems to have been always a surplus of girls, and since the social and economic structure of the tribe had no place for unmarried girls once they had passed a certain age, such surplus girls who failed to find a young man who wanted them as first or senior

9. Muriuki, *A History of the Kikuyu*, 133; Kenyatta, *Facing Mt. Kenya*, 310.

10. Fedders and Salvadori, *Peoples and Cultures of Kenya*, 119.

11. Kenyatta, *Facing Mt. Kenya*, 163–64.

12. Ibid., 178–79.

13. Ibid., 271.

14. Wanjohi and Wanjohi, *Social and Religious Concerns of East Africa*, 41–42.

15. Kenyatta, *Facing Mt. Kenya*, 13.

wife had to be content with becoming second or third wives in a polygamous household.[16]

The reasons for polygamy presented above are far from the erroneous misconception that non-Africans may hold of polygamy being the result of man's lust. In many cases, the second wife was introduced to the husband by his first wife or the would-be second wife's family. In either case, the girl was not able to find a position as a senior wife. Such marriages were by no means unhappy, but accepted because there were no alternatives.[17]

One thing needing mention is dowry, also called bride price or marriage insurance. An agreed number of goats and sheep was handed over to the bride's family to demonstrate good faith by the groom's family that the young man would make a good husband in accordance with law and custom. On the other hand, the acceptance of the stock by the bride's family was equally a guarantee that they believed the girl would make a good wife. If the marriage later broke down as a result of the man's failure to behave properly, his family would lose all the marriage insurance, and his wife would be allowed to return to her own people. However, if the marriage failed by fault of the woman, her family would have to hand back the stock they received as marriage insurance, along with all the offspring from the stock. This system of marriage insurance was a great stabilizer of marriage in a society where divorce was strongly discouraged.[18]

The idea of sharing among the Kikuyu was so strong that it extended even to marital intimacy:

> If the visitors come from far away and they are to spend the night in the homestead, the arrangements for their accommodation are made according to the rules and customs governing the social affairs among the age-group. On these occasions the wives exercise their freedom, which amount to something like polyandry. Each wife is free to choose anyone among the age-group and give him accommodation for the night. This is looked upon as purely social intercourse and no feeling of jealousy or evil is attached to it on the part of the husband or wife. This is sort of collective enjoyment.[19]

The husband also enjoyed some measure of freedom in his own hut, but later informed his wives. This freedom given to both men and women in

16. Leakey, *Mau Mau and the Kikuyu*, 17.

17. Ibid.

18. Ibid., 15–16.

19. Kenyatta, *Facing Mt. Kenya*, 181.

the marriage context gave the Kikuyu a sense of social unity that they are one.[20]

Gender

Gender is a term that has psychological and cultural connotations rather than biological and has to do with learned or socially acquired patterns of behavior over time.[21] Cultural attitudes toward gender do not change easily, as Nawal El Saadawi contends: "Time and time again, life has proved that, whereas political and economic change can take place rapidly, social and cultural progress tends to lag behind because it is linked to the deep inner motive and psychic processes of the human mind and heart."[22]

In Africa, gender distinction has remained strong until recently. The man is the sole head of his family and provider of its material needs. He is the decision maker in the family, although the woman is the main food producer. Women as mothers also take the main responsibility for raising children and helping form their character. In regard to position of man and woman in traditional Africa, including the Kikuyu, the man was often placed above the woman and had more access to resources, opportunities, decision making, and other rights. For example, if a woman became widowed, the traditional practice was that the male in-laws assumed the ownership of the dead husband's land, and the wife was denied any access to the land. Men also believed that they owned their wives and had the "right" to discipline them in any way they found fit after the payment of dowry. That explains the prevalent practice of wife beating in African countries.[23]

In the case of the Kikuyu, their customary law recognized the freedom and independence of every member of the tribe, including females. Although their society was patriarchal and patrilineal, female children were looked upon as the connecting link between one generation and another and one clan and another through marriage, and thus they were valued.[24] Traditionally, boys followed their elder brothers herding the goats and sheep and learning necessary skills, while girls accompanied their mothers

20. Leakey, *Mau Mau and the Kikuyu*, 18.
21. Kamaara, *Gender, Youth Sexuality and HIV/AIDS*, 22.
22. El Saadawi, preface to *The Hidden Face of Eve*.
23. Chesaina, "Cultural Attitudes and Equality," 204–10.
24. Kenyatta, *Facing Mt. Kenya*, 174–75.

on the daily household and agricultural duties, learning all the skills they would need to become good wives and mothers.[25]

When it came to accepting appropriate gender awareness and behaviors on the part of boys and girls, the initiation process played a crucial role. Eunice Kamaara presents an excellent argument about how the role and function of initiation rites affected the initiates' specific gender roles afterward. She contends that since initiation occurred typically at the critical psycho-sexual stage of human development, it made the differences between male and female social and sexual roles explicit. Initiation rites also internalized the masculine and feminine roles in the initiates. In other words, men were the heads of their families and must be authoritative, and women must be submissive. Since the Kikuyu traditionally practiced circumcision for boys and clitoridectomy (removal of clitoris) for girls, these initiation rites promoted male dominance and diminished female power.[26] Kamaara's following statement explains the point well.

> Through the initiation process, the major male gender attribute of dominance and the female gender attribute of subordination are inculcated. The major cultural male gender attributes common to all traditional Kenyan societies were therefore, social and psychological dominance. From a very tender age, for instance, boys were made to feel that men are powerful and authoritative. Within the Kikuyu community male initiation process, boys were expected to dominate and to force girls into desired sexual action . . . On the other hand, girls were socialized on how to submit to men. Women who deviated or who questioned male authority were ridiculed and punished, while those who were unquestioningly obedient, were praised and rewarded.[27]

While sex is determined and naturally recognized at birth, initiation conferred gender on individuals.

Economic System

The traditional Kikuyu society was organized and functioned under the patrilineal system, so the father was the supreme ruler of the homestead, owner of everything, and the custodian of the family property. As

25. Ibid., 21–22.

26. Kamaara, *Gender, Youth Sexuality and HIV/AIDS*, 23–32.

27. Ibid., 31–32.

agriculturalists, the Kikuyu depended entirely on the land, and the soil was honored especially. In all social, economic, and political life of the tribe, therefore, the most important factor was land tenure. The land did not belong to the community, but to those individual founders of the various families who had the full rights of ownership and the control of the land. The boundaries were properly fixed, and everyone respected his neighbor's property. When land disputes arose, the council of elders intervened to solve the problems.[28]

Since land is the most important economic factor as agriculturalists, every Kikuyu had a great desire to own a piece of land on which to build his home and establish his livelihood. Each family consisting of a man, his wife or wives, and their children constituted an economic unit. In the economy of the Kikuyu, domestic animals also played an important part. The domestic animals were used not only for food sources but also for marriage insurance and religious rites. Thus, rearing of livestock had social, economic, and religious applications. A man was considered rich when he owned a number of cattle.[29]

Besides the issues of land and livestock, the Kikuyu work ethic and economic mindset were the momentum that brought the Kikuyu to their present economic status. They exploited their land to the full production of food far beyond what they needed.[30]

Political System

According to Kenyatta, the Kikuyu system of government prior to the arrival of the Europeans was based on the following democratic principles: (1) People were given freedom to acquire and develop land under a system of family ownership; (2) People were given universal tribal membership. Every member, after passing through the circumcision ceremony, should take an active part in the government. Males should go through the initiation ceremony between the ages of sixteen and eighteen, and females between the ages of ten and fourteen; (3) Socially and politically, all circumcised men and women should be equal, full members of the tribe; (4) The government should be in the hands of councils of elders chosen from all members of the community who had reached the age of eldership after

28. Kenyatta, *Facing Mt. Kenya*, 8–33.

29. Ibid., 53–66.

30. Fedders and Salvadori, *Peoples and Cultures of Kenya*, 119.

retiring from warriorhood; (5) All young men between the ages of eighteen and forty should form a warrior class and be ready to defend the country; (6) In times of need, the government should ask the people to contribute in rotation sheep, goats, or cattle for national sacrifices or other ceremonies performed for the welfare of the whole people; (7) To keep democracy, the government offices should be based on a rotation system of generations; (8) All men and women must get married, and no man should be allowed to hold a responsible position (other than warrior) or become a member of the council of elders unless he was married and had established his own home-stead. Women should be given the same social status as their husbands; (9) Criminal and civil laws were established and procedures were clearly defined.[31] As seen from the rules of the government mentioned above, the Kikuyu advocated democracy, and thus, to them, submission to a despotic rule of any particular man or group was the greatest humiliation.[32]

Andrew Fedders' and Cynthia Salvadori's comment summarizes the economic and political contribution of the Kikuyu to Kenya:

> In sum, it may be safe to generalise that in the traditional culture of the Kikuyu people one is able to detect, in microcosm, two features of life which are characteristic of contemporary Kenya: a basically egalitarian, democratic political system; and a produc-tive, expanding free market system of economy. Now, these two features are by no means exclusively Kikuyu. They are shared by most of the cultures of the peoples of Kenya. . . . At present, as the numerically largest group in Kenya, the Kikuyu people are the custodians of both these institutions.[33]

Changes

From the latter half of the nineteenth century, Africa started experiencing changes that would alter its course of life permanently. These changes were comprehensive, involving the primal areas of their lives: religious, social, economic, and political.[34] Christianity from Western Europe and America not only came with the gospel, but also with it brought Western culture, technology, medicine, schools, and politics. In the case of the Kikuyu, the

31. Kenyatta, *Facing Mt. Kenya*, 186–89.

32. Ibid., 196.

33. Fedders and Salvadori, *Peoples and Cultures of Kenya*, 119.

34. Mbiti, *African Religions and Philosophy*, 216.

coming of the British East Africa Company to Kikuyuland was followed by Christian missions such as the Church of Scotland Mission in Thogoto, the Church Missionary Society in Kabete, and the Catholic White Fathers at St. Austin's near Nairobi. Missionaries built schools, hospitals, and dispensaries and taught the Kikuyu improved methods of agriculture.[35] These schools that missionaries built became the nursery for changes since the students learned not only Christianity but also Western culture and civilization, which made them gradually detached from their tribal culture and customs. Changes were inevitable.

Social Realm

The area that has been most affected by this change is the family. Family used to be the nucleus of individual and corporate existence, but the introduction of formal Western education, religion, economy, politics, and social structures made permanent changes in the Kenyan family. Individuals were not connected to each other as before but lost in the mass, especially in urban settings. The form, structure, and function of the family changed. The concept of the family changed from the traditional extended family to the modern immediate family, where the parents and their children constitute the family unit.[36]

About urbanization and its consequences, Mbiti says the following: "One of the most serious problems precipitated by city life in Africa is the situation which forces the men to work in town while their wives and children remain in the country. . . . [T]he wife is both mother and father to the children."[37] Furthermore, when problems arose within the family, it became more difficult, since the protective cover under the traditional setting had disappeared. Leakey's observation and statement made half a century ago still makes sense:

> Again, under the present day condition . . . hundreds of young men go to work far from their homes and take their young brides with them. . . . [I]t often happens that the difficulties which face a young married couple are much more serious than in the olden

---

35. Leakey, *Mau Mau and the Kikuyu*, 58–59.
36. Kithinji, "The Individual in Society," 274–75.
37. Mbiti, *African Religions and Philosophy*, 226.

days, and the circumstances are far less conducive to a happy marriage, so that many of these marriages break up.[38]

Because of these changes, the family is no longer that close-knit entity that offered love, security, and a sense of belonging to its members. Traditional roles of men and women have also changed and been mixed up.[39]

John Mbae points out several other social changes in the area of family. According to him, even the concept of immediate family is changing. Family is no longer a man, his wife, and their children. A single mother and her children can constitute a family these days. Furthermore, compared to the traditional role of the father/husband, who took an active role in family affairs making sure that every member of the family performs his/her duty, today's fathers/husbands are no longer involved in family life. Many fathers are under the illusion that they have done their part as long as they pay their children's school fees and provide them with their material needs. In the context of modernization and urbanization, where a communal aspect of responsibility is gone, this absence of father due to employment, drinking, etc., brings forth all kinds of social problems such as street children, proliferating orphanages, delinquent youth, prostitution, and abortion.[40]

Marriage itself has become a private affair rather than the concern of families and communities. Along with it, the intention of dowry has lost its original meaning. Traditionally, the livestock of marriage insurance could not be sold until it was certain that the marriage would not break down. Nowadays, the marriage insurance is paid in cash. Dowry has become a terrible burden on young people, and "[T]oday . . . there is a tendency on the part of some people to be exploitative in this matter, thereby causing hardships to the newly-married couple."[41] The following statement reveals the present picture:

> Due to the individualism and selfishness which have accompanied modern life, some parents ask too much money as bride price. One very serious result of this is to make nonsense of the original aim of the institution of bride price, making it degenerate into a form of commodity exchange, a wife-buying activity.[42]

---

38. Leakey, *Mau Mau and the Kikuyu*, 75.
39. Kithinji, "The Individual in Society," 276.
40. Mbae, "The African family," 43–49.
41. Kibera, "That's Our African Culture," 35.
42. Wanjohi, "African Marriage," 40.

Another significant change in the social realm is the disappearance of the traditional meaning of initiation. Traditionally, the purpose of the initiation rites was to extend to the initiates proper citizenship and the responsibilities of adult life. They were linked to the tribal religious beliefs and practices. However, modernization reduced this most important tribal custom to nothing but a hurried performance of surgical operation without necessary character training. Young men and women were not restrained anymore by the old tradition that discouraged full sexual intercourse until marriage. The consequence was a steady increase of pregnant girls before marriage and the ensuing social problems.[43]

Under the present condition, young boys and girls get little education in the area of behavior and character training, which were all part of the organized tribal educational system. Mbiti observes:

> These schools spend more time teaching young people about dissecting frogs and about colonial history than they ever spend teaching them how to establish happy home and family lives. Unless this structure and system of education is changed, we are heading for tragic social, moral and family chaos whose harvest is not far away. . . . Education is perhaps the greatest cry in Africa today.[44]

Economic Realm

Economically speaking, colonization and westernization brought a monetary economy to the African continent. This new economic system also introduced the concept of time as a commodity to be sold and bought.[45] However, the most important economic issue was land, since the Kikuyu were traditionally attached to land as agriculturalists. Land was vital for their survival and sustenance. Kenyatta's claim makes sense when he says, "When the European comes to the Gikuyu country and robs the people of their land, he is taking away not their livelihood, but the material symbol that holds family and tribe together."[46] Leakey's explanation of the land issue between the Kikuyu and the settlers in the early 1900s is helpful to

43. Leakey, *Mau Mau and the Kikuyu*, 23, 76.

44. Mbiti, *African Religions and Philosophy*, 227.

45. Ibid., 220.

46. Kenyatta, *Facing Mt. Kenya*, 317.

understand the continued Kikuyu resistance to the colonialists in the twentiethth century until independence:

> The coming of missionaries and administrators was followed about 1902 by the arrival of the first settlers. . . . These men and their wives wanted land, land which they could call their own, where they could build their homes and rear their families. They saw the nearly empty country, which had once been part of the "vast garden" described by the early travellers in the previous century. . . . Although these settlers paid for the land they desired, for the Kikuyu these payments did not and could not even rank as purchase of the land; at best they could only rank as payments for the right to cultivate, subject always to the real owner being allowed to evict the occupier at some future date. . . . So from the Kikuyu point of view none of the rights acquired in Kikuyu land by the white settlers were considered as vesting ownership in the newcomers, while from the point of view of British law, and the country was now administered by the British, the transactions were wholly valid and had been made in absolute good faith. . . . So in 1922 there was born the first Kikuyu political organization, the Kikuyu Central Association, led by a band of young men fired with immense patriotism and armed with a little learning, who made the first slogan of their party "We must be given back the lands which the white man has stolen from us."[47]

Sharing was a virtue among traditional African societies. It provided them with a form of insurance against total impoverishment. When calamity struck, a man who shared his wealth was able to rebuild it again by receiving gifts from his relatives, age-mates, neighbors, and friends. Among the Kikuyu, this sharing was evident as well when the owner(s) of land granted farming rights to the less fortunate members of the community. As the following Kikuyu proverb indicates, "The land does not benefit the one who clears it but the newcomer/tenant-at-will."[48] However, people have tended to abuse this noble concept of sharing through the practice of *harambee* (pulling together). It is a Kenyan tradition of community self-help events, which have been used as ways to build and maintain communities by pulling resources together for personal and community events. Politicians used harambee to gain popularity in their constituencies by donating large sums of money to various harambee events. Despite all the positive

---

47. Leakey, *Mau Mau and the Kikuyu*, 63–67.

48. Karega-Munene, "Aspects of Sharing among Africans," 26–27.

effects of harambee, people are getting tired of those who abuse other people's kindness and generosity.[49]

Political Arena

In the political arena, the changes the Kikuyu experienced together with other tribes in Kenya was also immense. The traditional Kikuyu ruling system of the elder council was replaced by newly appointed chiefs under the colonial government. The Kikuyu had not had one single tribal chief but a council of elders who governed the tribe, although there was a spokesperson. The colonial government mistook this spokesperson as the chief and imposed an unfamiliar system on the Kikuyu.[50]

Kenyan politics cannot be discussed without Kikuyu politics. The Kikuyu tribe is not only the largest tribe in Kenya but also played a major role in bringing Kenya to independence. The first Kikuyu political organization, known as The Kikuyu Central Association (KCA), came into being in 1922 with a catch phrase regarding the recovery of the "lost lands" of the Kikuyu. Later, the Kikuyu Central Association took on the issue of female genital mutilation, which the Church of Scotland Mission objected to due to the familiarity among the young men and women after initiation, let alone the practice itself. The KCA attacked the white man, especially missionaries, by saying, "First the land has been taken from us—actually only a small part had been taken and that in good faith—and now they attack our most sacred customs; what will they do next?" This episode led to the establishment of many Kikuyu separatist churches and independent schools.[51]

Later, when the Kikuyu Central Association was banned by the colonial government, another political organization came into being called Kenya African Union (KAU), whose leadership was mainly Kikuyu from the banned Kikuyu Central Association, although other tribes were incorporated into the organization. The resistance of the Kikuyu to the colonial government, led by the radical members of the KAU, culminated in the Kikuyu revolt known as the Mau Mau Revolt (Rebellion, Uprising, or Kenya Emergency) from the late 1940s until the early 1950s.[52] After the revolt, Kenya moved further on to independence and attained freedom in 1963

49. Ibid., 30.
50. Leakey, *Mau Mau and the Kikuyu*, 35.
51. Ibid., 87–90.
52. De Jong, *Mission and Politics in Eastern Africa*, 60–61.

under the Kenya African National Union (KANU) led by Jomo Kenyatta (c. 1899–1978), the first president of independent Kenya.

It is beneficial to expand on the Mau Mau here. Welbourn writes, "Mau, Mau, when it came, was an expression of the determination of almost a whole tribe—even of many who disapproved the form which it took. It was a determination to be rid, once for all, of the 'new situation,' of the Europeans with whom it has proved impossible to come to terms."[53] The main issue was land, and they recruited members by force using secret oath taking. The Kikuyu feared the consequences of breaking the oath, and Mau Mau leaders took advantage of this fear to expand the support base of the revolt. One of the phrases in Mau Mau oath ceremony was "If I do anything to give away this organization to the enemy, may I be killed by the oath." After taking such an oath, no ordinary Kikuyu would go to the police because he would be breaking the oath and calling down supernatural penalties upon himself or his family members. However, according to Kikuyu traditional law, an oath taken against his will and without the consent of family members was not valid. Knowing this, the Kikuyu Christians who experienced genuine conversion had no fear of supernatural punishment for breaking the heathen oath which they took against their will, so they reported the case to the police. The Kikuyu also organized tribe-wide cleansing ceremonies and mass meetings to call upon people to resist and denounce the Mau Mau.[54]

There were several groups among the Kikuyu who refused to take the Mau Mau oath and who were regarded as its enemies by the Mau Mau: these were, first of all, government administrative staff, those who were loyal to the British administration for one reason or another; those who were committed Christians, especially the Revival brethren who knew the superior power of God; and the old guard traditional Kikuyu who did not recognize the Mau Mau oath as a true Kikuyu oath.[55] The evaluations of the Mau Mau are varied, depending upon who looks at the event and from what perspective. With whatever perspective one looks at the event, either religiously (Kikuyu tribal religion), socioculturally (cultural alienation), economically (economic deprivation), or politically (political oppression), one thing is certain. It affected Kenya, and especially the Kikuyu so significantly that it hastened the process of national independence. Furthermore,

---

53. Welbourn, *East African Christian*, 140.

54. Leakey, *Mau Mau and the Kikuyu*, 95–104.

55. Wilkinson, *The Story of Chogoria*, 133.

the role that religious belief played in the revolt is significant proof again that the Kikuyu are truly religious, whether they are pagan or Christian. This confirms that spirituality affects politics and vice versa. They are intertwined in African mindset.

Change of Worldview

The traditional Kikuyu worldview assumptions are as follows: (1) holistic perception of reality; (2) God- or spirit-centered universe; (3) group identity (kinship) of self; (4) past orientation; (5) cyclical time; (6) value of relationship; (7) respect of age; and (8) value of cooperation.

Among these categories, the worldviews that the research participants[56] confirmed they have are holistic perception of reality and God-centered or spirit-centered universe. These two worldview assumptions seem to be more foundational and fundamental than other assumptions since they have remained more intact through generations than other assumptions. For example, one of the participants shared a situation at his farm. He had two cows, and one night they were stolen. Sometime later a group of robbers broke in to his farm again and stole some household items. His initial understanding of the incidents was that he was being "attacked" and asked for prayer. Although he found out later that the incidents were caused by someone who wanted him to leave his farm because of a land dispute, my research participant interpreted it, first of all, as spiritual harassment. However, this God- or spirit-centered universe couldn't help being changed as well. Another research participant shared that it was both God and medicine that would heal her when she got sick. Traditionally, it was the medicine man and his herbs. Now due to education, medical knowledge, and Christian faith, people believe in the efficacy of medicine and also the power of God. It is still a God-centered universe, but with modification due to Western civilization and the introduction of Christianity.

The categories of worldview that underwent some change are those of social values: the group identity of self, value of relationship, respect of old age, and the value of cooperation. All the research participants have shifted toward the Western worldview paradigm, but they have not completely changed. Although they still strongly value group identity, they embrace individualism too—in traditional Kikuyu culture, individuals were

56. See note 53 of ch. 5.

not ignored anyway.[57] Human relationship and material value share equal importance now. Age is still respected, but only when it is partnered with responsibility. This was true in the past, and now the young are regarded as important as the old.

These social values are all interrelated. For example, since individualism crept into their society and individuals are not cared for by the group anymore, they must fend for themselves by accumulating wealth. Since the value of group identity has shifted to individualism somewhat, competition is also accepted. Despite all these social changes, the research participants have retained the virtues of generosity, hospitality, and respect for people. These values are all about relationship and are still strong in them, testifying that the research participants are still Kikuyu—the identity that cannot be denied.

The most changes occurred in the area of time. Research participants showed both future and linear time orientation, and they are also conscious of quantity of time. It seems that this area reflects more Western influence than other worldview areas. To modern Kikuyu, time is not just an event anymore, but something that is calculated. City dwellers are particularly conscious of time. Nevertheless, the old paradigm still lingers even with the changes. It is true that they have moved to modern time consciousness, but they still show flexibility. Once when I was conducting an interview with one of my research participants at his church office, one of his lay leaders came by. She had made an appointment with him at that time. I became a little bit anxious, but my research participant did not mind and continued to spend another hour with me while she was waiting outside his office!

In regard to the orientation of time, there is one Kikuyu social custom which is still observed. The naming practice shows the Kikuyu are not completely out of the cyclical time orientation. Children are still named after their grandparents. This is a reminder of cyclical time orientation; the older generation still survives through their grandchildren. Life continues. The past is not completely forgotten.

Worldview assumptions are tenacious and resist changes, as Charles Kraft argues:

> Even radical paradigm shifts, such as . . . the introduction of Christianity into previously unevangelized societies, permit a large measure of continuity with antecedent worldview assumptions

57. Kibicho, "The Kikuyu Conception of God," 39.

and the strategies built on them. . . . [M]any features of the old will continue on, often in modified form, into the new.[58]

As explained above, all basic worldview assumptions still exist in the minds of the Kikuyu either intact or modified. This means the retention of Kikuyu social structures in some degree and the preservation of their religious orientation of the universe with Christian adaptation. Modified time orientation reveals that the Kikuyu outlook of life has become progressive and futuristic due to the introduction of Western education and Christianity.

Contemporary Socioeconomic-Political Phenomena in Kenya

Socioeconomic-political phenomena in Africa are closely related to religion and spirituality as seen in the traditional Kikuyu society. Likewise, in contemporary Kenyan society, spirituality is affected by issues of its society.

Urbanization and Poverty

Urbanization has been one of the major sociological trends in Africa since the beginning of the twenty-first century. The moral, physical, social, practical, and individual problems associated with it are enormous. In 1920, about 14 percent of the world's population lived in the city. By 1980, the percentage had increased to 40 percent. By the dawn of the new millennium, half of the world's population was urban. By the year 2025, 60 percent of the world is projected to be living in cities. Africa's urban areas are composed of about 40 percent of its population, and the urban growth rate is twice that of the population growth rate.[59] In East Africa, the urbanization rate is 7 percent, the world's highest.[60]

Urbanization can be defined either as the proportion of the population living in urban places, the process by which these urban places grow, or the spread of a way of life and values which have come to be associated with such places. In this sense, urbanization occurs as a result of population growth in the country as a whole, and associated economic, social, and political factors that draw people to urban areas.[61] A voice from an in-migrant tells it:

58. Kraft, *Anthropology for Christian Witness*, 436.

59. O'Donovan, *Biblical Christianity*, 42, 53; Shorter, "Slums," 61.

60. Zanotelli, "A Grace Freely Given," 14.

61. Peli and Oyeneye, *Consensus, Conflict and Change*, 205–6.

> We came to towns to look for money/employment and to be near
> development projects which are not in the rural areas. All sources
> of employment are to be found in towns, good schools and proper
> medical attention. Some rural places do not have an in-patient
> hospital. So we are here not out of choice but out of necessity.[62]

As so many people are drawn to cities and towns from the country-
side, one great problem they face is unemployment and resultant poverty.
Simply, job seekers outnumber job opportunities. Labor becomes cheap,
while housing costs skyrocket. Housing has become a major problem in
cities and towns, resulting in the growth of slums, squatter villages, and
shantytowns. Nairobi's slums hold 60 percent of its population.[63] The slum
is a miniature society where all kinds of human activities, good or bad, are
done in a smaller scale, and they form a subculture. Poverty in the slum is
dire, and slum living is characterized by complex problems.

The World Bank's report on poverty lists the following as the characteristics of ill-being commonly associated with slum living: material
lack, bad social relations (exclusion, rejection, isolation, and loneliness),
powerlessness and helplessness, frustration and anger, humiliation (stigma
and shame), the politics of infrastructure (feeling of abandonment by their
government), and environmental risks.[64] Slum dwellers are exposed to in-
fectious diseases such as cholera and typhoid. Inadequate or no running
water, inadequate toilet facilities, no sewer system, and no electricity make
slum living desperate. Slum dwellers also experience insecurity, immorality
and sexual abuse, drug abuse and alcoholism, and domestic violence more
frequently than non-slum dwellers because of their environment, which is
simply too conducive to such troubles.[65] Urban poverty is more acutely felt
than rural poverty since the traditional support structure of a community
does not exist in the slum. The formation of slums is an ugly adverse effect
of African modernization and urbanization. Its existence reveals social,
economic, environmental, and political constraints of the society.

62. Marenya, "The Voice of the Women from the Slums," 57.

63. Shorter, "Slums," 65.

64. Narayan et al., *Crying Out for Change*, 31–36, 81–85.

65. Marenya, "The Voice of the Women from the Slums," 50–58.

HIV/AIDS

In the early- and mid-1980s, HIV/AIDS was largely unknown in Kenya, although HIV started infecting some Kenyans as early as 1981. A couple of decades later on November 25, 1999, Kenya's second president, Daniel arap Moi (1924–), declared AIDS a national disaster.[66] HIV/AIDS is a complex problem that affects all aspects of human life, and the causes of its spread are also complicated. One cannot deny the fact that HIV/AIDS is related to poverty. Urbanization produced the urban poor and the slum. While men tried to find manual jobs, women either found domestic jobs or were desperately driven to prostitution for survival. Sociologist/theologian Aylward Shorter explains the high prevalence of HIV/AIDS in the slum:

> Prostitution of women and children is one of the commonest ways of making a living in the slums. The preponderance of male migrants, the need for female economic independence, the phenomenon of street children and the reality of crowded living conditions all favour it. The absence of normal family relationships and the morally disorienting experience of the shanty towns favour sexual promiscuity. This also means that the incidence of sexually transmitted diseases and HIV/AIDS is high.[67]

Another sociologist Eunice Kamaara describes HIV/AIDS ramifications on gender:

> HIV/AIDS is a gender issue, but women suffer more from the scourge than men. This is because of the women's physiological make-up and the economic and socio-cultural factors. Economically, women are more vulnerable to HIV infection than men because most women are disadvantaged as far as access to property and control of resources is concerned.[68]

Kamaara continues to explain that cultural expectations in traditional Africa were for men to have sexual experiences before marriage, unlike women, and that this sociocultural expectation of male dominance and female subordination accounts for contemporary youth's sexual behavior and spread of HIV/AIDS. In addition, while the traditional value of male dominance or patriarchal system still lingers, individuals enjoy freedom

---

66. Kamaara, *Gender, Youth Sexuality and HIV/AIDS*, 50–51.

67. Shorter, "Slums," 68.

68. Kamaara, *Gender, Youth Sexuality and HIV/AIDS*, 63.

of action due to the introduction of westernization. Christian morals are taught but not as much practiced. In this process of social transformation, it is the most productive age group, those between 15–45 years of age, who are most affected with the HIV/AIDS pandemic. AIDS-related death is a daily Kenyan experience.[69]

Tribal Politics and Corruption

The 2007–8 presidential post-election violence, which killed more than 1,200 and displaced an estimated 600,000, was a pronounced sign of tribal differences that had been simmering beneath the surface. Unfortunately, the church was also divided along tribal lines and failed to lead Kenya through this dark time.

As tribalism has played itself out in areas of security, so has it shown itself in the political arena. After independence in 1963, the Kikuyu-dominated KANU was both a recognized political party and a tribal government.[70] However, the evolution of Kenyan politics from 1963 through the late 1970s saw a decline in the importance of the party and an increasing importance of the tribe as the first preoccupation of most political leaders. By the time President Kenyatta died in 1978, the tribal factor had almost completely overshadowed national considerations in the mind of most politicians, both inside and outside of government.

Most sober-minded Kenyans of whatever tribe would agree today that they have had enough of tribal politics. They feel that the concern of politicians is simply to have their turn to commit the same misdeeds as their predecessors and also avenge their suffering—whether real or imagined. According to Daniel Gachukia, most political leaders today not only talk tribal, but they actually think tribal, which is more dangerous. They are so concerned about their tribe that they have no time to think about the welfare of Kenya.[71] The following statement is almost hurtful: "Our plight as a country is not due to 'international situation' or 'forces beyond our control.' Our plight is due, first and foremost, to one factor: politics based on the premise: now it is the turn of my tribe to benefit."[72]

---

69. Ibid., 70–76.

70. Gachukia, "Government by Tribe," 103.

71. Ibid., 103–5.

72. Ibid., 106.

Even Christian loyalty has not been able to save politicians and religious leaders from tribalism. As noted earlier, initially, the East Africa Revival Movement spread across tribal barriers, but the faith of the Revival members became subject to tribal ideals.[73] However, the church played a crucial role in enlarging the field of political parties. Kenya gained independence in 1963 with a single party, but the government legalized multiparty politics in 1991. In the process, "The church not only ignited but also sustained the struggle for multiparty rule. It provided the moral rationale and base from which other movements mobilized. Had the church not opened the critical political space, Kenya would perhaps to date be a single party state."[74]

The church continued to influence politics in the ensuing years. The Ufungamano Initiative, led by religious groups for constitutional review, played significantly in unifying opposition parties to form the National Rainbow Coalition (NARC), which stopped KANU's thirty-nine years of rule in 2002 with the election of President Mwai Kibaki (1931–) to replace President Moi. The Ufungamano Initiative worked harmoniously until the second Bomas of Kenya constitutional review process, contributing to a draft which failed in the 2005 referendum. In the most recent constitutional referendum that passed in 2010, the church in Kenya opposed it because of the inclusion of Islamic Kadhi courts and abortion. The church articulated its positions clearly, but to no avail.

As the Kikuyu tribe has been at the heart of Kenya's church history, so have they also been at the core of Kenyan politics. Two of Kenya's three presidents, President Kenyatta and President Kibaki, have been Kikuyu. It is a well-known fact that the Kikuyu are hard-working. They have fertile soil and good rains. From early on, they have enjoyed advantages of contact with Western civilization. Their numbers and political and economic success have made them the most influential group in Kenya. Henry Okullu says the following:

> By virtue of this they became more politically conscious, commercially competent and educationally more advanced than any other tribe. . . . But what must be condemned as utterly evil is any attempt to perpetuate that position by using unjust means because of thinking that that particular community is a "chosen people."[75]

73. Okullu, *Church and Politics in East Africa*, 44.
74. Kamaara, "Religion and Socio-political Change," 131.
75. Okullu, *Church and Politics in East Africa*, 46.

Besides tribalism, there is another matter that concerns the whole country, and almost all countries in Africa are struggling with it. It is the matter of corruption. Corruption can be defined as an anti-social behavior that confers improper benefits contrary to legal and moral norms.[76] The dynamics of corruption come from leaders and civil servants on the one hand and ordinary citizens who need social services on the other. Bureaucratic procedural loopholes, greed, inadequate income, and the erosion of moral standards also fuel corruption.[77] Unlike corruption of low-ranking officials for the sake of survival, political corruption involves high-ranking public officials who run the affairs of the state. Their use of illegal and unethical means to exploit their official positions produces quite negative consequences as Aquiline Tarimo expands:[78]

> Politically, it misuses the power of the state, affects political stability, and hinders administrative development and the formation of a comprehensive socio-political organization. Economically, it stifles personal initiative, creativity, and commitment to the ideals of human rights and social justice. In the long run political corruption degrades the standard of public service, moral responsibility, and the sense of the common good.[79]

Although Niccolo Machiavelli (1469–1527) and Hans Morgenthau (1904–80) accepted prudence—the weighing of the consequences of alternative political actions—and opportunism as virtues in politics, politicians must exhibit integrity and honesty because of the far-reaching consequences of their conduct.[80] Paul Gifford argues that the church is also guilty:

> Although slavery, colonialism, geography and terms of trade are all significant, the main reason for Africa's plight is its elite. Africa, under regimes like Moi's, shot itself in the foot. . . . None of Kenya's Christians (apart from certain mainline churchmen and the Catholic hierarchy in the early 1990s) challenges the country's political elite. Church leaders are in many ways part of that elite themselves, sometimes equally lacking in transparency, accountability and attention to due process.[81]

76. Osoba, "Corruption in Nigeria," 371.

77. Tarimo, "The State and Human Rights," 60.

78. Gyekye, *Tradition and Modernity*, 203.

79. Tarimo, "The State and Human Rights," 61.

80. Orwa, "Politics and Integrity," 113.

81. Gifford, *Christianity, Politics and Public Life*, 250–51.

Tribalism, tribal politics, and deep-rooted political corruption in Kenya seem to be daunting obstacles to tackle and overcome soon.

African Culture and Christian Spirituality

African cultural aspects are an integral part of Christian spirituality in Africa. Many Africans have desired to become Christians without changing culture. It is also shown in the Scripture that when the gospel was preached to the Gentiles, the Jerusalem church decided not to impose Jewish cultural laws on Gentile Christians (Acts 15). When the gospel was brought to Kenyans, there were conflicts between the Christian message and African culture. As a result, separate churches were established to preserve African culture and customs, resulting in syncretistic practices.

Even now, the issues of traditional culture, Christian message, and their interactions to each other are critical. What is required is integration between culture and the Christian message. Culture is relative, not absolute, and should be transformed to reflect the glory of God through its forms and expressions. It is like a living organism whose parts cannot be separated one from another. For example, religion cannot be separated from society. We can hardly talk about social matters without mentioning economics. Without technology communication may not be effective, and so on. This integrated model of culture keeps people in balance as each subsystem of culture and underlying worldview assumptions hold a society together.

However, when this integration and balance are somehow disrupted, either by a new custom introduced externally or sprung up internally, cultural and worldview changes are inevitable. In the case of the Kikuyu, great disruption occurred when Europeans came to Kenya. When missionaries and British settlers brought the gospel and Western civilization to the Kikuyu, Kikuyu traditional customs broke down. Worldview assumptions were shaken. However, culture is a "coping mechanism," and it is resilient.[82] In their changed circumstances, the Kikuyu resisted, accommodated, adapted to, and integrated the changes into their system, and their present cultural patterns are quite different from the traditional ones they had before the arrival of Europeans.

The Christian sociologist H. Richard Niebuhr (1951) presents several different positions of relationship between God and culture: (1) God is the

---

82. Kraft, *Anthropology for Christian Witness*, 38.

product of culture; (2) God is against culture; (3) God endorses a culture or subculture; (4) God is above culture and unconcerned; (5) God is above culture and working through it.[83] Kraft argues for yet another position saying that God exists apart from culture; He relates to and interacts with human beings in terms of the cultural waters within which humans are immersed.[84] Therefore, in line with Kraft's position and in order to study spirituality, the study of culture is crucial since the reality and perception of God is transmitted through the medium of culture. Spirituality is formed as a product of theological (God) and anthropological (culture) reflection and integration. Thus, the configuration of Christian spirituality in Africa is a unique reflection and integration of both the Christian message and African cultural aspects. A total rejection of culture or indiscriminate acceptance of it is not recommended. What is desired is a "transformation of culture."[85]

With such foundational understanding of the interaction between culture and Christianity as mentioned above, it is time to turn to cultural issues in Kenya still needing transformation in relation to Christianity. As mentioned earlier in this chapter, the Kikuyu practiced circumcision as a rite of passage. Boys and girls transitioned into adulthood through circumcision ceremonies. Male circumcision has not been a serious issue, but female circumcision has drawn sharp criticism from missionaries. Some Kenyan communities still practice female circumcision secretly. The practice needs to be eliminated or transformed since it violates the fundamental sexuality God endowed upon women.

As a counter measure, some Kenyan churches have introduced an alternative ceremony that upholds both tradition and Christian spirituality. Boys and girls of circumcision age attend a retreat where morals and adult responsibilities are taught. The boys are then encouraged to go through circumcision at the hospital,[86] but girls are prohibited from it. Follow-up meetings and mentoring are sometimes held afterward. Through this alternative rite of passage, Christian boys and girls experience a different initiation ceremony that gives them an opportunity to give allegiance to God

83. Niebuhr quoted in Kraft, *Anthropology for Christian Witness*, 92–93.

84. Kraft, *Anthropology for Christian Witness*, 91.

85. Ibid., 440–41.

86. However, in some communities, there is a tremendous peer pressure on the boys and their parents to go through a more prestigious traditional ceremony, which also requires a huge expense. *Nation*, 26 Mar, 2011.

instead of to tribal and cultural customs. Churches have taken the initiative, and the Kenyan government has also supported it with proper legislation. In the case of circumcision, both the form and the meaning of the practice must to be transformed.

Polygamy is another area needing elimination. It is deeply ingrained in the African traditional mindset, not only for the Kikuyu but for many other tribes as well. Just as some communities say there is no cockerel with only one hen, so they say a man cannot be expected to have just one wife and be faithful to her. Other communities allow the husband to marry another wife or wives to discourage immorality. Still other communities allow the husband to have sexual relationships with the sister of his wife, saying it is like one and the same person. Even among some Christians, polygamy is condoned by both husband and wife. If the husband doesn't like his wife, he simply gets another wife or concubine instead of divorcing her. Even if the wife becomes aware of his deed, she simply accepts it according to tradition.

While the man is expected or allowed to have more than one partner and it is assumed normal, the woman is allowed only one husband in most communities, except the Maasai. Among the Maasai, a man will sleep with the woman of his choice as long as he arrives first and plants his spear outside the door as a sign. Whether it was man's sexual desire that needed to be satisfied or the love of children, this traditional mentality caused rampant sexual immorality in African societies, including in Kenya. In the past, the church condemned polygamy. Some African Christians who desired to keep this tradition, however, broke off from mission churches and established separate African Independent Churches. Presently, evangelical churches are strict against polygamy. Polygamists are prohibited from participating in the sacraments of the church including the Lord's Supper. They are also not allowed to take church offices such as deacon or elder.

The Scripture teaches a monogamous relationship between one man and one woman (Gen 1:27; 2:18–25). In the creation, God set a model for a male-female relationship, that is, one man and one woman. In the New Testament, when Paul admonishes Timothy and Titus to select elders and deacons, one of the qualifications was the "husband of but one wife" (1 Tim 3:2; 3:12; Titus 1:6). Although, there are many figures in the Bible who married more than one woman, including the patriarchs, the original plan of God for mankind was a monogamous relationship between a man and a woman as shown in the foundational Genesis narrative. A prominent

Kenyan church recently dismissed four of its pastors for the reason of extramarital affairs. It is appalling to imagine, with some pastors engaging in extramarital affairs, how much more lay Christians may be engaging in polygamy or in extramarital affairs. The sexual mores in Kenyan society are loose, and Christianity has to decisively deal with this traditional polygamous mindset for the transformation of the culture for Christ.

Still another area needing transformation is wife (widow) inheritance. This African custom is not congruent with Christian spirituality. Old Testament examples of wife inheritance are shown in the story of Judah and Tamar (Gen 38) and Ruth and Boaz (Book of Ruth). However, this type of union is not mentioned in the New Testament. Some Africans may try to legitimize the practice of wife inheritance using Old Testament incidents, but these cultural practices of the Israelites are not enough to establish the practice as a norm for contemporary Christians. In the New Testament, we see an example of elderly widows being taken care of by the church, while younger widows were encouraged to remarry (1 Tim 5:3–16). Christian teaching about marriage is that the marriage union ends with the death of the husband (Rom 7:2–3). Afterward, the wife is not obligated to marry her dead husband's brother or another relative. She is released from the law of marriage that bound her. In Africa, where AIDS is prevalent, this cultural practice should be transformed.

What about other cultural aspects? Are there any positive cultural aspects that are compatible with Christian spirituality? One such aspect is African music. Although the first missionaries condemned African music and dance, they are coming back strong in contemporary Kenyan society. Traditionally, moral messages were transmitted mostly through songs from generation to generation. This ancient method is still an effective means of communication even in modern Africa. In Kenya, vernacular radio stations air tunes in different tribal languages, and people like it! Therefore, it would be effective if Christian morals and messages could be taught and disseminated through African ethnic music. Kraft confirms this practice by stating:

> Music (often including drama and dance) is another important vehicle of enculturation. . . . Both in non-western and western societies, the words of songs are powerful conveyers of the values of the society. Something sung to a catchy tune or beat is much more likely to be repeated than something merely spoken. In addition, something sung to a catchy tune or beat is more likely to be regarded positively than something merely spoken. Knowing this,

those who want to influence young people regularly package their message in songs.[87]

Even in English worship services, when the music is switched from English to Kiswahili, the dynamic suddenly changes and people become more excited. Christian spirituality and African culture can find a common ground in the use of ethnic music.

Another area of positive ground between Christian spirituality and African culture is a holistic understanding of life. We have bodies to be clothed and fed, and we experience God through both body and spirit. Christian spirituality is essentially holistic, and the African culture and worldview is holistic as well, as seen in the Kikuyu culture. The Kikuyu do not separate the spiritual from the material. In Christian spirituality, we also experience God in all dimensions of life. As mission Christianity brought medicine and education to Africa along with the gospel, in the same way the African church needs to approach its own people socially, economically, and politically so that their lives can be developed holistically. Through such holistic approaches, Christian spirituality in Africa can be deepened and take firm root.

Summary

The Kikuyu cultural aspects that have been examined in this chapter—society, economy, and politics—are inseparably integrated into the religious/spiritual life of the Kikuyu. The comprehensive nature of spirituality encompasses all these subsystems and truly affects all realms of life. At the same time, all subsystems contribute to the development of spirituality by enriching, adding concrete dimensions and flavors, and working at times as constraints and other times as facilitators.

African culture has changed as a result of missions and the introduction of Western civilization. With the changes arrived a host of social issues as mentioned in this chapter. Urbanization, poverty, HIV/AIDS, and corruption are just a few of those social ills. Traditional culture and Christianity have been interacting with each other since Christianity was introduced to Africa, especially from the late nineteenth century onward. Desired is the transformation of culture when there are conflicts between Christianity and culture. Christian spirituality in Africa can find its authentic and contextual expressions only when African Christians transform some of

87. Kraft, *Anthropology for Christian Witness*, 265.

the traditional cultural practices that are not compatible to Christianity, so that the form and the meaning of those cultural practices reflect true biblical teachings. Christian spirituality can also utilize such positive African cultural aspects as music and a holistic worldview to develop further on the African soil.

8

African Traditional Religion

BEFORE MISSIONARIES BROUGHT CHRISTIANITY to Africa, each tribe had its own religious beliefs and practices, collectively called African Traditional Religion (ATR). ATR is essential to understanding the past on which the present stands. It is also almost imperative to mention ATR since religion permeates all areas of life in Africa. In Kenya, although those who follow ATR are only 1.6 percent,[1] it plays a significant part in people's lives since even Christians revert back to ATR in times of life crisis.

African Traditional Religion is still an important element in the spirituality of many Kenyans. According to Mbiti, Africans are "notoriously religious."[2]

> To ignore these traditional beliefs, attitudes, and practices can only lead to a lack of understanding African behavior and problems. Religion is the strongest element in traditional background, and exerts probably the greatest influence upon the thinking and living of the people concerned.[3]

Most African scholars, including Mbiti, who studied African religion as an insider, have agreed in recent times that African Traditional Religion is one in essence.[4] Although their religious expressions may be different from tribe to tribe, the underlying philosophy is one.[5] Jacques Maquet

---

1. Kenya National Bureau of Statistics, 2009 Kenya Population and Housing Census, 396.

2. Mbiti, African Religions and Philosophy, 1.

3. Ibid.

4. Magesa, African Religion, 26.

5. Mbiti, African Religions and Philosophy, 1.

explains that this unity of sub-Saharan African culture is due to similar adaptation to the natural environment and the diffusion of cultural traits.[6] This chapter deals with the underlying features of ATR, with the Kikuyu as a micro example.

Regarding the basic characteristics of ATR, it is primarily holistic. In ATR there is no distinction between the sacred and the secular. ATR permeates all areas of life.[7] "For Africans religion is quite literally life and life is a religion."[8] They do not know how to exist without religion, and "religion is in their whole system of being."[9] That is why religion is a middle stratum between worldview and surface culture, as shown below.

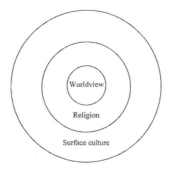

Second, ATR is communal. It is not for the individual primarily, but for the community.[10] Sociability, relationship, participation, and sharing are the central moral imperatives of African religion, and the unity of community is the paramount good.[11] The role of a religious leader is also to protect and prolong the life of the family and the community.[12] Third, ATR is more pragmatic or human centered: "To live here and now is the most important concern of African religious activities and beliefs."[13]

> The primary purpose of acts of worship and reverence is neither God nor the ancestors, but the well-being of the person or community concerned. African religion is human-centered, even

6. Maquet, *Africanity*, 16.

7. Mbiti, *African Religions and Philosophy*, 2.

8. Magesa, *African Religion*, 33.

9. Mbiti, *African Religions and Philosophy*, 2–3.

10. Ibid., 2.

11. Magesa, *African Religion*, 65–67.

12. Ibid., 68.

13. Mbiti, *African Religions and Philosophy*, 4.

overtly utilitarian in the communal rather than the individualistic sense.[14]

The beliefs of ATR can be classified into three basic components: belief in the Supreme Being, the spirit world, and mystical powers.[15] In beginning this discussion, one thing that needs to be pointed out is the apparent discrepancy between the supernatural worldview assumption and the human centeredness of African Traditional Religion. Although their understanding of the universe is supernatural, or God- or spirit-centered, the function of their religion was for the sake of humans. These two aspects co-exist in African Traditional Religion.

The Concept of God

The Attributes of God

In all societies of Africa, people have a notion of God as the Supreme Being, a concept that has been strongly influenced by the historical, geographical, social, and cultural background or environment. Thus, the basic understanding of African God is that he is both transcendent and immanent.[16] He is a distant Being, taking little interest in people's daily affairs, and yet at the crises of their lives, he can be called upon.[17] This notion of God is a reflection of the sociological structure of the African community where chiefs and kings were distant from people—beyond personal fellowship or communication.[18] Although "God is in relationship, or even better, in communion, with humanity and the entire world,"[19] "God should only be approached in case of a major problem."[20]

The Kikuyu name for God, *Ngai,* signifies that God is the creator and ruler of all things, and he distributes everything to his children everywhere.[21] He is also addressed by the Kikuyu as *MweneNyaga* (possessor of brightness) and associated with *Kere-Nyaga* (Mount Kenya), which means

14. Magesa, *African Religion,* 69.

15. Gehman, *African Traditional Religion in Biblical Perspective,* 9.

16. Mbiti, *African Religions and Philosophy,* 29–30.

17. Kenyatta, *Facing Mount Kenya,* 234.

18. Gehman, *African Traditional Religion in Biblical Perspective,* 230.

19. Magesa, *African Religion,* 46.

20. Kirwen, *African Cultural Knowledge,* 13.

21. Kibicho, "*The Kikuyu Conception of God,*" 59.

"that which possesses brightness or mountain of brightness." The traditional Kikuyu believed that *Kere-Nyaga* was *Ngai's* official resting place.[22] Another name for God used especially in public prayers is *Githuri* (Great Elder), which emphasizes God's wisdom, love, care of his children, and approachableness in confidence without fear. Still another name *Murungu* suggests his mystery, power, and otherness. *Murungu* was commonly used in combination with *Ngai* as in *Ngai-Murungu*.[23] According to the Kikuyu, "God lives in heaven and he is everywhere"; "God is great"; "God ultimately prevails."[24] According to Mbiti, the Kikuyu believed that God has

> *No father nor mother, nor wife nor children;*
> *He is alone.*
> *He is neither a child nor an old man;*
> *He is the same today as He was yesterday.*[25]

Mbiti goes on to explain that "God is self-sufficient, self-supporting and self-containing, just as He is self-originating. . . . He is truly self-dependent, absolutely unchangeable and unchanging."[26]

As seen above, the Kikuyu God *Ngai* is both transcendent and immanent. Kibicho summarizes the character of *Ngai* as follows:

> The Kikuyu has a clear conception of God as the creator and sustainer of all things. Although transcendent in all ways, yet he is immanent with and for his children, and they can approach him with confidence and trust. He helps men through the talents he has given them if they are used in the proper way. He is the God of justice and mercy above everything else and demands of all men that they pursue the same for the enhancement of life and the welfare of all his children.[27]

---

22. Kenyatta, *Facing Mount Kenya*, 234.

23. Kibicho, "*The Kikuyu Conception of God,*" 58–59.

24. Ibid., 11.

25. Mbiti, *African Religions and Philosophy*, 34.

26. Ibid.

27. Kibicho, "*The Kikuyu Conception of God,*" 61.

Worship of God

Kibicho treats Kikuyu communication with God in three categories: individual, family, and public in regard to prayer, worship, and sacrifice.[28]

Individual

As mentioned before, the Kikuyu emphasize the welfare of family and community more than individuals, but individuals are not ignored. Actually, they are the ultimate objects of concern. In religious matters, it is the same. Although communal approach to God is more emphasized, individuals can approach God alone in prayers when they feel such need.[29] Leakey says that those individual prayers are usually short, and a good Kikuyu adult would say such short prayers daily: "God keep me through this night," and "God you have kept me through this night."[30]

Family

In traditional African culture, family means extended family, including the living and the dead, and it is the most important worship unit in the Kikuyu culture. The Kikuyu identify four important occasions in life: birth, initiation, marriage, and death. According to Kenyatta, communication with God is established in all these occasions, and it is done by the family group: "No individual may directly supplicate the Almighty. . . . [A]lthough the crises are in the life of the individual, he may not make supplication on his own behalf; his whole family group must pledge their interest in his life."[31] Other events where the family is involved for communication with and supplication to God, besides the main events mentioned, are disease in the family or domestic animals, adoption ceremony of a man from a different tribe, and various cleansing and purification ceremonies.[32] Again, the following saying of the Kikuyu describes the importance of family as a basic religious unit. "God lives in the heavens and he does not bother with

28. Ibid., 39.
29. Ibid.
30. Leakey, *Mau Mau and the Kikuyu*, 40.
31. Kenyatta, *Facing Mt. Kenya*, 235.
32. Kibicho, "*The Kikuyu Conception of God*," 45.

the work or affairs of one man alone. He looks after the affairs of a whole people or a homestead group. There is no one man's religion or sacrifice."[33]

Public

In every region of Kikuyuland, there is one big fig tree set aside as a special place of communal worship of and sacrifice to God. Other subsidiary fig trees grow around the main one to form a "sacred grove."[34] This one big tree symbolizes Mount Kenya and four other minor sacred mountains of the Kikuyu. Under these sacred trees the Kikuyu worship, pray, and make their sacrifices to God. In the Christian sense, it is like the "House of God."[35]

The following public prayer was offered to God in all public assemblies in Kikuyuland. An elder led and the assembly responded:

> Elder: *Say ye, the elders may have wisdom and speak with one voice.*
>
> People: *Praise ye Ngai. Peace be with us.*
>
> Elder: *Say ye that the country may have tranquility and the people may continue to increase.*
>
> People: *Praise ye Ngai. Peace be with us.*
>
> Elder: *Say ye that the people and the flocks and the herds may prosper and be free from illness.*
>
> People: *Praise ye Ngai. Peace be with us.*
>
> Elder: *Say ye the fields may bear much fruit and the land may continue to be fertile.*
>
> People: *Peace be with us.*[36]

Kenyatta goes on to say that no sacrifice was involved in these kinds of prayers. The Kikuyu offered sacrifices to God only in such serious matters as drought, outbreak of an epidemic, and great distress, as with a serious illness. On such occasions, elders took up the duty of offering the sacrifices to God.[37] According to Mbiti, the Kikuyu made sacrifices on great occasions

---

33. Kenyatta, *Facing Mt. Kenya*, 236.

34. Leakey, *Mau Mau and the Kikuyu*, 40.

35. Kenyatta, *Facing Mt. Kenya*, 236.

36. Kenyatta, *Facing Mt. Kenya*, 238–39.

37. Ibid., 239–42.

such as at the rites of passage, planting time, before crops ripen, and at the harvest of the first fruits, and, in the case of a severe drought, they even sacrificed a child whom they buried alive in a shrine.[38] What is noteworthy in Kikuyu traditional religion is that elders were leaders of the community including religious matters, and that there was no class called "priests." Religion is so closely interwoven with traditions and social customs of the people that all the members were considered to have acquired necessary knowledge about their religion and customs.[39]

Spirit World

Ancestors and the Living-Dead

It is impossible to grasp the meaning of the religious foundations of Africa without going through the "thought area" occupied by the ancestors.[40] The worship and placating of the departed ancestral spirits is a major religious concern.[41]

There are two categories of ancestral spirits according to Mbiti: those whose names and identities have been forgotten, and those who have died recently up to five generations ago. The first category is called just spirits, and the second, living-dead. There are also spirits of children, brothers and sisters, barren wives, and other members of the family who were not necessarily the "ancestors." Since spirits have sunken into *Zamani* (the past), they have no family or personal ties with human beings, and are no longer living-dead. On the other hand, the living-dead are still in the *Sasa* (now) period, and their process of dying has not been completed yet.[42] It is these living-dead that Africans are most concerned about:

> It is through the living-dead that the spirit world becomes personal to men. They are still part of their human families, and people have personal memories of them. . . . The living-dead are still "people," and have not yet become "things," "spirits" or "its." They return to their human families from time to time, and share meals with them, however symbolically. . . . They are the guardians of family affairs, traditions, ethics and activities . . . Because they

38. Mbiti, *African Religions and Philosophy*, 59.

39. Kenyatta, *Facing Mt. Kenya*, 241.

40. Parrinder, *African Traditional Religion*, 57.

41. Leakey, *Mau Mau and the Kikuyu*, 41.

42. Mbiti, *African Religions and Philosophy*, 78–85.

are still "people," the living-dead are therefore the best group of intermediaries between men and God.[43]

Research shows African people's understanding of the role of the living-dead as follows: The living-dead intercede for the living, influence the decisions of the living, apportion blessings and property, and act as a link between the living, the dead, and the spiritual world. They are the guardians and protectors of the living and also cultural guardians. They give solutions to crises in life, and control personal, social, and communal life.[44]

Magesa's definition of ancestors is a little different. While Mbiti makes a distinction of ancestors in terms of how long ago they passed away, Magesa puts emphasis on ancestorship that is ascribed to the founders of the clan who "originated the lineage, clan or ethnic group and who provided the people with their name(s)." Ancestors maintain the norms of social action as authority figures and cause trouble when these are not obeyed. They are present and continue to influence earthly life, although they can be scolded if there is evidence of jealousy or unjust behavior on their part. When the living feel that the ancestors are behaving unjustly, they say to them in a ritualistic way, "Why are you doing this to us? What have we done? What have we not given you that was our duty to give?"[45]

Whether it is the living-dead or ancestors, the dominant viewpoint of ATR toward them is one of fear and interdependence.[46] Mbiti's remark also conveys this ambivalent attitude of Africans towards their ancestors: "The food and libation given to the living-dead are paradoxically acts of hospitality and welcome, yet of informing the living-dead to move away. The living-dead are wanted and yet not wanted."[47]

Other Spirits

Besides ancestors, there are other spirits in the African spiritual world. First, there are human spirits or ghosts,[48] termed "ghost-spirits" by Bolaji Idowu.[49] The human spirits are the spirits of children who died without

43. Ibid., 83.

44. Kirwen, *African Cultural Knowledge*, 39.

45. Ibid., 52–53.

46. Gehman, *African Traditional Religion in Biblical Perspective*, 136, 140.

47. Mbiti, *African Religions and Philosophy*, 84.

48. Magesa, *African Religion*, 56.

49. Idowu, *African Traditional Religion*, 175.

proper initiation or without children of their own, or people who did not receive a proper burial upon death. Other human spirits include those who died an unhappy death by hanging, drowning, being struck by lightning, or in pregnancy, or those who were accursed while living. These ghost-spirits were not accepted to ancestorship but wander aimlessly in the forests, mountains, and rivers—molesting and harming people. Second, there are non-human created spirits that inhabit the woods, forest, rivers, rocks, and mountains. They can also inhabit animals and birds.[50] Regarding the omnipresence of spirits in African religion, Idowu says, spirits are "ubiquitous; there is no area of the earth, no object or creature, which has not a spirit of its own or which cannot be inhabited by a spirit."[51]

Kikuyu Communion with Ancestors

Kenyatta argues that while the Kikuyu worshiped God, *Ngai,* they did not worship ancestors on the same plane. Rather, they had communion with ancestors. Although the Kikuyu word *Kuruta magongona* (sacred offerings) was applied to both God and ancestors, they worshiped God (*guthaithaya Ngai*) but communed with ancestors (*guitangera ngoma njohi*—to pour out or to sprinkle beer for spirits), which was carried out constantly through ceremonies. These ceremonies brought back the memory and glory of an ancestor and pleased ancestral spirits to whom the same honor and courtesy were due as to living members of the community.[52]

There are three main groups of ancestral spirits: (1) parental spirits, which communicate advice or reproach to their living children the same way they did during their lifetime; (2) clan spirits, which act collectively for the welfare and prosperity of the clan according to the behavior of the clan or its members; (3) age-group spirits, also known as tribal spirits, having interest in particular age-groups and entering into tribal affairs.[53] While Kenyatta claims that the Kikuyu do not worship ancestors but have communion with them, Idowu argues that human psychology makes it difficult to distinguish between ancestor worship and veneration (respect mingled with awe) of them because of the delicate emotional make-up of the human

50. Ibid., 174–75.

51. Ibid., 174.

52. Kenyatta, *Facing Mt. Kenya*, 231–68.

53. Ibid., 266–67.

mind. Emotional pressure or spiritual climate at the moment could easily lead a person to give undue homage to ancestors.[54]

Specialists and Mystical Powers

Specialists

Specialists are those who connect the physical world to the spiritual world. They are the symbols of African religious universe. Without them, African religious phenomena lose meaning. In other words, African religiosity requires their presence and appreciates their functions. Although their functions may overlap, there are several specialists that are recognized.

Medicine Men

In African societies, there are well-known religious specialists called medicine men. They are also called herbalists, traditional doctors, or *waganga* in Kiswahili, and they are the most useful religious people. They are also wrongly called witch doctors. They go through formal or informal training to prepare to serve as medicine men. The main duty of the medicine man is to deal with sickness, disease, and misfortune religiously, psychologically, and physically. Since African people view suffering, misfortune, disease, and accident as being caused mystically, it requires a religious approach to deal with these issues. Psychological help is as vital to comforting the people as physical help.[55] Mbiti further clarifies the people's dependence on medicine men:

> Modern hospitals may deal with the physical side of diseases, but there is the religious dimension of suffering which they do not handle, and for that purpose a great number of patients will resort to both hospitals and medicine-men, without a feeling of contradiction, although if they are Christian or "educated" they might only go secretly to the medicine-man or follow his treatment.[56]

Kraft calls this dependence on medicine man by Christians as *dual allegiance.*[57]

54. Idowu, *African Traditional Religion*, 182.

55. Mbiti, *African Religions and Philosophy*, 166–69.

56. Ibid., 170.

57. Kraft, *Anthropology for Christian Witness*, 453.

Another important duty of the medicine man is that he takes preventive measures against magic, witchcraft, sorcery, "evil eye," or bad words. Having access to the force of nature and other forms of knowledge unknown or little known to the public, medicine men purge witches, detect sorcery, remove curses, and control the spirits and the living-dead. Essentially, as pastors, psychiatrists, and doctors of traditional African communities, they are the hope of society and are likely to continue exerting their influence since people's belief in the practice of medicine men goes deep in their belief system.[58]

Mediums and Diviners

The main duty of mediums is to link humans with the living-dead and the spirits. They function as mediums only when they are "possessed" by a spirit. Otherwise, they are normal people without special abilities. Diviners are chiefly concerned with acts of divination, interpreting the message and instruction received from spirits or divinities through mediums or acts of divination. Thus diviners function as intermediaries between the human and spiritual world for the benefit of the community.[59] Diviners provide the reasons and causes of suffering, illness, anger, discord, floods, drought, poverty, barrenness, impotence, and all kinds of loss and death. They provide not only this deep knowledge but also power to eliminate or neutralize them. However, in many African societies, although diviners are publicly known, they are not distinguished from the rest of society except during actual performance.[60]

Priests

Priests are religious servants performing their duties in temples, shrines, sacred groves, or elsewhere. While diviners are mainly called to restore the disturbed relations with supernatural powers through spells and material objects, priests are generally expected to influence spirits through prayers and rituals.[61] However, the priest may also function as a medium and contact the spiritual world. While the duties of priests are mainly religious,

58. Mbiti, *African Religions and Philosophy*, 170–71.
59. Ibid., 171–78.
60. Magesa, *African Religion*, 215.
61. Von Furer-Haimendorf, "Priests," 87–88.

they demonstrate the African integration of religion with the rest of life by also serving as political heads, judges, and ritual experts in some contexts. It is often the priests who officiate at sacrifices, offerings, and ceremonies. In Kikuyu, they are called *muthingiri*. On a national level, the priest is the chief intermediary between God and humans. Elders function as priests in each community, and in a household, the head of family functions as a ritual leader in making family offerings, libation, and prayers.[62]

Rainmakers

Rainmakers are some of the most important individuals in most African societies, especially where rain is sparse. Although both people and rainmakers know that only God can "make" rain, rainmakers study the sky and the signs of weather and intercede for people. In rainmaking rituals, rainmakers make sacrifices, offerings, and prayers to God directly or through the living-dead or other spiritual agents. They also use magical chants and materials.[63]

All these specialists—medicine men, mediums, diviners, priests, and rainmakers—are mediators between God and men in African Traditional Religion.

Mystical Powers

Traditional Africans have a belief in mystical power. To them it is not fiction, but a reality that they have to deal with in every life. This mystical power is particularly manifested as magic, sorcery, and witchcraft.

Good Magic (White Magic)

Traditional Africans believe good magic is beneficial to society. It is used in treating diseases, counteracting misfortunes, and warding off or destroying evil power or witchcraft by medicine men, diviners, and rainmakers. The diviner or the medicine man uses charms, amulets, powder, rags, feathers, figures, special incantations, or cuttings on the body for the protection of homesteads, families, fields, cattle, and other property as well as for bringing health, fortune, or prosperity. For Africans, spiritual power functions

62. Mbiti, *African Religions and Philosophy*, 188–89.
63. Ibid., 179–81; Gehman, *African Traditional Religion in Biblical Perspective*, 77.

through physical means, and both the physical and the spiritual world are one universe.[64] Mbiti goes further to say:

> These objects represent and symbolize power which comes from God. This power may directly be supplied by God, or it may be through the spirits, the living-dead or as part of the invisible force of nature in the universe. At this point religion and the magic merge, and there is no clear way of separating them, any more than magic has been separated from Christianity or Islam at certain points. . . . The older a person is, and the higher his social status is, the more he is thought or expected to have this mystical power, either in himself or through the possession of the necessary objects in which it may be stored.[65]

Evil Magic (Black Magic or Sorcery)

Evil magic involves using mystical power to harm humans and their property. In this magical practice, mystical power is used maliciously against the welfare of society. Therefore, sorcerers are the most feared and hated people in the community, along with witches, since African people feel and believe that they use mystical power to cause illnesses, misfortune, accidents, tragedies, sorrows, and dangers. To counteract the evil use of mystical force, people turn to medicine men and diviners to supply them with objects of protection and cure, and to perform cleansing rituals of people and homestead.[66] Although this is not scientifically explained, for the majority of Africans, this mystical experience of a deeply religious nature is a reality.

Witchcraft

Witchcraft is the most popular term used to describe all kinds of evil use of mystical power in a secret way. It is an integral part of traditional African belief systems, along with sorcery and magic.[67] While sorcery is a skill to be learned, witchcraft is an inherent power residing in witches. According to anthropologists, African society does not make such academic distinctions

---

64. Mbiti, *African Religions and Philosophy*, 198–99.

65. Ibid., 199.

66. Ibid., 199–201; Gehman, *African Traditional Religion in Biblical Perspective*, 69–72.

67. Lehman and Myers, *Magic, Witchcraft and Religion*, 189.

between witchcraft, sorcery, evil magic, evil eye, and other ways of employing mystical power to harm people and their properties.[68] The Kiswahili term for witchcraft, *uchawi,* includes a wide variety of such practices that involves harmful employment of mystical power in all its different manifestations. While Mbiti argues that "African peoples believe there are individuals who have access to mystical power which they employ for destructive purposes,"[69] Magesa claims "the power of witchcraft is not a prerogative of only certain individuals," but "every human being is potentially witch."[70] Regarding witchcraft and sorcery, Magesa further explains:

> Witchcraft is not only a symptom of the diminishment of the power of life (as wrongdoing and illness may be perceived to be), it is also seen to be the very embodiment of evil in the world . . . In a very particular way, then, it is essential that witches and witchcraft be detected and dealt with if life in the community is to continue and flourish.[71]

The ubiquitous presence of mystical power, permeating all areas of life and being manifested through magic, sorcery, and witchcraft, reveals the religious understanding of African people of the universe. It is part of the religious corpus of beliefs. This understanding permeates all dimensions of their life such as social, political, psychological, and economic.[72]

Prayers, Sacrifices, and Offerings

Mystical powers, whatever they are, can be also implored through prayers, sacrifices, and offerings, which are prominent features of African Traditional Religion. Prayer emphasizes dependence on God and ancestors. Apart from individual prayers, all the other prayers accompany rituals, that is, sacrifice or offerings. Sacrifices are usually bloody, whereas offerings are bloodless. Through sacrifices and offerings, unity and balance are restored to human life.[73] "In this sense, rituals are symbolic re-enactments of the primordial relationship between human life and the mystical sources of life."[74]

68. Mbiti, *African Religions and Philosophy,* 202.

69. Ibid.

70. Magesa, *African Religion,* 167.

71. Ibid., 175.

72. Mbiti, *African Religions and Philosophy,* 203.

73. Magesa, *African Religion,* 177–208.

74. Ibid., 211.

Kikuyu Practice

In Kikuyuland there is a magician "who has acquired the profession heredi-
tarily and has gone through long years of training, at the end of which he
has been initiated into the cult through payment of some sheep and goats
or a cow . . ."[75] This magician is called the "medicine man," or *mundu mugo*
in the Kikuyu language.[76] Leakey defines the role of the medicine man:

> His role in tribal organization was a composite one; he was the
> doctor who diagnosed and treated diseases and ailments, some-
> times by herbal remedies, sometimes by magic rites and purifi-
> cation ceremonies and sometimes by a combination of both. He
> was also the seer who was consulted as to whether the occasion
> was propitious for marriage, for a long journey, or for the holding
> of an initiation ceremony, and he was the person whose help was
> sought against the workers in black magic or witchcraft who tried
> to destroy people and property and who were known as *murogi*.[77]

Although medicine men were not given any special rights otherwise,
they were accorded with honor and opportunities to officiate in important
religious ceremonies because of their wisdom and outstanding abilities.
They were specialists in such areas as herbs, diagnosis of illnesses due to
spiritual causes, or protective magic. Kikuyu's belief in the power of the
medicine man was so absolute that if there was a failure on the part of a
medicine man, it was not his fault but some superior force which was at
work against his magic.[78]

While the medicine man works openly in broad daylight, the worker
in black magic or witchcraft, the *murogi*, usually works secretly by night.
He prepares evil charms for the victim and hides them in or near the victim's abode, or uses something that belongs to the victim to cast an evil
spell causing fear in the victim. Besides white magic or black magic, there is
also an implicit belief that harmful magic known as "evil eye" may emanate
from ordinary people.[79] According to Maloney, evil eye means "someone
can project harm by looking at another's property or person." It is a belief

---

75. Kenyatta, *Facing Mt. Kenya*, 281.

76. Leakey, *Mau Mau and the Kikuyu*, 47.

77. Ibid.

78. Ibid., 47–49.

79. Ibid., 49–51.

that power emanates from the eye or mouth and strikes an object or person, and the destruction or injury is sudden. Envy is considered a factor.[80]

Anthropologists who study African culture and religion normally do not differentiate religion and magic since these two overlap and the distinction is thin. The Kikuyu are not an exception either. They do not separate magic from religion, especially when they deal with good magic.[81] Leakey comments in the same way as follows: "It is not easy to draw a dividing line between religion and magic in Kikuyu society, nor between white magic which is beneficial and black magic or witchcraft which is anti-social."[82] Kenyatta enumerates eleven different Kikuyu magical practices: (1) charms or protective magic—the majority of the Kikuyu carried a charm against a particular danger to be protected from; (2) hate or despising magic—used to destroy friendship between individuals or between a group of people; (3) love magic—intended to seek the love of one or many; (4) defensive magic—used in court cases or other disputes with hypnotic power; (5) destructive magic, witchcraft—an antisocial practice; (6) healing magic—through connection with supernatural power or ancestral spirits; psychological influence; (7) enticing and attracting magic; (8) silencing and surprising magic; (9) fertilizing magic; (10) wealth and agricultural magic; and (11) purifying magic. As seen above, the Kikuyu used magic for many different purposes, and their practice was based on the fear of the absolute power of magic.[83]

African Morality

Morality depends on religion. While religious beliefs are internal factors, morality deals with conduct.[84] In African traditional societies, morals are God given[85] and preserved in customs, regulations, taboos, proverbs, myths, signs, and symbols.[86] Morals guide people in doing what is right and good for their own sake and for their community. It is morals, customs, laws, and traditions that keep society harmonious and keep it from disintegration,

---

80. Maloney, Introduction to *The Evil Eye*.

81. Kenyatta, *Facing Mt. Kenya*, 280.

82. Leakey, *Mau Mau and the Kikuyu*, 47.

83. Kenyatta, *Facing Mt. Kenya*, 280–81.

84. Mbiti, *Introduction to African Religion*, 174.

85. Mwikamba, "Changing Morals in Africa," 87.

86. Ansah, "The Ethics of African Religious Tradition," 241.

with the main pillar being morals. Something that does not feel right will not readily become a custom or law.[87] Thus morals take a central place in African society: "African religious beliefs, values, rituals and practices are directed towards strengthening the moral life of each society. Morals are the food and drink which keep society alive, healthy and happy."[88]

Hannah Kinoti, who studied Kikuyu traditional morality, argues that the role of morality is to keep the fundamental unity among the different realms of the African cosmos, that is, supernatural and spiritual realities, the human society, animals, and plants and all other realities. For example, the totemic relationship of animals and plants with the human kinship system restrained the African society from plundering nature indiscriminately. Taboos exist to keep the moral structure of the universe for the good of humanity. In traditional African thought, if man and nature are intertwined as above, human beings belonged to each other more.[89] Louis Leakey, who lived and studied the Kikuyu in the mid-1930s, explains the perception of human relationships in the Kikuyu society:

> A man and his sisters and half-sisters were really one and the same person except that they differed in sex[,] . . . a woman was part of her husband, being merely a female part of him. Therefore, fundamentally, a person's mother and mother's brothers were one person, her brothers being male mothers to her children.[90]

This realization of relationship between the individual and the community is the central, moral, and ethical imperative of African Traditional Religion. Thus, participation and sharing are essential principles for human existence.[91] About this communal aspect of African traditional morality, Friday Mbon says, "In African traditional society, one person's 'sin' could have serious socio-economic consequences for the entire society."[92] Individual members of the society, therefore, did not go about behaving as if it was only they who lived in the community. They had to be careful not to do anything that would bring suffering to other members of the society.[93]

87. Mbiti, *Introduction to African Religion*, 177.

88. Ibid., 179.

89. Kinoti, "African Morality," 76–78.

90. Leakey quoted in Kinoti, "African Morality," 78.

91. Magesa, *African Religion*, 65–67.

92. Mbon, "African Traditional Socio-religious Ethics," 102.

93. Ibid., 105.

Evil is that which conflicts with the interests of the community.[94] Sin is an offence against one's neighbor and punishable here and now.[95] From this perspective, it is understood why witchcraft is viewed as the greatest wrong by virtue of its antisocial connotation. It is the ultimate enemy of life on earth.[96]

Another important aspect of African morality is its religious basis. Kinoti says, "Traditionally African peoples have held a strong belief that spiritual powers are deeply concerned about the moral conduct of individuals and communities alike."[97] God is thought to be the ultimate guardian of human morality. God gave humans laws and rules, and humans were accountable not only to the society but also to supernatural powers, who were believed to intervene when natural order or justice were violated.[98] However, it is not God but the patriarchs, ancestors, elders, priests, and even spirits who are the guardians of human morality on a daily basis.[99] More precisely, "the principal moral actors are the living; by their behavior they determine what is to befall them and the universe."[100]

There is still another element that is noteworthy in African morality. In the African moral system, man is not innately good or bad, but judged in terms of what he does or does not do.[101] This behavior-oriented African morality is not only passive restraining of evil behaviors, but active pursuing of righteous actions.[102] Thus, African morality actively seeks such virtues as honesty, reliability, sharing, participation, generosity, temperance, humility, and justice. African morality is socioreligious, involving the whole spectrum of social, economic, and political life, and spiritual entities in purely utilitarian and anthropocentric senses in order to maintain balance and harmony in the universe.

The following chart shows the elements of African traditional spirituality.

---

94. Gehman, *African Traditional Religion in Biblical Perspective*, 254.

95. Adeyemo, *Salvation in African Tradition*, 70.

96. Magesa, *African Religion*, 69.

97. Kinoti, "African Morality," 79.

98. Ibid., 79–80.

99. Mbiti, *African Religions and Philosophy*, 213.

100. Magesa, *African Religion*, 67.

101. Mbiti, *African Religions and Philosophy*, 214.

102. Magesa, *African Religion*, 155.

African Traditional Spirituality
• The intrinsically spiritual world
• Communal spirituality
• Pragmatic spirituality

African Traditional Religion and Christianity

The relationship between ATR and Christianity is both positive and negative. It is positive because ATR's religious worldview made Africans accept Christianity with relative ease. However, ATR contributed to Christian syncretism. Thus, it is essential to discuss ATR's relationship with Christian spirituality.

The importance of understanding the proper place of ATR in Christianity is shown as Jehu Hanciles argues:

> The emergence of African Christianity as a popular religious movement owes much to continuity with African primal religions; notably in the widespread use of vernacular names for the Christian God, the preoccupation with spiritual power, and the centrality of healing . . . [T]he encounter between the message of the gospel and the primal tradition . . . has proven to be indispensable for the emergence of dynamic Christian movement.[103]

The recent charismatic movement in Africa, including Kenya, is an example of this dynamic Christian movement as discussed in chapter 6. The charismatic movement is pneumatocentric spirituality and appeals to those with a spirit-centered universe. Emphasizing healing, deliverance, and miracles, charismatic Christianity resonates with the African worldview and religiosity.

African Traditional Religion's communal aspect is also compatible with Christian spirituality. ATR is not for the individual primarily, but for the community. Sociability, relationship, participation, and sharing are the central moral imperatives of African religion, and the unity of community is the paramount good; the role of a religious leader is also to protect and prolong the life of the family and the community.[104]

103. Hanciles, *Beyond Christendom*, 129–30.

104. Magesa, *African Religion*, 65–68.

Christian spirituality is also communal spirituality. The Old Testament spirituality treats community as an authentic expression of spirituality. Both the law and the prophets are for the sake of people. There was no such thing as a private spiritual advancement. The patriarchs, judges, prophets, kings, and priests were all for the people. There was no understanding of faith and life apart from the community. An important characteristic of New Testament spirituality is also its communal character. "Early Christian spirituality was conceived, nurtured, and realized within the body of Christ."[105] The Spirit was given to edify the body of Christ: "When the Spirit blows the result is never to create good individual Christians but members of a community. This became fundamental for Christian spirituality in the New Testament and was in direct line with the Old Testament mentality."[106] Bowe states:

> Christian identity is a corporate identity and there is no such thing as "an *individual Christian*" . . . To be a Christian is to be a member of the body of Christ. Paul's insistence on the corporate character of the body and his exhortations to communal living are key to his preaching of the gospel and to the way he responded to almost every pastoral question.[107]

African religiosity entails the socioeconomic-political-spiritual dimensions of life, and so does Christian spirituality. From the beginning, mission Christianity was holistic. Welbourn states, "By African standards a missionary was the greatest known farmer, carpenter, smith, doctor, dentist, linguist and story teller."[108]

Despite the beneficial aspects of ATR on Christian spirituality as discussed above, African Traditional Religion and culture have been a cause of syncretism in Christian spirituality in Africa. Syncretism is defined as "the process by which elements of one religion are assimilated into another religion resulting in a change in the fundamental tenets or nature of those religions."[109] When missionaries came to Kenya in late 1800s or early 1900s, some condemned African culture as a whole, including ATR, while others were more lenient to them. For example, Presbyterians were against the Kikuyu culture and religion, and, as a result, those who became Christians

105. Saunders, "Learning Christ," 158.

106. Zizioulas, "The Early Christian Community," 27.

107. Bowe, *Biblical Foundations of Spirituality*, 158.

108. Welbourn, *East African Christian*, 81.

109. Imbach, "Syncretism," 1062–63.

separated themselves rather completely from African traditional rituals and sacrifices. High Anglicans and Catholics, however, were more accepting of local cultures resulting in syncretistic practices among their followers. Polygamy, tribal dances, and female circumcision were some of the major cultural practices that were opposed by missionaries.

In the contemporary Kenyan society, it is well known that even confessing Christians revert to ATR in times of crises. Christians visit medicine men; they attend traditional ceremonies which involve spirits and ancestors. It is not unusual either to find a Christian holding a black chicken at night visiting a witchdoctor and on Sunday carrying a big black Bible to church. A Kenyan pastor in Nairobi says about some of the African traditional elements that are still problematic to Christians in Kenya:

> I believe that some of these include wife inheritance, female genital mutilation (FGM) and practices related to birth, marriage, and death. . . . Christian widows in rural Kenya face lots of hostilities and communal sexual harassment. The widow in most cases is threatened with dire consequences including excommunication from the society if she refuses to be inherited. . . . Female circumcision is also a major challenge in Kenya. In some communities in Kenya it is a mandatory rite of passage for girls. Some parents secretly facilitate circumcision of their daughters. . . . Regarding birth, a child belongs to the community. The community even names the child. Christian parents struggle with this because it prohibits them from naming their child their own preferred names.[110]

Among African traditional practices, rites related to death are the most complex and complicated issues. The pastor quoted above continues:

> The treatment of the body and actual burial is defined by complex traditional rites. To begin with the body must be buried in the ancestral land. The traditional elders have a major say on how the death rites are done. . . . In most African communities people are Christians until they die. After their death, the community dictates how the burial ceremony is conducted.[111]

Although ATR per se does not attract much attention from people in modern Kenyan society, African Traditional Religion and practices can

---

110. Paper submitted to Spiritual Formation Class at Nairobi International School of Theology, Nov. 2010.

111. Ibid.

easily lead Christians away from their devotion to Christ and the message of the Scriptures.

Summary

African Traditional Religion is intrinsically spiritual, communal, and pragmatic. The supernatural orientation of ATR is, however, fundamentally for humans. African morality is also religiously based in that spiritual powers are deeply concerned about the moral conduct of individuals and communities. Humans are not intrinsically good or bad in African morality, but morality is determined by behavior.

ATR's spirit-centered universe and communal spirituality is compatible with Christian spirituality and has appealed to the recent charismatic movement. As Richard Gehman claims, the virtues and values of the traditional culture and religion formed the bedrock of Christianity in Africa, and remained as such.[112] But as Paul Hiebert states, since "All Christians live with two traditions, cultural and Christian,"[113] ATR has also contributed to syncretism in Christian spirituality. Although African Traditional Religion is not being practiced as before, it remains hidden in the minds of Africans. While ATR with its practices cannot be endorsed by the serious Christian, it is worthwhile at the conclusion of this section to quote an early evangelical missionary's statement about African Traditional Religion.

> No matter how strange this may sound, I have frequently found God in the soul of the African Bantu. Certainly, it is not the full revelation of the Father. But nevertheless, God Himself is the One who lies hidden behind a curtain as a shadowy figure, but the main outline is visible. A surprising and glorious experience! And when I experienced the moment that a soul surrenders, I understand the Master had been there earlier.[114]

---

112. Gehman, *African Traditional Religion in Biblical Perspective*, 259.

113. Hiebert, *Anthropological Insights for Missionaries*, 189.

114. Barvinck, *The Impact of Christianity*, 227.

9

Secularization and Spiritual Formation[1]

Western Secularism in Kenyan Society

KENYAN SOCIETY HAS BEEN in a state of constant change from a traditional society to a modern one since colonial times. It has been slowly moving away from a religious orientation to a worldly orientation, as in the West. While Christianity seems to have replaced much of traditional religion outwardly, Western secular influence has increasingly been affecting Kenyan society. This influence from the West is mainly been reflected in urban areas through urbanization, modernization, and the media, but it is also taking roots in rural areas. A recent study of Gifford reveals: "Now all Kenyans experience the unrelenting pressures of modernity."[2]

Secularization is the process through which religion loses its hold both at the level of social institution and human consciousness. It is a worldview that denies in theory and/or practice the immanence of God.[3] Secularism also exposes Christians to religious indifferentism and materialism.[4] In an ideological sense, secularization connotes "a shift in ways of thinking and living away from God and toward this world."[5] Secularism along with humanism, as an approach to life and thought, individual and society, glorifies the creature and rejects the Creator. This "disenchantment" of

1 The voices of the Kenyan pastors in this chapter, unless stated otherwise, are those of students at NIST (Nairobi International School of Theology) in 2010.

2. Gifford, *Christianity Politics and Public Life*, 103.

3. Shorter, "Secularism," 253.

4. Ibid., 254.

5. Gill, "Secularism, Secular Humanism," 996–97.

the modern world, as Max Weber termed it, was attributed to Renaissance humanism, Enlightenment rationalism, the rising power and influence of science, the breakdown of traditional structures (e.g., the family, the church, the neighborhood), the rise of a technology-driven society, and so on.[6]

Secularization traces its roots further back to the Reformation, which stripped the medieval church of its domination and authority over individuals by introducing the priesthood of every believer. This made way for reason and science to claim their authority in the society over faith. When the church's hierarchy was disclaimed, feudal hierarchy was questioned by the public, hence the demolition of the feudal system and the beginning of democratic, industrialized society. Thus rationalization, increasing cultural diversity, and social and structural differentiation undermined religion. As societies have become more diverse, urban, and industrialized, so they have become secular.[7]

What should be noted is that Kenyan society has not been completely secularized as per the definition and processes that occurred in Europe. In Kenya, the religious worldview is still prevalent in society, whether traditional or Christian. However, the influence of Western cultural secularism is affecting society more and more in the forms of materialism, individualism, nominalism, and the decay of moral conducts. Demerath III calls this kind of secularization "diffused secularization", or that which is caused by external forces and which spreads more by diffusion than direction or coercion. He argues, "These are often the unintended consequences of culture contacts. They result from transmitted cultural innovations that become hegemonic in new locales, and in the process serve to displace old practices, rituals, and beliefs, whether formally or informally sacred."[8]

A Kenyan pastor laments, "It's my humble view that in Kenya the church is not effectively influencing our society. I believe that attending church in Kenya has become like a social phenomenon. It's socially and politically correct to attend church." Another one states, "Society is not being transformed by the presence of the church in Kenya as it should be. Secular ideals from the West seem to have taken over the society, both the Christian and non-Christian. Christianity is influencing society to a

---

6. Ibid.

7. Bruce, "The Social Process of Secularization," 249–58.

8. Demerath III, "Secularization Extended," 219–26. Demerath III distinguished four different forms of secularization: "emergent" (internal and non-directed), "coercive" (internal but directed), "imperialist" (external and directed), and "diffused" (external and non-directed).

very negligible level." The retired bishop of Christ Is the Answer Ministries (CITAM), Bonifes Adoyo, questions whether the Christian population in Kenya is really 82 percent in light of the 2007 post-election violence, saying if that is the case, then the Christian community has failed miserably in its mandate to spread the love of God.[9] These are but a few voices, but they represent the growing concern and frustration of evangelical Kenyan Christians regarding the waning influence of the penetrating power of the gospel in society under the increasing weight of secularism.

The most serious impact of secular humanism on the Kenyan society is that of materialism. Being rooted in Western capitalism, materialism proclaims the overriding importance of economic factors and assumes an exclusively economic interpretation of reality.[10] In Kenya, the craving of wealth and power has become so entrenched in the system that it has also resulted in corruption and other forms of social crimes. Christian businessmen and women must contend with corruption and double dealings in their business endeavors, as they try to remain steadfast in their faith. Political leaders buy their way into the parliament; the amount of money they spend on campaigns determines the leader, as opposed to their integrity and leadership abilities.

Materialism has also found its way into the church through the preaching of the "faith gospel" commonly known as the "prosperity gospel." The prosperity gospel advances the dubious claim that faith makes one prosperous not only in the spiritual, but also in the material sense.[11] It originated from Kenneth Hagin of Tulsa, Oklahoma in 1934, who taught that prayers for heath and wealth were answered without fail. The basic teaching is that God wants Christians to be wealthy and that poverty is an indication of personal sin. Naturally, the poor are attracted to the prosperity gospel only to be disillusioned after continuous failures to acquire wealth as proclaimed from the pulpit. However, pastors of such churches attribute those failures to a lack of faith or personal sin.[12] These churches preach that Christianity is invariably related to wealth/success/victory. What stands out among these is material success.[13] Shorter's statement is pointy:

9. Adoyo, Radio broadcast, Nov. 28, 2010.

10. Shorter, "Secularism," 254.

11. Bloesch, *Spirituality Old & New*, 147.

12. Shorter, "Secularism," 262–64.

13. Gifford, *Christianity Politics and Public Life*, 123.

It is difficult to avoid the conclusion that the faith gospel formula is a child of modern secular materialism emanating from the Americas, and that for many of its exponents religion is simply a way of making money. It is, in fact, a religious form of economic rationalism. . . . Such emerging religious movements are part and parcel of the secular global phenomenon.[14]

In the context of absolute poverty the gospel of material blessing and success thrives and captivates the poor to the neglect of other aspects of Christian spirituality. As Gifford states, "Economic demands have determined the form of the Christianity preached."[15] However, a materialistic understanding of the Christian gospel is not only influenced by Western culture; it is also embedded in the African traditional worldview. According to the African worldview, salvation means seeking the spiritual powers of ancestors, divinities, and ultimately God, to overcome impediments towards the fullness of life, that is, material well-being.[16] Bediako's "grassroots theology"[17] fosters "human material well-being, thus promoting the tendency already latent in the understanding of salvation in African traditional religious culture."[18]

Charismatic/Pentecostal spirituality, which has gained prominence in the African context within the past decades, emphasizes the power of the Holy Spirit to ward off other forces or powers in the spirit-centered African context. It was a natural but superior choice for Africans. As Anderson argues:

Pentecostalism purports to provide for much more than the "spiritual" problems of life. The important role given to divine healing and exorcism, the particular emphasis on the power of the Spirit . . . represent a new and vigorous spirituality offering help to human problems. This spirituality is a holistic approach to Christianity that appeals more adequately to popular worldviews than older Christian traditions had done, and in some respects was also more satisfying than "traditional" religions had been.[19]

14. Shorter, "Secularism," 264.

15. Ibid., 171.

16. Ngong, "Salvation and Materialism," 3.

17. The grassroots theology is theology that comes from where the faith lives in the conditions of life of the community of faith, the theology of the living church reflecting faith as present reality in daily life. Bediako, "Jesus and the Gospel," 8–9.

18. Ngong, "Salvation and Materialism," 9–10.

19. Anderson, *Introduction to Pentecostalism*, 201–2.

However, this charismatic/Pentecostal brand of Christianity is also the very one that fosters the material dimension of Christianity through the preaching of the prosperity gospel, to the detriment of the whole gospel.

It is not just the state of poverty that has spread materialism within Kenyan Christianity. In Nairobi, there are other types of churches that target the middle class. They do not fall into the category of charismatic/Pentecostal churches necessarily, but they are basically of the same strand. Gifford refers to them as "middle class Pentecostalism." He argues that these churches—Nairobi Pentecostal Church (NPC), Nairobi Baptist Church (NBC), and Nairobi Chapel—are at root not totally different from other Pentecostal churches because in these churches, their preoccupation rests with making it in the modern globalized world.[20] Preoccupied with the modernization and globalization of their ministries, these churches serve the urban middle class with appropriate programs that meet its needs, such as premarital counseling, marriage enrichment seminars, workshops for entrepreneurs, etc. Nairobi Chapel, which has attracted young professionals, has also been seeking global partnerships aggressively. A pastor of one of these churches, however, comments, "Materialism affected the lives of [these] Christians so believers are no longer defined in terms of who they are in Christ but what they own, the car they drive, the estate they live in, and the school their children attend." Whether the gospel is interpreted from the perspective of prosperity for the poor, or through promotion of the interests of growing middle-class Christians, their agenda is basically the same. It is about success, victory, and achievement in modern, urban Kenya.

The charismatic church is not the only church that has been affected by materialism; mainline churches have been affected as well. A pastor of the Presbyterian Church of East Africa (PCEA), one of the mainline denominations in Kenya, stated recently, "Religion has become a big business. As a result, the line between religion and the profane has become blurred. There are those who choose to model their churches after businesses, which could lead to better church management or to an invitation to corruption."[21] Mainline churches own land, guest houses, and hotels that generate income for church activities.[22]

20. Gifford, *Christianity Politics and Public Life*, 112–15.

21. "Seek Ye First the Kingdom," *Nation*, Jan. 30, 2011.

22. PCEA owns a guesthouse right next to their headquarters in Nairobi South C area; Methodists also run a guesthouse in Kilimani area, Nairobi; Anglicans have their

It should be noted, however, that an emphasis on material blessing is more prominent among charismatic churches than mainline churches. Many evangelical/charismatic churches in Kenya follow the principles of modern business and become a corporate church with separate administrative and investment arms.[23] A reputable pastor of a large Pentecostal church in Nairobi said recently that many pastors no longer teach the gospel, but encourage people and give them hope through the prosperity gospel, for fear that they will run away. Indeed, a large number of believers flock to churches where the prosperity gospel is the key message. This trend can be observed in both urban and rural settings.

Manipulation of giving is another way in which the prosperity gospel has taken root in some churches. The gospel has become extremely commercialized, being reduced to sowing a seed and then waiting for a big financial blessing from God. In most cases, the pastors are the channels of blessing and some ministers charge believers for praying for them. It also happens that some disenchanted members of charismatic/Pentecostal churches have moved to more stable mainline churches where the gospel is preached without undue stress being placed on material success. Overall, however, one can hardly escape from the sting of materialism in modern Kenyan society.

Secular humanism has affected Kenyan society in the area of values and morals as well. In traditional African contexts, polygamy was practiced. Polygamy is still practiced as a different form in modern Kenya. According to a recent poll, 35 percent of married people were involved in an affair with two other partners besides their spouse. It is argued that "in Kenya, 'modern polygamy' is gaining currency in the form of extramarital affairs commonly called *mpango wa kando*" (plan on the side).[24] It is well known that even some Christians are engaged in extramarital affairs without incurring much guilt. Having a concubine(s) or girlfriend(s) is not uncommon among married men, and these same women don't see a problem in sharing their men with other women.

Sexual degradation is becoming one of the most deadly realities of modernity in Africa.[25] A Kenyan pastor observes, "There is extreme obsession with the body and sex. Sex has become a key topic of discussion in

---

own guesthouse in Upper Hill area.

23. *Nation*, Jan. 30, 2011, Lifestyle section.

24. "Why Your Partner Could Stray," *Nation*, Feb. 12, 2011.

25. O'Donovan, *Biblical Christianity*, 96.

our entire social infrastructure. This revolution has resulted in some social problems, such as disease, single parenthood, prostitution, and so on." Infidelity, ensuing HIV/AIDS infection, marriage breakups, and pornography are social ills associated with modern, secular influences. The media play a significant role here.[26] Mass media in Kenya—print media, television, and videos—are closely connected to the secularization of the society. For example, locally produced obscene literature offers direct encouragement toward sexual promiscuity; television airs material not suitable for children during prime viewing time; and video shops are everywhere, exposing Kenyans to Western videos indiscriminately. The youth are especially vulnerable to these influences.

Music is also heavily influenced by secularism, especially in regard to gospel music. Tremendous growth of Pentecostal and charismatic churches in Kenya in the 1990s encouraged the proliferation of gospel music.[27] However, the face of gospel music has changed greatly with the crossover into it by many secular musicians, either because of its popularity or their own conversions. Gospel music, by definition, should promote Christian worship, and is also used in public domain to bring about positive social and political changes in Kenyan society.[28] Many conservative Kenyan Christians find the actual outcome questionable, arguing that many gospel singers have turned their ministry into mere entertainment for financial gain. Some musicians employ worldly language having little spiritual effect on listeners. Bars in urban centers comfortably play these songs while people drink and dance to them. Corporate organizations also woo popular gospel singers to advertise their products. An example would be "Tusker Project Fame," a singing competition for East African countries, aired by Citizen Television and sponsored by the East Africa Breweries Ltd. and a South African company. It promotes alcoholic products and features many gospel singers. Gospel singers attract the youth, especially as they dance to the tune and dramatize the songs. A Kenyan pastor says that a good number of

26. Kenya's prominent newspaper, *Nation*, deals with this topic frequently in their Saturday edition. These articles sometimes are not just informative but provocative, leading to more sexual promiscuity.

27. Parsitau, "Sounds of Change and Reform," 56.

28. Ibid., 70. Parsitau states that Kenyan politicians frequently use gospel music in their political campaigns as a mobilizing factor for change. In these political campaigns, popular gospel songs acquire new meanings altogether and strike a chord or evoke certain emotions to win the battle.

these gospel singers do not subscribe to membership of any local church, pastoral care, or authority.

Growing individualism in modern Kenyan society also deserves our attention. Danièle Hervieu-Léger differentiates religious individualism from modern individualism. He argues that Calvinism has pushed religious individualism the furthest in developing the idea that everyone must confirm his/her personal destiny and salvation in every aspect of everyday life in the world. While religious individualism finds the meaning of the individual in the service of the kingdom, modern rational individualism as the true offspring of the Enlightenment claims individual autonomy.[29] Individualism here refers to the latter kind. A Kenyan pastor observes, "Western individualistic approach to life has infiltrated Kenyan society to the extent that it is almost destroying the relational approach to life." Another one confesses, "Self-centeredness has taken over people's lives and one would be ready to do anything to get fame. The church has not been spared either. Many church leaders have established empires which they rule until 'death-do-us-part' so to speak."

Individualism over communal spirit is not conducive to a healthy spirituality, but modern Kenyans are prone to be more individualistic in their approaches to life and religion. Bryan Wilson argues that, through secularization, external communal surveillance gives way to the internalization of moral sense, and that a secularized concept of salvation surrenders community for the sake of the survival of the self.[30] The danger of this modern individualism is well expressed by Richard Fenn:

> Modern individualism, as Hervieu-Léger describes it, puts a high value on the goods of this world, on achievements and satisfactions, as opposed to an ethic or spirituality of responsible self-renunciation. It is as if individuals were suffering from a form of spiritual amnesia in which they forgot not only their traditions but . . . who they truly are. Their souls are thus in perennial danger because they lack a spiritual and social context in which to thrive and against which to discover their own limitations. Narcissism replaces spirituality.[31]

The end result of secular humanism is the entrenchment of secular ideologies and philosophies in social structures; hence affecting the

29. Hervieu-Léger, "Individualism," 161–64.

30. Wilson, "Salvation, Secularization, and De-moralization," 39–51.

31. Fenn, "Editorial Commentary: Religion and the Secular," 15.

conservative approach to religion and faith. Self-actualization, self-help, and self-realization are all products of the modern individualistic approach to religion. Religion becomes self-centered, and its approach becomes similar to ATR's. Although Christianity is the *de facto* religion in Kenyan society, nominal practices of faith, Western secularism, and the African traditional mindset, along with other contextual factors, are the forces that negatively affect Christian spirituality in Kenya—whether they are development-oriented mainliners, success-oriented charismatics, or tradition-oriented AICs. Therefore, the need of spiritual formation is essential in the midst of confusion and the identity crisis of Christians in Kenya.

Spiritual Formation in Kenya

In this book I have tried to describe Christian spirituality in the Kenyan context. The components that make up or contribute to Christian spirituality in Kenya have been discussed. African cultural and religious perspectives are the foundational blocks of spirituality in Kenya except, perhaps, for the younger generation. African worldviews still linger in the minds of Kenyans, although there is a degree of difference according to the exposure and upbringing of each individual. The biblical narratives have been taught and Christians have embraced biblical values, at least nominally. The Christian movements in Kenya—East Africa Revival Movement and charismatic movement—have contributed to Christian spirituality in Kenya significantly. Western secular influences, as well as Kenyan contextual forces, are also powerful elements that are shaping the contours of Christian spirituality in Kenya. The future of Christian spirituality in Kenya depends on how these dynamics will play out in the hearts and minds of Kenyan Christians.

As I have discussed the subject of Christian spirituality in this book, I have taken a descriptive process, as the definition of Christian spirituality emphasizes "the lived experience of Christian faith and discipleship." However, as I conclude this book I would like to argue for the intentional formation of Christian spirituality. The Scripture admonishes us to be conformed to the likeness of Jesus Christ (Rom 8:29–30), and we are being transformed into his likeness through the Spirit (2 Cor 3:18). Christian spiritual formation refers to "the *Holy Spirit-driven process* of forming the inner world of the human self in such a way that it becomes like the inner being of Christ himself."[32]

32. Willard and Simpson, *Revolution of Character*, 16.

Willard points out two crucial elements in the process of spiritual formation—divine grace and our responsibility—by saying, "Spiritual formation is both a profound manifestation of God's gracious action through his Word and Spirit *and* something we are responsible for before God and can set about achieving in a sensible, systematic manner."[33] The Scripture verses and Willard's statement are sufficient to give the reader some basic idea of spiritual formation. Compared to *Christian spirituality* we have discussed so far, *spiritual formation* encompasses our deliberate effort for transformation; it involves spiritual disciplines. What we need desperately is not mere transmission of information from pulpit to pew, or from lecture podium to student, but the process of spiritual transformation of every Christian.

In his book *Celebration of Discipline,* Richard Foster talks about the necessity of spiritual disciplines for spiritual formation, such as meditation, prayer, fasting, study, simplicity, solitude, submission, service, confession, worship, guidance, and celebration. He groups these disciplines into the inward, outward, and corporate disciplines, but these groupings can change. According to Foster, "God has given us the Disciplines of the spiritual life as a means of receiving his grace. The Disciplines allow us to place ourselves before God so that he can transform us."[34] Spiritual disciplines themselves are not the goal but the means which can be used to draw closer to God. What we need to understand, though, is that spiritual formation or transformation is ultimately God's work with our participation in the process.

For the last two years, I have had the privilege of teaching the Spiritual Formation course at Nairobi International School of Theology (NIST), and I have witnessed changes taking place in the lives of most of the students who took the class. I myself was also sharpened as I conducted the class. Through lectures, small group discussions, readings, reading responses, devotions, journal writings, research, and so on, we experienced the grace of God. Students themselves confessed the necessity of spiritual disciplines for spiritual formation. Kenyan Christians are already familiar with some spiritual disciplines such as prayer, fasting, and worship. Prayer seems to be the one discipline that Christians practice the most of all spiritual disciplines. One student commented, "Prayer is the most relevant in the African context because Africans have been praying from time immemorial, though not necessarily to Jehovah. They would pray, especially for rain, and the rain would fall."

33. Ibid., 19.
34. Ibid., 7.

Africans value prayer so much and pray for so much that prayer has become like a lifestyle to many families. Even non-believers ask for prayer in meetings and hospitals. However, with every spiritual discipline comes abuse, and prayer is not an exception. For example, Africans traditionally prayed to their ancestors and were governed by the law of "give and take." They would ask for protection from sickness, death, and evil spirits, and for gifts of children, longevity, and material blessings. These traditional prayers were for fulfillment of man's desires rather than God's will.[35] Therefore, prayer was not guided by thirst for God, but for material benefits. This traditional concept of prayer, coupled with the dissemination of the prosperity gospel, could easily distort the genuine practice of prayer as a spiritual discipline that enhances intimacy with God.

Another area of spiritual discipline that Africans are accustomed to is worship. African worship is vibrant, especially in Pentecostal and charismatic churches. Christians sing and dance as they praise and worship God. As a non-African, this is one of the moments I enjoy the most. African worship is both individual and communal, although Africans seem to enjoy corporate worship more than individual worship. One particular aspect of worship needing attention in the African context is its participatory nature. It is a common phenomenon, especially in Pentecostal and charismatic churches, to see people engaged in many expressive actions such as singing, dancing, and raising hands. As mentioned earlier, the rapid growth in Pentecostal and charismatic churches in terms of worship and styles is due to the introduction of gospel music and dance from 1990s.[36] However, it is to be remembered that the object of our worship is God himself. Through worship, believers are ushered in to the glorious presence of God. The act of praise and worship is a medium to this presence of God.

Notwithstanding the wide practice of prayer and worship as spiritual disciplines, there are some spiritual disciplines that Kenyan Christians are not familiar with, such as study, submission, meditation, and solitude. In contemporary Kenya, especially in urban areas, people are always surrounded by noise. It is a challenge to find a quiet place to practice the discipline of solitude. Of course, their traditional communal spirit also makes the practice of solitude difficult. However, students confess the necessity and value of this discipline to restore the presence of God in their lives. Meditation has been avoided possibly for fear of engaging in Eastern

35. Adeyemo, *Salvation in African Tradition*, 36.
36. Parsitau, "Sounds of Change and Reform," 58.

meditation practices, such as Transcendental Meditation or yoga. Perhaps Christian meditation is relatively new to African Christians, but they are well aware of the foundational benefit of meditating on the Scripture.

Submission is the area with which most people struggle. In a culture where mentorship is lacking and leaders suppress the younger generation rather than raise them up, submission to authority is a challenge. Also, in a male-dominated culture where women's rights are not fostered, it is challenging for the wife to submit to the authority of the husband. The Scripture, however, teaches mutual submission.

One last area worth mentioning is the discipline of study. One student commented on the lack of this discipline among Africans. The reasons he put forth are quite interesting: fatalistic thinking (e.g., "Africans are not good readers because they were created that way," or, "We can't change it, for it has always been that way."), poverty, and ignorance (e.g., "Education, especially theological education, is evil!"). Pastors are discouraged from attending Bible schools or training centers. Many pastors, especially from Pentecostal and charismatic denominations, don't believe in education, and are also told by their seniors to rely on the Holy Spirit only for preaching rather than to prepare sermons. I have encountered many of these people myself. However, this wrong concept is being expelled slowly through the teaching of educated pastors and Christian scholars. One student confesses, "The discipline of study is paramount, especially to a believer."

Spiritual formation involves spiritual disciplines that believers need to practice for the transformation of their lives. Then the transformation of our lives is not for us but for others. The nature of spiritual formation is the process of being conformed to the image of Christ *for the sake of others*.[37] This aspect of Christian spirituality is well summarized by the following statements of Donald Bloesch:

> True spirituality will be anchored in biblical revelation. . . . True spirituality will also resist the allurement of secularism. . . . True spirituality is not trying to make ourselves spiritual through faith, but it is living out our faith in service to God and neighbor. It is not the adornment of the soul that should command our primary attention but hearing the cries of the oppressed and deprived of the world and coming to their aid. . . . True spirituality signifies . . . obedience to God through the power of the Spirit. This obedience, which consists of works of love, is a manifestation and

37. Mulholland Jr., *Invitation to a Journey*, 15–40.

demonstration of a salvation already accomplished in the life, death, and resurrection of Jesus Christ.[38]

The nature of a spiritual journey is fluid. Spirituality deals with life, which is flexible. We don't always keep growing spiritually; sometimes we go off track or regress in our spiritual journey. We experience ups and downs in our spiritual life. So spirituality is different from theology; while theology is the articulation of Christian faith, spirituality is the lived experience of that faith. Of course, these two are related and overlap. We understand spiritual formation as a journey. For us to successfully negotiate this journey, we need to accept ourselves and others, understanding human limitations and frailty and not be so critical of ourselves and others. While not satisfied with our current spiritual status, we push forward toward a higher summit. If we continue our journey without giving up, we will experience the presence, power, and glory of God not only in the future but also through the journey.

38. Bloesch, *Spirituality Old & New*, 142–48.

Bibliography

Abeledo, Yago. "The Slums: The Challenge of a Crucified People." In *The Slums: A Challenge to Evangelization*, edited by Pierli, F. and Y. Abeledo, 109–32. Nairobi, Kenya: Paulines Publications Africa, 2002.

Adeyemo, Tokunboh. *Salvation in African Tradition*. Nairobi, Kenya: Evangel Publishing House, 1997.

Adoyo, Bonifes. Radio broadcast (Hope FM, 93.3), Nov. 28, 2010.

Anderson, Allan. *An Introduction to Pentecostalism*. Cambridge: Cambridge University Press, 2004.

Anderson, William B. *The Church in East Africa*. Nairobi, Kenya: Uzima, 1977.

Ansah, J. K. "The Ethics of African Religious Tradition." In *World Religions and Global Ethics*, edited by S. Cromwell Crawford, 241–65. New York: Paragon House, 1989.

Barabas, S. "Keswick Convention." In *Evangelical Dictionary of Theology* 603–4.

Barrett, David. "The Worldwide Holy Spirit Renewal." In *The Century of the Holy Spirit: 100 Years of Pentecostal and Charismatic Renewal*, edited by Vinson Synan, 381–414. Nashville: Thomas Nelson, 2001

Barrett, David B., et al., editors. *Kenya Churches Handbook*. Kisumu, Kenya: Evangel Publishing House. 1973.

Barton, John. "The Old Testament." In *The Study of Spirituality*, edited by Cheslyn Jones et al., 47–57. Oxford: Oxford University Press, 1986

Barton, Stephen C. *The Spirituality of the Gospels*. Eugene, OR: Wipf & Stock, 1992.

———. "Synoptic Gospels, Spirituality of." In *The New Westminster Dictionary of Christian Spirituality*, edited by Philip Sheldrake, 608–10. Louisville: WJK, 2005.

Barvinck, J. H. 1948. *The Impact of Christianity on the Non-Christian World*. Grand Rapids: Eerdmans, 1948.

Bass, Diana B., and Joseph Stewart-Sicking. "Christian Spirituality in Europe and North America since 1700." In *The Blackwell Companion to Christian Spirituality*, edited by Arthur Holder, 139–55. Oxford: Blackwell, 2005.

Bavinck, Herman. *In the Beginning: Foundations of Creation Theology*. Edited by J. Bolt. Translated by J. Vriend. Grand Rapids: Baker, 1999.

———. *Reformed Dogmatics*. Vol 2. Edited by J. Bolt. Translated by J. Vriend. Grand Rapids: Baker Academic, 2004.

Beck, Brian E. *Christian Character in the Gospel of Luke*. London: Epworth, 1989.

Bediako, Kwame. *Christianity in Africa: The Renewal of a Non-Western Religion*. New York: Orbis, 1995.

Beetham, Thomas A. "Co-operation between the Churches." In *Kenya Churches Handbook*, edited by David B. Barrett et al., 149–53. Kisumu, Kenya: Evangel Publishing House, 1973.

Benedict. *Saint Benedict's Rule*. Translated by P. Barry. Malwah, NJ: Hiddenspring, 2004.

Bibliography

Berling, Judith. "Christian Spirituality: Intrinsically Interdisciplinary." In *Exploring Christian Spirituality: Essays in Honor of Sandra M. Schneiders*, edited by Bruce H. Lescher and Elizabeth Liebert, 35–52. New York: Paulist, 2006.

Bloesch, Donald G. *Spirituality Old & New: Recovering Authentic Spiritual life*. Downers Grove, IL: InterVarsity, 2007.

Bouyer, Louis. *The Spirituality of the New Testament and the Fathers*. Minneapolis: Seabury, 1963.

Bowe, Barbara E. *Biblical Foundations of Spirituality: Touching a Finger to the Flame*. Lanham: Rowman and Littlefield, 2003.

Bruce, Steve. "The Social Process of Secularization." In *The Blackwell Companion to Sociology of Religion*, edited by Richard K. Fenn, 249–63. Oxford: Blackwell, 2003.

Brueggemann, Walter. *An Introduction to the Old Testament*. Louisville: Westminster John Knox, 2003.

———. *The Psalms: The Life of Faith*. Edited by P. D. Miller. Minneapolis: Fortress, 1995.

Burgess, Stanley M. "Neocharismatics." In *The New International Dictionary of Pentecostal and Charismatic Movements*, revised and expanded ed., edited by Stanley M. Burgess and Eduard M. van der Maas, 928. Grand Rapids: Zondervan, 2003.

Burgess, Stanley M., and Eduard M. van der Mass, editors. *International Dictionary of Pentecostal and Charismatic Movements*. Revised and expanded ed. Grand Rapids: Zondervan, 2003.

Carney, G., and W. Long. "Job." In *The Renovaré Spiritual Formation Bible*, edited by Richard J. Foster, 721–24. San Francisco: HarperSanFrancisco, 2005.

Chesaina, Ciarunji. "Cultural Attitudes and Equality of the Sexes." In *Social and Religious Concerns of East Africa: A Wajibu Anthology*, edited by Gerald J. Wanjohi and G. Wakuraya Wanjohi, 203–11. Nairobi, Kenya: Wanjohi, 2005.

Collins, Kenneth, editor. *Exploring Christian Spirituality: An Ecumenical Reader*. Grand Rapids: Baker Academic, 2000.

Davies, O. "Ruysbroeck, à Kempis and the *Theologia Deutsch*." In *The Study of Spirituality*, edited by Cheslyn Jones et al., 321–24. Oxford: Oxford University Press, 1986.

De Jong, Albert. *Mission and Politics in Eastern Africa*. Limuru, Kenya: Paulines Publications Africa, 2000.

Deidun, Tom. "Pauline Spirituality." In *The New Westminster Dictionary of Christian Spirituality*, edited by Philip Sheldrake, 479–81. Louisville: Westminster John Knox, 2005.

Demerath III, Nicholas J. "Secularization Extended: From Religious 'Myth' to Cultural Commonplace." In *The Blackwell Companion to Sociology of Religion*, edited by Richard K. Fenn, 211–28. Oxford: Blackwell, 2003.

Dent, C. M. "Zwingli." In *The Study of Spirituality*, edited by Cheslyn Jones et al., 346–49. Oxford: Oxford University Press, 1986.

Dockery, David S. "An Outline of Paul's View of the Spiritual Life: Foundations for an Evangelical Spirituality." In *Exploring Christian Spirituality: An Ecumenical Reader*, edited by Kenneth J. Collins, 339–51. Grand Rapids: Baker Academic, 2000.

Donahue, John R. "Jesus as the Parable of God in the Gospels of Mark." *Interpretation* 32 (1978) 369–86.

———. "The Quest for Biblical Spirituality." In *Exploring Christian Spirituality: Essays in Honor of Sandra M. Schneiders*, edited by Bruce H. Lescher and Elizabeth Liebert, 73–97. New York: Paulist, 2006.

Downey, Michael. *Understanding Christian Spirituality*. New York: Paulist, 1997.

Dunn, James D. "Models of Christian Community in the New Testament." In *Strange Gifts?: A Guide to Charismatic Renewal*, edited by David Martin and Peter Mullen, 1–18. Oxford: Blackwell, 1984.

Dysinger, Luke. "Early Christian Spirituality." In *The New Westminster Dictionary of Christian Spirituality*, edited by Philip Sheldrake, 256–59. Louisville: Westminster John Knox, 2005.

El Saadawi, Nawal. *The Hidden Face of Eve: Women in the Arab World*. Translated and edited by S. Hetata. London: Zed, 1980.

Endres, J. C. "Psalms and Spirituality in the 21st century." *Interpretation* 56 (2002) 143–54.

Elwell, Walter A, editor. *Evangelical Dictionary of Theology*. Grand Rapids: Baker, 1984.

Faust, Clarence H. and Thoams H. Johnson, editors. *Jonathan Edwards*. New York: American, 1935.

Fedders, A., and C. Salvadori. *Peoples and Cultures of Kenya*. Nairobi, Kenya: Transafrica Book Distributors, 1979.

Fenn, Richard K. "Editorial Commentary: Religion and the Secular; the Sacred and the Profane: The Scope of the Argument." In *The Blackwell Companion to Sociology of Religion*, edited by Richard K. Fenn, 3–22. Oxford: Blackwell, 2003.

Foster, Richard. *Celebration of Discipline: The Path to Spiritual Growth*. Rev. and exp. ed. San Francisco: HarperSanFrancisco, 1988.

———, editor. *The Renovaré Spiritual Formation Bible*. San Francisco: HarperSanFrancisco, 2005.

———. *Streams of Living Water: Celebrating the Great Traditions of Christian Faith*. San Francisco: HarperSanFrancisco, 1998.

Gachukia, Daniel. "Government by Tribe or Government by Political Parties?" In *Social and Religious Concerns of East Africa: A Wajibu Anthology*, edited by Gerald J. Wanjohi and G. Wakuraya Wanjohi, 101–7. Nairobi, Kenya: Wanjohi, 2005.

Garrard, D. J. "Kenya." In *The New International Dictionary of Pentecostal and Charismatic Movements*, edited by Stanley M. Burgess and Eduard M. van der Maas, 150–55. Revised and expanded ed. Grand Rapids: Zondervan, 2003.

Gehman, Richard J. *African Traditional Religion in Biblical Perspective*. Nairobi, Kenya: East African Educational Publishers, 1989.

George, A. Raymond. "John Wesley and the Methodist Movement." In *The Study of Spirituality*, edited by Cheslyn Jones et al., 455–59. Oxford: Oxford University Press, 1986.

Gerrish, Brian A. *The Old Protestantism and the New*. Chicago: University of Chicago Press, 1982.

Gifford, Paul. *Christianity, Politics and Public Life in Kenya*. London: Hurst, 2009.

Gill, D. W. "Secularism, Secular Humanism." In *Evangelical Dictionary of Theology*, edited by Walter A. Elwell, 996–97. Grand Rapids: Baker, 1984.

Githii, David M. "The East African Revival Movement and the Presbyterian Church of East Africa." ThM thesis, Fuller Theological Seminary, 1992.

———. "The Introduction and Development of Western Education in Kenya by the Presbyterians, 1891–1991." DMiss diss., Fuller Theological Seminary, 1993.

Green, M. "Abba Worshipers." In *Living the Story: Biblical Spirituality for Everyday Christians*, edited by R. Stevens and M. Green, 3–15. Grand Rapids: Eerdmans, 2003.

Gregory the Great. *Dialogue*. Translated by O. J. Zimmerman. New York: Fathers of the Church, 1959.

Guthrie, Donald. *New Testament Theology*. Leicester, UK: InterVarsity, 1981.

Bibliography

Guthrie, Harvey H. "Anglican Spirituality: An Ethos and Some Issues." In *Exploring Christian Spirituality: An Ecumenical Reader*, edited by Kenneth J. Collins, 158–71. Grand Rapids: Baker Academic, 2000.

Gyekye, K. *Tradition and Modernity*. New York: Oxford University Press, 1997.

Habig, M., editor. *St. Francis of Assisi: Writings and Early Biographies*. 4th rev ed. Quincy, IL: Franciscan, 1991

Hageman, Howard 2000. "Reformed Spirituality," In *Exploring Christian Spirituality: An Ecumenical Reader*, edited by Kenneth J. Collins, 138–57. Grand Rapids: Baker Academic, 2000.

Hanciles, Jehu J. *Beyond Christendom: Globalization, African Migration, and the Transformation of the West*. Maryknoll, NY: Orbis, 2008.

Handy, Robert. "Some Patterns in American Protestantism." In *The Study of Spirituality*, edited by Cheslyn Jones et al., 473–80. Oxford: Oxford University Press, 1986.

Hanson, Bradley. "Lutheran Spirituality." In *The New Westminster Dictionary of Christian Spirituality*, edited by Philip Sheldrake, 415–17. Louisville: Westminster John Knox, 2005.

Harper, J. S. "Old Testament Spirituality." In *Exploring Christian Spirituality: An Ecumenical Reader*, edited by Kenneth J. Collins, 311–26. Grand Rapids: Baker Academic, 2000.

Hervieu-Léger, Danièle. "Individualism, the Validation of Faith, and the Social Nature of Religion in Modernity." In *The Blackwell Companion to Sociology of Religion*, edited by Richard K. Fenn, 161–75. Oxford: Blackwell, 2003.

Heschel, Abraham J. *The Prophets: An Introduction*. New York: Harper & Row, 1969.

Hiebert, Paul G. *Anthropological Insights for Missionaries*. Grand Rapids: Baker, 1985.

Hocken, P. D. "Charismatic Movement." In *The New International Dictionary of Pentecostal and Charismatic Movement*, revised and expanded ed., edited by Stanley M. Burgess and Eduard M. van der Maas, 477–519. Grand Rapids: Zondervan, 2003.

Hoffman, Bengt. "Lutheran Spirituality." In *Exploring Christian Spirituality: An Ecumenical Reader*, edited by Kenneth J. Collins, 122–37. Grand Rapids, Baker Academic, 2000.

Holder, Arthur, editor. *The Blackwell Companion to Christian Spirituality*. Oxford: Blackwell, 2005.

Holt, Bradley P. *Thirsty for God: A Brief History of Christian Spirituality*. Minneapolis: Fortress, 2005.

Idowu, E. Bolaji. *African Traditional Religion*. Maryknoll, NY: Orbis, 1973.

Ignatius. *Epistle to the Romans*. Translated and annotated by James A. Kleist. New York: Paulist, 1946.

Imbach, S. R. "Syncretism." In *Evangelical Dictionary of Theology*, edited by Walter A. Elwell, 1062–63. Grand Rapids: Baker, 1984.

Jones, Cheslyn, et al., editors. *The Study of Spirituality*. New York: Oxford University Press, 1986.

Justin Martyr. *The First and Second Apologies*. Translated by L. W. Barnard. New York: Paulist, 1997.

Kabira, Wanjiku M., and Karega Mutahi. *Gikuyu Oral Literature*. Nairobi, Kenya: East Africa Educational Publishers, 1988.

Kamaara, Eunice K. *Gender, Youth Sexuality and HIV/AIDS: A Kenyan Experience*. Eldoret, Kenya: AMECEA Gaba Publications, 2005.

———. "Religion and Socio-political Change in Kenya 1978–2003." In *Church-State Relations: A Challenge for African Christianity*, edited by J. N. K. Mugambi and Frank Kuschner-Pelkmann, 125–38. Nairobi, Kenya: Acton, 2004.

Karega-Munene, K. "Aspects of Sharing among Africans." In *Social and Religious Concerns of East Africa: A Wajibu Anthology*, edited by Gerald J. Wanjohi and G. Wakuraya Wanjohi, 25–31. Nairobi, Kenya: Wanjohi, 2005.

Kenya National Bureau of Statistics. *2009 Kenya Population and Housing Census*. Vol. II, Population and Household Distribution by Socio-Economic Characteristics, 2010.

Kenyatta, Jomo. *Facing Mount Kenya: The Traditional Life of the Gikuyu*. Nairobi, Kenya: Heinemann Kenya, 1978.

Kibera, Valerie. "'That's Our African Culture' Thoughts on Selective Cultural Preservation." In *Social and Religious Concerns of East Africa: A Wajibu Anthology*, edited by Gerald J. Wanjohi and G. Wakuraya Wanjohi, 32–37. Nairobi, Kenya: Wanjohi, 2005.

Kibicho, S. G. "The Kikuyu Conception of God, Its Continuity into the Christian Era, and the Question It Raises for the Christian Idea of Revelation." PhD diss., Vanderbilt University, 1972.

Kinoti, Hannah W. "African Morality: Past and Present." In *Moral and Ethical Issues in African Christianity*, edited by J. N. K. Mugambi and A. Nasimiyu-Wasike, 73–82. Nairobi, Kenya: Acton, 2003.

Kirwen, Michael, editor. *African Cultural Knowledge: Themes and Embedded Beliefs*. Nairobi, Kenya: Maryknoll Institute of African Studies, 2005.

Kithinji, Ciriaka. "The Individual in Society: Focus on the African Family." In *Social and Religious Concerns of East Africa: A Wajibu Anthology*, edited by Gerald J. Wanjohi and G. Wakuraya Wanjohi, 273–78. Nairobi, Kenya: Wanjohi, 2005.

Kraft, Charles H. *Anthropology for Christian Witness*. New York: Orbis, 1996.

————. *Christianity in Culture: A Study in Biblical Theologizing in Cross-cultural Perspective*. 2nd ed. Maryknoll, New York: Orbis, 2005.

Kushner, Lawrence. *Jewish Spirituality: A Brief Introduction for Christians*. Woodstock, VT: Jewish Lights, 2001.

Leakey, L. S. B. *Mau Mau and the Kikuyu*. London: Routledge, 1952.

Leclercq, J., et al. *The Spirituality of the Middle Ages*. Vol. II, *A History of Christian Spirituality*. Minneapolis: Seabury, 1968.

Lehman, Arthur C., and James E. Myers. *Magic, Witchcraft and Religion*. 4th ed. Mountain view, CA: Mayfield, 1997.

Lescher, Bruce, and Elizabeth Liebert, editors. *Exploring Christian Spirituality: Essays in Honor of Sandra M Schneiders*. New York: Paulist, 2006.

Longman III, Tremper, "Song of Solomon." In *The Renovaré Spiritual Formation Bible*, edited by Richard J. Foster, 963–65. San Francisco: HarperSanFrancisco, 2005.

Lotz, David W. "Continental Pietism." In *The Study of Spirituality*, edited by Cheslyn Jones et al., 448–52. Oxford: Oxford University Press, 1986.

Louth, Andrew. "Augustine." In *The Study of Spirituality*, edited by Cheslyn Jones et al., 134–45. Oxford: Oxford University Press, 1986.

Lovelace, Richard F. "Evangelical Spirituality." In *Exploring Christian Spirituality: An Ecumenical Reader*, edited by Kenneth J. Collins, 214–26. Grand Rapids: Baker Academic, 2000.

Luther, Martin. *Luther's Spirituality*. Edited by Philip D. W. Krey and Peter D. S. Krey. New York: Paulist, 2007.

Macpherson, Robert. *The Presbyterian Church in Kenya*. Nairobi, Kenya: Kenya Litho, 1970.

Magesa, Laurenti. *African Religion: The Moral Traditions of Abundant Life*. Limuru, Kenya: Paulines Publications Africa, 1998.

———. "Charismatic Movements as "Communities of Affliction." In *Charismatic Renewal in Africa: A Challenge for African Christianity*, edited by Mika Vähäkangas and Andrew A. Kyomo, 27–44. Nairobi, Kenya: Acton, 2003.

Magoti, Evaristi. "Charismatic Movement in the Context of Inculturation." In *Charismatic Renewal in Africa: A Challenge for African Christianity*, edited by Mika Vähäkangas and Andrew A. Kyomo, 91–110. Nairobi, Kenya: Acton, 2003.

Maloney, Clarence, editor. "Introduction" to *The Evil Eye*. New York: Columbia University Press, 1976.

Mambo, George K. "The Revival Fellowship (Brethren) in Kenya." In *Kenya Churches Handbook*, edited by David B. Barrett, 110–17. Kisumu, Kenya: Evangel, 1973.

Marenya, Neddy, editor. "The Voice of the Women from the Slums." In *The Slums*, edited by Francesco Pierli and Yago Abeledo, 50–58. Nairobi, Kenya: Paulines Publications Africa, 2002.

Marquet, Jacques. *Africanity: The Cultural Unity of Black Africa*. Translated by J. R. Rayfield. New York: Oxford University Press, 1972.

Mbae, John. "The African Family: Where Are the Fathers?" In *Social and Religious Concerns of East Africa: A Wajibu Anthology*, edited by Gerald J. Wanjohi and G. Wakuraya Wanjohi, 43–49. Nairobi, Kenya: Wanjohi, 2005.

Mbiti, John S. *African Religions and Philosophy*. Nairobi, Kenya: East African Educational Publishers, 2002.

———. "Diversity, Divisions and Denominationalism." In *Kenya Churches Handbook*, edited by David B. Barrett, 144–48. Kisumu, Kenya: Evangel Publishing House, 1973.

———. *Introduction to African Religion*. 2nd ed. Nairobi, Kenya: East African Educational Publishers, 1991.

Mbon, Friday M. "African Traditional Socio-religious Ethics and National Development: the Nigerian Case." In *African Traditional Religions in Contemporary Society*, edited by Jacob K. Olupona, 101–9. St. Paul, MN: Paragon House, 1991.

McCarthy, Marie. "Spirituality in Postmodern Era." In *The Blackwell Reader in Pastoral and Practical Theology*, edited by James Woodward and Stephen Pattison, 192–206. Oxford: Blackwell, 2000.

McDonald, Lee M. *The Biblical Canon: Its Origin, Transmission, and Authority*. Peabody, MA: Hendrickson, 2007.

Moffatt, Ron, editor. *The Presbyterian Church of East Africa Handbook*. Nairobi, Kenya: Jitegemea, 1974.

A Monk of the Eastern Church. "The Essentials of Orthodox Spirituality." In *Exploring Christian Spirituality: An Ecumenical Reader*, edited by Kenneth J. Collins, 108–21. Grand Rapids: Baker Academic, 2000.

Moorman, John R. H. "The Franciscans." In *The Study of Spirituality*, edited by Cheslyn Jones et al., 301–8. Oxford: Oxford University Press, 1986.

Morrice, William G. *Joy in the New Testament*. Exeter, UK: Paternoster, 1984.

Mugambi, J. N. K. "Evangelistic and Charismatic Initiatives in Post-colonial Africa." In *Charismatic Renewal in Africa: A Challenge for African Christianity*, edited by Mika Vähäkangas and Andrew A. Kyomo, 111–44. Nairobi: Acton, 2003.

Mugambi, J. N. K., and A. Nasimiyu-Wasike, editors. *Moral and Ethical Issues in African Christianity: Explorative Essays in Moral Theology*. 3rd ed. Nairobi, Kenya: Acton, 2003.

Mugambi, J. N. K., and Mary N. Getui, editors. *Religions in Eastern Africa under Globalization*. Nairobi, Kenya: Acton, 2004.

Mugo, E. N. *Kikuyu People.* Nairobi, Kenya: Kenya Literature Bureau, 1982.

Muita, Isaiah W. *Hewn from the Quarry.* Nairobi, Kenya: The Presbyterian Church of East Africa, 2003.

Mulholland, M. Robert, Jr. *Invitation to a Journey: A Road Map for Spiritual Formation.* Downers Grove, IL: InterVarsity, 1993.

Muriuki, G. *A History of the Kikuyu 1500–1900.* Nairobi, Kenya: Oxford University Press, 1974.

Murray, Jocelyn. "Varieties of Kikuyu Independent Churches." In *Kenya Churches Handbook,* edited by David B. Barrett, 128–34. Kisumu, Kenya: Evangel, 1973.

Mwaura, Philomena N. 2004. "African Instituted Churches—a Perspective from Kenya." In *Religions in Eastern Africa under Globalization,* edited by J. N. K. Mugambi and Mary N. Getui, 101–20. Nairobi: Acton, 2004.

Mwikamba, C. M. "Changing Morals in Africa." In *Moral and Ethical Issues in African Christianity: A Challenge for African Christianity,* edited by J. N. K. Mugambi and A. Nasimiyu-Wasike, 83–106. Nairobi: Acton, 2003.

Narayan, D., et al. *Crying Out for Change: Voices of the Poor.* New York: Oxford University Press, 2000.

Nasuti, H. P. "The Sacramental Function of the Psalms in Contemporary Scholarship and Liturgical Practice." In *Psalms and Practice: Worship, Virtue, and Authority,* edited by S. B. Reid, 80–81. Collegeville. MN: Liturgical, 2001.

Ndiokwere, Nathaniel I. *Prophecy and Revolution.* London: SPCK, 1981.

Ngong, David T. "Salvation and Materialism." *Studies in World Christianity* 15 (2009) 1–21.

Niebuhr, H. Richard. *Christ and Culture.* New York: Harper and Row, 1951.

Nthamburi, Zablon. "The Beginning and Development of Christianity in Kenya." In *A Handbook of Christianity in East Africa,* edited by Zablon Nthamburi, 1–36. Nairobi, Kenya: Uzima, 1991.

———. "Mainline Christian Churches—a Historical Survey." In *Religions in Eastern Africa under Globalization,* edited by J. N. K. Mugambi and Mary N. Getui, 72–83. Nairobi: Acton, 2004.

O'Donovan, Wilbur. *Biblical Christianity in Modern Africa.* Carlisle, UK: Paternoster, 2000.

Okite, Odhiambo W. "Politics of Africa's Independent Churches." In *Kenya Churches Handbook,* edited by David B. Barrett, 118–23. Kisumu, Kenya: Evangel Publishing House, 1973.

Okullu, H. *Church and Politics in East Africa.* Nairobi, Kenya: Uzima, 1974.

Orwa, D. Kaketete. "Politics and Integrity: A Challenge in Political Leadership." In *Social and Religious Concerns of East Africa: A Wajibu Anthology,* edited by Gerald J. Wanjohi and G. Wakuraya Wanjohi, 108–15. Nairobi: Wanjohi, 2005.

Osoba, S. O. "Corruption in Nigeria: Historical Perspectives." *Review of African Political Economy* 23.69 (1999) 371–86.

Parrinder, Geoffrey. *African Traditional Religion.* Westport, CT: Greenwood, 1976.

Parsitau, Damaris S. "Sounds of Change and Reform: The Appropriation of Gospel Music and Dance in Political Discourses in Kenya." *Studies in World Christianity* 14 (2008) 55–72.

Peli, M., and O. Oyeneye. *Consensus, Conflict and Change: A Sociological Introduction to African Societies.* Nairobi, Kenya: East African Educational Publishers, 1998.

Peterson, Doug. *Not by Might Nor by Power: A Pentecostal Theology of Social Concern in Latin America.* Oxford: Regnum, 1996.

Peterson, Eugene H. "Saint Mark: The Basic Text for Christian Spirituality." In *Exploring Christian Spirituality: An Ecumenical Reader,* edited by Kenneth J. Collins, 327–38. Grand Rapids: Baker Academic, 2000.

Pierard, R. V. "Holiness Movement, American." In *Evangelical Dictionary of Theology,* edited by Walter A. Elwell, 516–18. Grand Rapids: Baker, 1984.

Pierli, F., and Y. Abeledo, editors. *The Slums: A Challenge to Evangelization.* Nairobi, Kenya: Paulines Publications Africa, 2002.

Principe, Walter. "Toward Defining Spirituality." In *Exploring Christian Spirituality: An Ecumenical Reader,* edited by Kenneth J. Collins, 43–59. Grand Rapids: Baker Academic, 2000.

Raitt, Jill. "European Reformations of Christian Spirituality (1450–1700)." In *The Blackwell Companion to Christian Spirituality,* edited by Arthur Holder, 122–38. Oxford: Blackwell, 2005.

Rice, Howard L. *Reformed Spirituality: An Introduction to Believers.* Louisville, KY: Westminster/John Knox, 1991.

Saunders, Stan P. "'Learning Christ': Eschatology and Spiritual Formation in New Testament Christianity." *Interpretation* 56 (2002) 155–67.

Schaeffer, Francis. *True Spirituality.* Wheaton, IL: Tyndale, 1971.

Schneiders, Sandra M. "Approach to the Study of Christian Spirituality." In *The Blackwell Companion to Christian Spirituality,* edited by Arthur Holder, 15–33. Oxford: Blackwell, 2005.

———. "Biblical Spirituality." *Interpretation* 56 (2002) 133–42.

———. "Christian Spirituality: Definition, Methods and Types." In *The New Westminster Dictionary of Christian Spirituality,* edited by Philip Sheldrake, 1–6. Louisville: Westminster John Knox, 2005.

———. "Johannine Spirituality." In *The New Westminster Dictionary of Christian Spirituality,* edited by Philip Sheldrake, 385–87. Louisville: Westminster John Knox, 2005.

———. "The Study of Christian Spirituality: Contours and Dynamics of a Discipline." *Christian Spirituality Bulletin* 6.1 (1998) 1, 3–12.

Seifert, Harvey. *Explorations in Mediation and Contemplation.* Nashville: The Upper Room, 1981.

Sheldrake, Philip, editor. *The New Westminster Dictionary of Christian Spirituality.* Louisville: Westminster John Knox, 2005.

———. *Spirituality & History.* Rev. ed. Maryknoll, NY: Orbis, 1995.

———. "Spirituality and Its Critical Methodology." In *Exploring Christian Spirituality: Essays in Honor of Sandra M. Schneiders,* edited by Bruce H. Lescher and Elizabeth Liebert, 15–34. New York: Paulist, 2006.

Shorter, Aylward. "Secularism and Emerging Religious Movements." In *Religions in Eastern Africa under Globalization,* edited by J. N. K. Mugambi and Mary N. Getui, 253–67. Nairobi: Acton, 2004.

———. "Slums: A Social Analysis." In *The Slums,* edited by Francesco Pierli and Yago Abeledo, 61–70. Nairobi: Paulines Publications Africa, 2002.

Smith, A. C. S. *Road to Revival: The Story of the Ruanda Mission.* London: The Church Missionary Society, 1946.

Smith, Cyprian, and Oliver Davies. "The Rhineland Mystics." In *The Study of Spirituality*, edited by Cheslyn Jones et al., 315–20. Oxford: Oxford University Press, 1986.

Spearritt, Placid. "Benedict." In *The Study of Spirituality*, edited by Cheslyn Jones et al., 148–56. Oxford: Oxford University Press, 1986.

Spittler, R. P. "Spirituality, Pentecostal and Charismatic." In *The New International Dictionary of Pentecostal and Charismatic Movements*, revised and expanded ed., edited by Stanley M. Burgess and Eduard M. van der Maas, 1096–1102. Grand Rapids: Zondervan, 2003.

Stanley M. Burgess, editor. *The New International Dictionary of Pentecostal and Charismatic Movements*. Rev. and Exp. ed. Grand Rapids: Zondervan, 2003.

Stewart, Columba. "Christian Spirituality during the Roman Empire (100–600)." In *The Blackwell Companion to Christian Spirituality*, edited by Arthur Holder, 73–89. Oxford: Blackwell, 2005.

Strayer, R. W. *The Making of Mission Communities in East Africa*. London: Heinemann, 1978.

Synan, Vinson. *The Century of the Holy Spirit: 100 years of Pentecostal and Charismatic Renewal*. Nashville, TN: Thomas Nelson, 2001.

———. "Pentecostalism." In *Evangelical Dictionary of Theology*, edited by Walter A. Elwell, 835–39. Grand Rapids: Baker, 1984.

Tarimo, Aquiline. "The State and Human Rights in Africa." In *Church-State Relations: A Challenge for African Christianity*, edited by J. N. K. Mugambi and Frank Küschner-Peklmann, 51–72. Nairobi, Kenya: Acton, 2004.

Thomas à Kempis. *Imitation of Christ*. Translated by J. McCann. New York: The New American Library, 1957.

Thornton, Martin. "The Caroline Divines and the Cambridge Platonists." In *The Study of Spirituality*, edited by Cheslyn Jones et al., 431–37. Oxford: Oxford University Press, 1986.

Thurston, Bonnie. "The New Testament in Christian Spirituality." In *The Blackwell Companion to Christian Spirituality*, edited by Arthur Holder, 55–70. Oxford: Blackwell, 2005.

———. *Spiritual Life in the Early Church: The Witness of Acts and Ephesians*. Minneapolis, MN: Fortress, 1993.

Tripp, D. H. "Calvin." In *The Study of Spirituality*, edited by Cheslyn Jones et al., 354–56. Oxford: Oxford University Press, 1986.

———. "Luther." In *The Study of Spirituality*, edited by Cheslyn Jones et al., 343–46. Oxford: Oxford University Press, 1986.

———. "The Protestant Reformation." In *The Study of Spirituality*, edited by Cheslyn Jones et al., 342–43. Oxford: Oxford University Press, 1986.

Tugwell, Simon. "The Dominicans." In *The Study of Spirituality*, edited by Cheslyn Jones et al., 296–300. Oxford: Oxford University Press, 1986.

———. "The Mendicants." In *The Study of Spirituality*, edited by Cheslyn Jones et al., 294–95. Oxford: Oxford University Press, 1986.

Vähäkangas, Mika, and Andrew A. Kyomo, editors. *Charismatic Renewal in Africa: A Challenge for African Christianity*. Nairobi, Kenya: Acton, 2003.

Von Furer-Haimendorf C. "Priests." In *Magic, Witchcraft, and Religion: An Anthropological Study of the Supernatural*, 4th ed., edited by Arthur Lehman and James Myers, 86–90. Mountain View, CA: Mayfield, 1997.

Wakefield, Gordon S. "The Puritans." In *The Study of Spirituality*, edited by Cheslyn Jones et al., 437–44. Oxford: Oxford University Press, 1986.

Wanjohi, Gerald J. "African Marriage, Past and Present." In *Social and Religious Concerns of East Africa: A Wajibu Anthology*, edited by Gerald J. Wanjohi and G. Wakuraya Wanjohi, 40. Nairobi: Wanjohi, 2005.

Wanjohi, G. J., and G. W. Wanjohi, editors. *Social and Religious Concerns of East Africa: A Wajibu Anthology.* Nairobi, Kenya: Wanjohi, 2005.

Wanyoike, E. N. *An African Pastor.* Nairobi, Kenya: East Africa Publishing House, 1974.

Ward, Benedicta. "Gregory the Great." In *The Study of Spirituality*, edited by Cheslyn Jones et al., 277–80. Oxford: Oxford University Press, 1986.

———. "The New Orders." In *The Study of Spirituality*, edited by Cheslyn Jones et al., 283–91. Oxford: Oxford University Press, 1986.

Ward, K. "'Tukutendereza Yesu' the Balokole Revival in Uganda." In *A Handbook of Christianity in East Africa*, edited by Zablon Nthamburi, 113–44. Nairobi, Kenya: Uzima, 1991.

Ware, Kallistos. "The Origins of the Jesus Prayer: Diadochus, Gaza, Sinai." In *The Study of Spirituality*, edited by Cheslyn Jones et al., 175–84. Oxford: Oxford University Press, 1986.

———. "The Spirituality of the Icon." In *The Study of Spirituality*, edited by Cheslyn Jones et al., 195–98. Oxford: Oxford University Press, 1986.

Watson, David Lowes. "Methodist Spirituality." In *Exploring Christian Spirituality: An Ecumenical Reader*, edited by Kenneth J. Collins, 172–213. Grand Rapids: Baker Academic, 2000.

Welbourn, F. B. *East African Christian.* London: Oxford University Press, 1965.

Wesche, K. P. "Eastern Orthodox Spirituality: Union with God in *Theosis*." *Theology Today* 56 (1999) 29–43.

Wiethaus, Ulrike. 2005. "Christian Spirituality in the Medieval West (600–1450)." In *The Blackwell Companion to Christian Spirituality*, edited by Arthur Holder, 106–21. Oxford: Blackwell, 2005.

Wilkinson, John. *The Story of Chogoria.* Tillicoultry, UK: Handsel, 1994.

Willard, Dallas. *The Spirit of the Disciplines: Understanding How God Changes Lives.* New York: HarperCollins, 1988.

Willard, Dallas, and D. Simpson. *Revolution of Character.* Colorado Springs, CO: NavPress, 2005.

Wilson, Bryan. "Salvation, Secularization, and De-moralization." In *The Blackwell Companion to Sociology of Religion*, edited by Richard K. Fenn, 39–51. Oxford: Blackwell, 2003.

Wolters, Clifton. "The English Mystics." In *The Study of Spirituality*, edited by Cheslyn Jones et al., 329–37. Oxford: Oxford University Press, 1986.

World Health Organization 2000. "Fact Sheet No 241." World Health Organization. Online: http://www.who.int/mediacentre/factsheets/fs241/en/

Zanotelli, A. "A Grace Freely Given." In *The Slums*, edited by Francesco Pierli and Yago Abeledo, 13–19. Nairobi: Paulines Publications Africa, 2002.

Zizioulas, John D. "The Early Christian Community." In *Christian Spirituality: Origins to the Twelfth Century*, vol. 1, edited by Bernard McGinn et al., 23–43. New York: Crossroad, 1985.

Zwingli, Huldrych. "Of the Clarity and Certainty of the Word of God." In *Zwingli and Bullinger*, vol. xxiv, edited and translated by G. W. Bromiley, 59–95. Philadelphia: Westminster, 1953.

——. "An Exposition of the Faith (I)." In *Zwingli and Bullinger*, vol. xxiv, edited and translated by G. W. Bromiley, 245–79. Philadelphia: Westminster, 1953.

Index

Index

Index